School Smarts

More than 2,000 Things Students Need to Know in School

Edited by Jay Amberg

Illustrated by Amy O'Brien Krupp
and Rebecca Hershey

 GoodYearBooks

An Imprint of ScottForesman
A Division of HarperCollins*Publishers*

School Smarts is a trademark of Work/Family Directions, Inc., used with permission.

GoodYearBooks
are available for most basic curriculum subjects plus many enrichment areas. For more
GoodYearBooks, contact your local bookseller or educational dealer. For a catalog with
information about other GoodYearBooks, please write:

GoodYearBooks
ScottForesman
1900 East Lake Avenue
Glenview, IL 60025

Book design by Amy O'Brien Krupp.

All cover illustrations by Amy O'Brien Krupp except illustrations of head profile and lightning
diagram by Rebecca Hershey.

Illustrations for pages 2, 10, 13, 17, 22, 23, 27, 30, 31, 33, 34, 37 bottom, 39, 43 top, 44, 46, 48,
50, 55 bottom, 58, 60, 62, 66, 72, 73, 74 top, 78, 79, 83, 85, 90, 93, 98, 99, 100, 101, 102, 110,
111, 115, 116, 118, 119, 121, 125, 126, 129, 132 left, 133, 141, 142, 147, 149, 150, 154, 157, 159,
160, 161, 164, 167, 171, 174, 175, 176, 178, 179, 180, 181, 182, 183, 191, 192, 198, 201, 202,
203, 204, 205, 209, 212, 213, 220, 222, 227, 230, 231, 234, 235, 236, 238, 239, 241, 242, 246
right, 252, 255, 256, 257, 258, 266, 270, 274, 275, 283, 284, 290, 293, 300, 312, 320, 324, 326,
327, 331, 333, 334, 339, 341, 349, 351 left, 355, 356, 361, 363 right, 371, 372, 373, 376, 379,
382, 384, 386, 397, 399, 405, 407, and 408 by Amy O'Brien Krupp.

Illustrations for pages 4, 7, 15, 21, 26, 37, 41, 43 bottom, 55 top, 56, 68, 70, 71, 74, 77, 80, 81,
103, 111, 121, 127, 131, 132 right, 136, 139, 143, 144, 150 bottom, 155, 166, 186, 188, 207, 208,
228, 237, 246 left, 253, 255, 261, 267, 273, 279, 285, 294, 296, 298, 306, 328, 350, 351 right,
357, 363 left, 369, 381, and 385 by Rebecca Hershey.

ISBN 0-673-36136-5

1 2 3 4 5 6 7 8 9 - DP - 01 00 99 98 97 96 95 94

Preface

Who was Marie Curie?
What is the Pythagorean Theorem?
Where is Seoul?
When was the Jamestown settlement founded?

School Smarts answers these questions and thousands of others students need to answer in order to succeed in school. The more than 2,000 items in *School Smarts* have been carefully selected to provide students with the terminology and information needed to understand the subjects they take in school.

In fact, most of the entries in *School Smarts* have been gathered from civics, geography, health, history, language arts, mathematics, and science textbooks used by hundreds of thousands of students across the country. The key points and boldface terms have been gleaned from each of these texts and included here. Still more entries are related to art, music, computers, library science, and other areas for which students need to understand the technical language to develop further their talents and skills.

The clear advantage *School Smarts* provides students is a single source in which to find key information promptly and easily. *School Smarts* is designed as a ready reference. It is not only easy to use but will also prove helpful across the curriculum. Further, entries are cross-referenced, enabling students to quickly discover related information. The entry for the *Koran*, for example, leads to *Islam* and then to *Muhammad*, which in turn leads to *Mecca* and then *Saudi Arabia*. The entry for *Henry David Thoreau* leads to both *Mohandas K. Gandhi* and *Martin Luther King, Jr.*, and then to *civil rights. Volcano* leads to both *magma* and *lava*. Art and photography are used to explain with a single visual image what it would take many words to explain. Finally, the index provides a quick review of all of the information presented.

Whether for classwork or homework, students will find *School Smarts* to be an invaluable reference tool that gives them immediate help for their school courses and insight into the roots of our learning.

Acknowledgements

My thanks to Mona Kahney for providing the foundation for the history entries, and to Professor Anthony D. Fredericks of York College for his work on many of the science entries found here. In addition, other material was culled from the following sources:

America: The People and the Dream. Glenview, IL: Scott, Foresman, 1991.

America Reads, Grade 7. Glenview, IL: Scott, Foresman, 1989.

America Reads, Grade 9. Glenview, IL: Scott, Foresman, 1989.

Civics for Americans. Glenview, IL: Scott, Foresman, 1991.

Exploring Mathematics, Grade 3. Glenview, IL: Scott, Foresman, 1994.

Exploring Mathematics, Grade 5. Glenview, IL: Scott, Foresman, 1994.

Exploring Mathematics, Grade 7. Glenview, IL: Scott, Foresman, 1994.

Health for Life. Glenview, IL: Scott, Foresman, 1994.

People on Earth: A World Geography. Glenview, IL: Scott, Foresman, 1986.

ScottForesman Earth Science. Glenview, IL: Scott, Foresman, 1990.

ScottForesman Life Science. Glenview, IL: Scott, Foresman, 1990.

ScottForesman Physical Science. Glenview, IL: Scott, Foresman, 1990.

ScottForesman World Geography. Glenview, IL: Scott, Foresman, 1989.

Transition Mathematics. Glenview, IL: Scott, Foresman, 1992.

Thanks, too, to the diligent people who checked the facts in this book: Lois-Eve Anderson, Willet Ryder, and Scott Thomas.

Important Dates

1066

The Norman conquest of the Saxons in the Battle of Hastings in England occurred in 1066. William the Conqueror, the Norman leader, united England, making all landowners swear allegiance to him as their leader, and founded a strong English monarchy.

1492

The year 1492 marked the first voyage of Christopher Columbus to the New World. Columbus believed that he had found a new route from Europe to Asia. Actually, he laid the foundation for Spain's colonial empire in America. *See Christopher Columbus.*

1607

In 1607 in Jamestown, Virginia, the first permanent English colony in America was founded. Of the 105 original colonists, more than half survived the first seven months.

1776

In 1776 the thirteen American colonies declared their freedom from England. The Continental Congress adopted the Declaration of Independence on July 4, 1776. The date marked the official start of the Revolutionary War and is now the holiday called Independence Day.

1861–65

The years 1861–65 mark the period of the Civil War in America. War between the northern and southern states split the United States for four years. Victory by the North saved the Union and abolished slavery. *See civil war.*

1914–18

World War I spanned the years 1914–18. Fought mainly in Europe, World War I pitted Germany and its allies against Britain, France, Russia, and the United States. Germany surrendered on November 11, 1918, a date commemorated in the United States as Veterans Day.

1939–45

The years 1939–45 are the dates usually given to mark the beginning and end of World War II. Germany, Japan, Italy, and six other countries, known as the Axis Powers, fought the Allies (Britain, France, the Soviet Union, the United States, and their allies). The war ended in Europe in June 1945 when the Axis Powers surrendered after the Allies defeated Adolf Hitler's army. The war in Asia ended in August of that same year after the United States dropped atomic bombs on two Japanese cities. *See Adolf Hitler and World War II.*

1945

The United Nations was founded in 1945. After World War II, fifty nations joined together to protect the hard-won world peace. Today, most independent countries belong to the United Nations.

365 days

The Egyptians were the first to develop a calendar related to the sun. It had twelve 30-day months, plus five extra days. But that still was one-quarter of a day less than a full year. At the advice of Sosigenes in 46 B.C., the Romans adopted a calendar of three 365-day years, followed by one 366-day leap year. *See calendar and Egypt.*

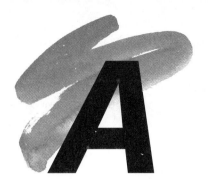

a cappella

The term *a cappella* is an Italian phrase describing singing without instrumental accompaniment.

A.D.

Anno domini, or A.D., means "in the year of the Lord." Most historians date events from the birth of Jesus. A.D. before a date means "after the birth of Jesus." *See B.C.*

a lot/allot

▷ The phrase *a lot* means "much or many."

▷ *Allot* means to "give out or distribute." *Alot* is not a word; it is never correct.

Example:

The foundation allotted a lot of money to the charity.

abacus

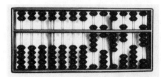

The abacus is a frame with beads for counting. It was probably invented by ancient Sumerians in Mesopotamia and was widely used by ancient Greeks, Romans, and the Chinese. The abacus was developed to solve arithmetic problems quickly. Many people still use abacuses today and find them as quick and easy to use as modern calculators.

abbreviation

An abbreviation is a shortening of a word, usually by writing a part of the word. An abbreviation is followed by a period.

Examples:

- Mr.   Mister
- Mrs.   Missus
- Dr.   Doctor
- P.M.   prime meridian (a term used in designating time)
- Ave.   Avenue

See period.

abdicate

To abdicate means "to give up or renounce power or authority." In 1936, King Edward VIII of Great Britain abdicated his throne. His brother became the new king, George VI.

abdomen

In mammals, the abdomen is the part of the body between the thorax and pelvis. It is the belly. The rear or lower body region of crustaceans is also called the abdomen. The back or tail end of an ant is the abdomen.

Abdomen

abolition

To destroy or eliminate something completely is to abolish it. The abolition of slavery in the United States occurred in 1865. Sojourner Truth and Frederick Douglass were important abolitionists—that is, people who spoke out against slavery and worked to abolish it. *See Frederick Douglass.*

absolute zero

Absolute zero is what scientists think is the coldest temperature possible. It is set at -273.15° Celsius (about -459.67° Fahrenheit). In theory, at this temperature, all atoms and molecules of a substance would stop moving completely. The scientist who formulated this theory was named William Kelvin.

abstain

To abstain from something means "to choose not to do it." Someone who abstains from voting chooses not to vote on some issue.

abstract noun

An abstract noun is a noun that names an idea, a quality, or a characteristic.

Examples:

- hatred
- bravery
- loveliness

See noun.

acceleration

The rate of change of velocity in a given time period is acceleration. A car, for example, accelerates when it begins to move from a stop sign. The rate at which the car gains speed is its rate of acceleration. The rate of acceleration can be given in meters per second, feet per second, miles per hour, or in any number of similar ways.

accent mark

An accent mark (´) is used in a dictionary to demonstrate which syllable in a word is emphasized when that word is pronounced. For example, the word *fiction* has an accent mark on the first syllable (fic´-tion).

accept/except

▷ *Accept* is used as a verb meaning "to receive."

Example:

He will accept the award this evening.

MORE

▷ *Except* is used as either a verb or a preposition. As a verb, it means "to omit or exclude."

Example:

I have finished all of my homework except the geography report.

▷ As a preposition, *except* means "excluding."

Example:

To except the student because he is a freshman is unfair.

accidental

In music, an accidental is a sharp, flat, or natural written before a note to raise or lower it one note from its usual tone in the key, for that measure only. Measures are divided by bar lines.

accompaniment

A musical accompaniment is a supporting part of the music, such as the chords in the left hand of a piano part for the melody played by the right hand. It is also the music played by orchestra, piano, organ, or other instruments in support of a soloist or chorus.

accordion

An accordion is a musical instrument. It is made up of two boxlike boards with a bellows in between. The bellows fills with air and compresses when the instrument is played. One side of the accordion looks like a piano keyboard. The other side has buttons that the player pushes to produce single notes and chords.

acid

An acid is a chemical compound that produces hydrogen ions when dissolved in water. Acids have a sour taste, and acidic fruits such as lemons have a sour, tart taste. Some strong acids can severely burn the skin.

acid rain

Acid rain forms when certain acids mix with water molecules in the air. When coal and oil are burned, they create chemical compounds consisting of sulfur dioxide and nitrogen oxides, which mix with the water molecules in clouds. The rain that falls then becomes more acidic than usual. On a PH scale of 0–14, normal rain is about a PH of 5.5 to 6.5, but acid rain has a PH between 4 and 4.5. Acid rain causes a great deal of damage to crops and forests, as well as to plant and animal life in rivers and lakes. *See PH scale.*

acoustics

The science of sound is called acoustics. In the world of music, the term *acoustics* describes how well sounds can be heard in a room or building. For example, a musician might say that a concert hall has good acoustics. This means that sounds bounce well off the walls and ceilings so they can be heard well. A concert hall with poor acoustics would absorb sounds so they would not be clear and crisp.

acronym

An acronym is a word formed from the beginning letters or syllables of other words. SCUBA, for instance, is an acronym for self-contained underwater breathing apparatus. Some acronyms like NOW (National Organization for Women) are formed from the abbreviations of companies or organizations. Acronyms are pronounced as words rather than as a series of letters.

Acropolis

An acropolis is a walled fortress and religious center built on a hill in the center of ancient Greek communities. Townspeople moved inside an acropolis during an attack. The best-known acropolis is now the site of the Parthenon and ruins of other ancient temples in Athens, Greece. *See Athens.*

acute angle

An acute angle is any angle that measures less than 90°.

ad misericordium

Ad misericordium is a logical fallacy in which a person appeals to sympathy instead of reason.

Example:

I know I cheated on the exam, but please don't flunk me because my dog was sick last night, and I really couldn't study because I was just so worried about poor Fifi.

See logical fallacy.

adagio

Adagio is a musical term that means "a slow tempo."

adapt/adopt

▷ *Adapt* is a verb that means "to adjust (to)" or "to modify (for or from)."

▷ *Adopt* is a verb that means "to take," "to use as one's own," "to accept," or "to choose."

Example:

In order to adapt to her new job, Tanu decided to adopt a policy of working hard and speaking little.

Addams, Jane

Jane Addams, a social worker, opened a settlement house for immigrants in Chicago in 1889. The medical care, food, and English lessons she offered helped the immigrants adjust to their new country and its customs.

addend

An addend is simply another name for a number that is added.

Example:

adhesion

Adhesion is a force that attracts particles of one substance to particles of another. Tape, for example, creates adhesion between the tape and the surface on which it is put. Likewise, glue creates adhesion.

adjective

An adjective is a word that modifies a noun or pronoun. An adjective may tell what kind, which one, or how many. An adjective usually comes before the word it modifies. In the phrase "the big green truck," for example, both *big* and *green* are adjectives.

adjective clause

An adjective clause is a subordinate (dependent) clause that, like an adjective, modifies a noun or pronoun. An adjective clause begins with a relative pronoun, such as *that* or *which*.

Example:

The highway that runs through the city is under construction.

adjective clause

See adjective, clause, and relative pronoun.

adobe

Adobe is Spanish word for "sun-baked bricks." Native Americans of the Southwest made houses of adobe. A community of adobe houses is called a *pueblo*, the Spanish word for "village."

adrenal gland

The adrenal gland produces hormones that help the body adjust to stress, regulate the use of digested foods, regulate the kidneys, and produce sex hormones.

Adriatic Sea

The Adriatic Sea is an arm of the Mediterranean Sea bordered by Italy, Yugoslavia, and Albania.

adverb

An adverb is a word that modifies a verb, an adjective, or another adverb. An adverb may tell how, when, where, how often, or how much. Most adverbs end in *-ly*.

Examples:
- slowly
- quickly
- supremely

Exceptions:
- fast
- hard

See adjective and verb.

adverb clause

An adverb clause is a subordinate (dependent) clause that gives a notion of time, place, or cause and effect. An adverb clause begins with a subordinating conjunction, such as *when, as,* or *since.*

Example:

When she finally found time, Beth baked an apple pie.

adverb clause

See adverb, clause, and subordinating conjunction.

advice/advise

▷ *Advice* is a noun that means "recommendation" or "counsel."

▷ *Advise* is a verb that means "to give advice" or "to inform or recommend."

Example:

Mrs. Mueller advised Ralph to think over her advice.

Aegean Sea

The Aegean Sea is a section of the Mediterranean Sea bordered by Greece, Turkey, and the island of Crete. The islands of the Aegean Sea became well known because of ancient Greek legends and history. The Aegean was also an important trade route for ancient civilizations.

aerobic exercise

Aerobic exercise is steady exercise that promotes taking in and processing large amounts of oxygen. This aids the body in production of energy and lessens the risk of heart disease. *See anaerobic exercise.*

Aeschylus

Aeschylus (525–456 B.C.) was the first of the great Greek writers of tragedy. He made important innovations in drama that Sophocles and Euripides later used and developed further. He is said to

MORE

have been the first dramatist to use dialogue for individual actors. Of his ninety plays, only seven survive. His *Oresteia* is the only Greek trilogy or related themes to be preserved from ancient times.

Aesop

Aesop (620–560 B.C.?) was the assumed author of many animal fables. Although Aesop may never have existed, there is a legend that he was a Greek slave who was freed and who then traveled around Greece telling his fables. Aesop's fables were combined with other ancient fables and written into Greek verse by Valerius Babrius, a Greek writer in about 230 A.D. *See fable.*

aesthetics

Aesthetics is a philosophy of art concerned with the study of beauty. It focuses on artistic sensitivity and the connection of art to other cultural topics. Throughout the ages numerous theories have been proposed about aesthetics by philosophers. Some artists, though, have thought that whatever is beautiful is modeled after forms that are found in nature.

affect/effect

▷ *Affect* is usually used as a verb meaning "to influence."

Example:

The error affected the outcome of the baseball game.

▷ *Effect* is generally used as a noun meaning "result."

Example:

The effect of the error was that three runs scored.

Much of the confusion between these two words stems from the fact that *affect* is sometimes used as a noun to mean "feeling" or "emotion," and *effect* is occasionally used as a verb to mean "to cause" or "bring about" a change.

Examples:

The way he is talking is just an affect.

Coaches sometimes effect changes during games.

affirmative action

Affirmative action is the term used for any laws encouraging or requiring government agencies, businesses, and universities to hire or admit women, minorities, and physically challenged individuals.

Afghanistan

Afghanistan is a mountainous country in southwest Asia between Pakistan and Iran. It is one of the world's least developed nations. The people of Afghanistan are Muslims.

Africa

Africa is the world's second largest continent. It is located south of Europe and southwest of Asia. Africa's population is about 706 million people.

Afrikaner

An Afrikaner is a person born in South Africa of Dutch descent. The white-minority-controlled government has until recently followed a policy of apartheid, or racial apartness, in South Africa, which also has a large black population. *See apartheid and South Africa.*

Agassiz, Jean Louis

Jean Louis Agassiz (1807-1873) was a world-famous naturalist and authority on both zoology and geology. He was Swiss by birth, and during vacations he used to explore the mountains and nearby glaciers. By discovering glaciers move, Agassiz showed that glaciers once covered large areas of Europe. He learned this by driving

stakes into the ground near a cabin that was built on a glacier. After more than a decade, he noticed that the stakes had moved in a U-shaped pattern as the glacier itself melted and reformed, moving, over time.

Age of Reason

The Age of Reason was a period (1600s-late 1700s) in which thinkers stressed that the use of reason was the best way to discover truth. Knowledge, they believed, was power. The scientific method and experimentation were emphasized. During this time in Europe, scientists made great strides in astronomy, chemistry, medicine, and mathematics. Literature and the arts flourished. It was a time of great philosophers, such as Voltaire and Rousseau, and great musicians, such as Bach and Mozart. Paris, in particular, became the model of taste and fashion. *See Enlightenment and Paris.*

agenda

A list of items of business to be discussed at a meeting is an agenda. In a broader sense, agenda can also mean "a plan or program." If someone has a "hidden agenda," he or she has a plan or program that has not been revealed to others.

agreement

In English, two words agree when they have the same person, number, gender, or case. A verb agrees with its subject in person and number. A pronoun agrees with its antecedent in person, number, and gender. *See antecedent, case, gender, and number.*

agribusiness

The term *agribusiness* is used for farming and other businesses that have to do with farm products. An example is the manufacture of fertilizers and tractors. Agribusiness is especially important in the midwestern United States.

agriculture

The growing of crops and raising of livestock is called *agriculture.* As early as 8,000 B.C., people began to farm. This meant that people no longer were dependent for survival on what food they could gather or hunt.

AIDS

AIDS is an acronym for Acquired Immune Deficiency Syndrome. It is a disease spread by a virus in bodily fluids. AIDS decreases the body's ability to fight disease. It is transmitted through the exchange of bodily fluids from a blood transfusion or sexual contact.

ain't

In nonstandard English, *ain't* is sometimes used to mean "am not," "is not," "are not," "has not," or "have not." Avoid the use of *ain't*. *See Nonstandard English.*

air pollution

Air pollution is the ruining of air quality by pollutants, harmful chemicals, and other contaminants. The quality of the Earth's air began to decline in the 1800s. This is when factories became more common. By the early 1920s, automobiles were adding to the levels of air pollution. In 1952, air pollution caused more than 4,000 deaths in London, England. This and other tragedies brought the problem of air pollution to the attention of the world.

air pressure

Air has pressure that pushes down on the surface of the Earth, even though people can't feel it. It results from the Earth's gravitational pull on its atmosphere. Another term for air pressure is "atmospheric pressure."

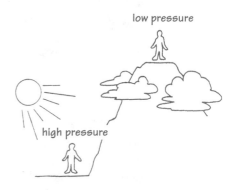

Air pressure changes with the temperature. When the Earth is heated, warm air rises. As the air rises, there is less pressure in that area of the Earth. This is what is called a "low pressure" area. If air is cooled, it sinks to the Earth's surface. This causes more pressure on the Earth, or a high-pressure area. Air pressure also varies according to altitude. The higher a person goes, the lower the air pressure is. Yet, at sea level, there are 2,000 pounds of air pressure on each square foot of a person's body area.

air resistance

The force of air molecules rubbing against the surface of something as it moves through the air is air resistance. Airplanes fly
because their wings rely on air resistance to keep them airborne.
Baseball pitches curve because of the air resistance from the baseball and its seams.

Akbar

A Mogul emperor, Akbar the Great (1542–1605) reigned in India
for forty-nine years during the late sixteenth and early seventeenth
centuries. Although it was customary for an emperor to make his
people follow his religion, Akbar allowed his subjects to practice
whatever religion they wished. During his time in power, the arts
and learning flourished in India.

Alamo

The Alamo is an abandoned mission
that was used in 1836 as a fort by
Texans rebelling against Mexico.
Refusing to surrender, the group of
Texans fought to the end, and
"Remember the Alamo" became the
Texas battle cry. Texas later won its
independence from Mexico.

Alcott, Louisa May

Louisa May Alcott (1832–1888) was an American writer whose
most famous novel was *Little Women*. Based on Alcott's personal
experience, *Little Women* was about a family of girls growing up.
Alcott's teachers included Ralph Waldo Emerson and Henry
David Thoreau. *See Ralph Waldo Emerson and Henry David Thoreau.*

Alexander the Great

King of the ancient country of Macedonia, Alexander the Great
(356-323 B.C.) was educated by the great philosopher Aristotle. As
son of King Philip of Macedonia, he ascended to the throne and
extended his father's empire from Greece to Egypt to India. *See
Aristotle.*

Alexandria

Alexandria is a city in northern Egypt on the Mediterranean Sea. Alexandria was founded by and named for Alexander the Great in the fourth century B.C. In ancient times, it was known for its great library and huge lighthouse. *See Alexander the Great.*

algae

Algae is among the simplest groups of plant life. Algae can be found both in fresh water and salt water. Usually, algae is identified by color—blue-green, brown, green, and red. Some algae are so small that they can only be seen under a microscope. Other algae are so big they may reach lengths of 200 feet or more. Seaweed is an example of this kind of algae. It provides food for many kinds of animals that live in water.

Algeria

Algeria is a country in north Africa on the Mediterranean Sea. Algeria is Africa's second largest country, but because the Sahara Desert covers the southern four-fifths of its area, almost the entire population lives near the Mediterranean Sea. *See Africa.*

all ready/already

▷ *All ready* means "prepared."
▷ *Already* is an adverb that means "before or previously."

Example:
The cakes are all ready to be served, and the pies have already been baked.

all right/alright

▷ *All right* can mean "yes" or "everything is satisfactory."
▷ *Alright* is not considered proper English. It should not be used in formal or informal writing.

Example: ➜

all together/altogether

▷ The expression *all together* is used to describe all of the members of a group gathered together.

▷ *Altogether* is an adverb that means "completely" or "wholly."

Example:
The team decided all together that Ralph's singing was altogether nutty.

allegory

An allegory is a story in which the plot and characters represent general ideas or morals. One example of an allegory is George Orwell's *Animal Farm*.

allegro

Allegro is an Italian word meaning "brisk" or "lively." It is also the term used to describe the first and last sections, or movements, of a symphony or sonata.

alliance

An alliance is a joining of countries to protect or further their mutual interests. Great Britain, Russia, and the United States formed an alliance during World War II to defeat their common foe, Germany.

alliteration

Alliteration is the repetition of sounds, usually at the beginning of words.

Examples:
baby buggy bumper
slimy, slippery, slithering snake

allusion

In a piece of writing, an allusion is a brief reference to a person, place, thing, or event that is familiar to most readers. A writer might, for example, make an allusion to Lincoln's Gettysburg Address.

ally

A person, group, or nation that is united with another to form a common purpose is an ally. Countries that joined with the United States to fight in World War I and World War II were our allies.

almanac

An almanac is a reference book published every year. Almanacs include a great deal of information, such as astronomical data, weather forecasts, names of cities and countries, and biographical notes about famous people. *See reference.*

alphabet

An alphabet is a name given to the letters of a language arranged in order. Experts say that one difference between humans and animals is that humans have the ability to use language. The invention of an alphabet was an important step in developing our use of language.

About 1000 B.C., the ancient Phoenicians invented a system of twenty-two signs for the sounds of their language. They based the system on early symbol writing. Our alphabet comes from that early Phoenician alphabet.

alphabetizing

Alphabetizing involves placing words and phrases in alphabetical order. There are three general rules to follow:

1. Names are listed with the last name (surname) first (Shakespeare, William).
2. Titles are listed according to the first word that is not an article (*Killer Angels, The*).

MORE

3. In an index an item is listed according to its first important word (Groups, capitalizing names of).

Alps

The Alps are the highest mountains in Europe. This mountain range extends from eastern France through northern Italy and Switzerland into southern Germany, Austria, and Yugoslavia. *See Europe*.

although/though

Although and *though* have the same meaning and can be used interchangeably.

▷ *Although* is more likely to introduce a clause that precedes the main clause.

▷ *Though* is usually used to introduce a clause that follows the main clause.

Examples:

Although Allan is an excellent organist, he does not sing well.

Bob remembers names very well though he has no idea how he does it.

alto

An alto, or contralto, is the the lowest woman's voice, or the second part of a four-part vocal composition or choral group.

Amazon River

The Amazon River is the world's second longest river. Located in South America, it carries more water than any other river in the world. *See South America*.

amendment

An amendment is a change made in a law, bill, or motion by adding, taking out, or altering the language. The Constitution of the United States has more than twenty amendments. The Bill of Rights is made up of the first ten amendments to the Constitution. *See Constitution*.

American Revolution

The American Revolution (1775–1783) is also known as the American War for Independence and the Revolutionary War. In this war, American colonists thought British taxes and trade rules were unfair because the colonists did not have a vote in the government decisions that affected them. They rebelled, fought for their independence, and won—thus creating the United States of America.

amino acid

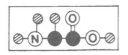

O oxygen N nitrogen
hydrogen carbon

Any of twenty organic acids that combine to form proteins in human beings and higher animals are amino acids. They are the end product of the digestion of protein foods.

among/between

▷ Although the two words are sometimes used interchangeably, *among* is usually used with three or more items.

▷ *Between* is usually used with two items.

Examples:

The clerk split the money among the five workers.

Bill and I split the bag of cookies between us.

amount/number

Amount is used with things in bulk, such as money, time, and homework. *Number* is used with things that can be counted, such as dollars, hours, or assignments.

Example:

The teacher gave such a huge amount of homework that the students could not imagine the number of hours it would take to complete.

See fewer/less.

ampere

An ampere is a unit of measurement used to measure the amount of electrical current. It was discovered by Andre Marie Ampere.

ampersand

An ampersand (&) is the sign and that is sometimes substituted for the word *and* in business and technical writing and in charts and graphs. The ampersand is generally used to save space. Its use is not appropriate in most writing.

amphetamine

An amphetamine is a stimulant—that is, a drug that charges up the body, seemingly giving it energy, and hiding fatigue. Amphetamines can cause anxiety, depression, and violent behavior.

amphibians

An amphibian is a cold-blooded animal with scaleless skin that usually begins its life in water breathing with gills. Later, amphibians develop lungs and live on the land. Frogs are one type of amphibian.

amplifier

Like the word *magnify*, to *amplify* means "to make stronger." An amplifier is an electrical device that increases the strength of electrical signals. Another kind of amplifier can also increase the strength of the music heard through a stereo system.

Amundsen, Roald

Roald Amundsen (1872-1928), a Norwegian explorer, led the expedition that first reached the South Pole in 1911. He was also the first person to reach both the North and the South Poles. He also commanded the first European expedition to sail the Northwest Passage through the Arctic Sea.

anabolic steroid

Anabolic steroids are dangerous substances that cause muscles to become more bulky. If misused, anabolic steroids can cause bodily harm.

anaerobic exercise

Anaerobic exercise is exercise done in short, fast bursts in which the heart cannot supply blood and oxygen as fast as muscles use it. Football plays, for example, provide anaerobic exercise. *See aerobic exercise.*

analogy

An analogy is a comparison based on a particular similarity between two words or pairs of words.

Example:

Skin is to apple as shell is to peanut.

anarchy

Absence of any official government or law is anarchy. An anarchist believes that government is harmful. In an anarchy, cooperation among people would take the place of governmental law. Anarchy is often feared because it can lead to lawlessness and crime.

ancestor

An ancestor is a person from whom one is descended. One's grandparents and great-grandparents are one's ancestors. A person is a descendant of his or her ancestors.

Ancient Greece

Ancient Greece is a civilization that arose around the Aegean Sea about 2000 B.C. Referred to simply as Hellas, it lasted until it was conquered by Rome in 146 B.C. Greco-Roman culture is the main source of Western civilization.

Ancient Persia

Ancient Persia was once a great empire in western Asia. Persians conquered Babylon in 539 B.C. and ruled until they were overcome by the Greeks. Darius, an important Persian leader, extended Persian culture and government into southeastern Europe and what is now Pakistan.

Ancient Rome

Ancient Rome was an empire centered in present-day Italy. At its height of power and prosperity between A.D. 96–180, the Roman empire included all of Europe south and west of the Danube and Rhine rivers and parts of Africa and Asia. It developed a strong government and many public works.

Andes

The Andes are mountains in South America that run north and south near the Pacific Ocean for 4500 miles. They make up the world's longest mountain range and the second tallest range after the Himalayas. *See Pacific Ocean and South America.*

anemometer

Wind speed is measured with an instrument called an *anemometer.* It has a series of small cups that look like Ping Pong balls cut in half. These cups are mounted sideways on a rotating wheel. As the wind pushes the cups, it makes the anemometer spin. The faster the wind blows, the faster the anemometer spins. The spinning part of the anemometer is connected to a dial that measures the wind speed.

Angelou, Maya

Maya Angelou (b. 1928), a writer, dancer, and actress, is best known for her autobiographical novel *I Know Why the Caged Bird Sings.* She has also written collections of poetry, plays, and scripts for TV programs about African heritage in the United States.

angle

The figure formed by two rays with the same endpoint is an angle. *See endpoint and ray.*

annex

To annex means to join or add something to a larger or more important thing, such as when a country adds a territory to itself. In its early days, America annexed new territories to increase the size of the nation.

anorexia nervosa

Anorexia nervosa is an emotional disorder in which a person severely limits food intake. *See bulimia.*

antagonist

In a play or story, the antagonist is the opponent of the main character. In *To Kill a Mockingbird*, for instance, Bob Ewell is the antagonist. *See protagonist.*

Antarctica

Antarctica is an ice-covered continent that makes up approximately 8.75 percent of the world's land. Antarctica includes and surrounds the South Pole. The land in Antarctica is almost completely devoid of plant life due to ice and cold. *See continent.*

antecedent

In language, an antecedent is a noun, noun phrase, or clause to which another pronoun or adverb refers.

Example:

When the truck turned left, it hit the fire hydrant.

The noun *truck* is the antecedent of the pronoun *it*.

See pronoun.

antennae

antennae

Antennae are sensory structures on the heads of insects such as flies and bees, and most other arthropods. Antennae help these arthropods gain information through their senses of touch, smell, and sound.

Anthony, Susan B.

A nineteenth-century activist, Susan B. Anthony (1820–1906) campaigned for the abolition of slavery and for women's rights. When freed slaves were granted the vote, some women expected, but did not receive, the same privilege. Anthony continued to work for reforms until she was eighty years old.

anthropologist

A scientist who studies cultures is an anthropologist. Anthropologists read historical background and observe and interview people. The American anthropologist Margaret Mead lived with and studied the Samoans in the Pacific to learn about their customs and way of life.

antibiotics

An antibiotic is a drug produced from a living organism, such as bacteria or fungi, that fights other microbes that cause disease. It literally means "against life." The important thing about an antibiotic is that each one kills a certain kind of life—one particular bacteria—without harming any other part of the body. Thousands of people used to die each year from infections in their bodies. Now a person can go to a doctor and receive an antibiotic that attacks a particular infection.

antibody

An antibody is a protein substance produced by the body that destroys or weakens foreign bacteria, viruses, or poisons inside the body. When people catch colds, the antibodies in their bodies attack the cold virus.

anticlimax

In writing, an anticlimax is a sudden change from an expected climax. The writing builds toward a climax but presents instead something unimportant or ironic. An anticlimax can be used for a humorous effect. *See climax.*

Anti-Federalist

At the time of the U. S. Constitutional Convention and the Constitution's ratification (1787–1788), those in favor of the new Constitution were called Federalists and those who were opposed to it were called Anti-Federalists. Anti-Federalists favored the liberties of individuals and the states over those of a strong federal government. *See American Revolution.*

antiseptics

An antiseptic is a substance used to kill germs on living tissue. Before performing surgery, doctors make sure that the patient and all of the instruments are completely free of germs. This is called making things "sterile." This was not done until it was proven in the mid-1800s that antiseptics could check the spread of infection. Up to that time, patients sometimes died as a result of infections they acquired in the operating room.

antonym

An antonym is a word that has a meaning opposite to the meaning of another word. *Bright* and *dull,* for example, are antonyms, as are *top* and *bottom.*

ants

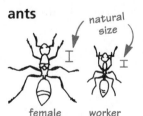

natural size

female   worker

Ants are probably the most numerous insects in the world. Ants are also legendary workers that seem never to tire. The average ant can lift about ten times its own weight with its mouth.

apartheid

Apartheid comes from a word in the Afrikaans language for "separateness." The South African government has practiced

MORE

apartheid in dealing with the black population, making blacks live and eat in areas separate from whites. *See Afrikaner and South Africa.*

Aphrodite

In Greek mythology, Aphrodite was the goddess of love and beauty. Her Roman name was Venus.

Apollo

In Greek mythology, Apollo was the god of light, poetry, music, purity, and healing. His Roman name was Phoebus Apollo.

apostrophe

An apostrophe (') is a punctuation mark most often used to show possession. The rules for adding apostrophes in words are simple:

1. For a singular noun, an apostrophe and an *s* are usually added (Sarah's book).
2. For a plural noun, an apostrophe is usually added after the *s* (girls' books).

Other uses of the apostrophe include showing that one or more letters have been left out of a contraction (*don't, they're*) and making the plurals of letters and numbers (four A's, six 8's). Apostrophes are not used to show possession in personal pronouns like *its, his, hers, ours,* and *theirs. See contraction and personal pronoun.*

Appalachian Mountains

The Appalachians are a mountain range in eastern North America. They extend from Canada to the southern United States. *See North America.*

appendix

An appendix is an addition to the end of a book. An appendix may contain definitions of key terms, mini-biographies, maps, charts, tables, documents, and other useful information.

Appian Way

The Appian Way was a military road that was part of an extensive network of roads that linked Rome to the rest of its empire. It was so well built about 2,300 years ago that parts of it are still used today. In ancient times, Roman highways covered a distance of 50,000 miles or twice around the equator. *See Rome.*

Appomattox Court House

On April 9, 1865, the Civil War officially ended when Confederate General Robert E. Lee surrendered to Union General Ulysses S. Grant. This historic event took place in the village of Appomattox Court House, Virginia.

appositive

▷ An appositive is a noun or pronoun that stands next to another noun or pronoun and renames or explains it.

Example:

The two of us, John and I, went to the movies.

John and I is an appositive because it renames *The two of us.*

▷ An appositive can be used in an appositive phrase consisting of an appositive and modifiers.

Example:

Marlee Matlin, the deaf actress, won an Academy Award for her performance in *Children of a Lesser God.*

arabesque

Arabesque is a style of decoration derived from forms found in Islamic art. Often this style has numerous interwoven lines with geometric patterns and designs of flowers, leaves, or animals. An arabesque design has a lacy and elaborate appearance.

arachnid

Arachnid is a scientific class to which spiders belong. Ticks (tiny bugs found in wooded areas) and scorpions are also arachnids.

MORE

The main distinguishing feature of arachnids is their four pairs of legs and a two-part body, including an abdomen. Most arachnids, which are not nearly as frightening as they look, help humans by eating a lot of insects.

spider

arc

An arc is part of a curve. It is, for example, a segment of a circumference of a circle.

arc of the circle

arch

An arch is a curved structure that supports the weight above it. The early Romans used arches to build bridges and aqueducts. Fourteeenth-century Moors used horseshoe-shaped arches when building the Alhambra Palace in Spain.

archaeologist

An archaeologist studies human cultures of the past when there were few, if any, written records. He or she researches and writes about ancient life from the remains of buildings, tools, pottery, and other artifacts. *See artifact.*

archaism

An archaism is a word or phrase that was once commonly used in English but is no longer used widely (for example, hark and ye). Because they are old-fashioned and outmoded, archaisms should be avoided in writing.

Archimedes

Archimedes (287?-212 B.C.) was a Greek mathematician. He figured out a formula to measure the outside of a circle. He also invented a water-lifting machine, still used today in some countries, to irrigate fields. He is thought to have said, "Give me a place to stand on, and I will move the earth." He supposedly made this remark in connection with one of his best discoveries, the lever. He showed how, with a lever, a large weight such as a boulder can be moved. *See Archimedes principle.*

Archimedes principle

The Archimedes principle is the key to understanding buoyancy—that is, the amount of weight an object seems to lose when placed in liquid. Legend has it that Archimedes discovered this principle one day when he noticed how much water flowed over the tub as he sat down in his bath. He was so excited that he jumped out, completely naked, and ran through the streets shouting, "Eureka! I've got it!" *See Archimedes.*

archipelago

A sea containing a large group of islands is an archipelago. The islands themselves are sometimes also referred to as an archipelago.

architect

An architect designs buildings. Builders use the architect's plans in construction. Ancient Greek architecture, or style of building, has influenced architects throughout history.

architecture

The character and style of a building is its architecture. This term also refers to the profession of designing buildings. *See architect.*

Arctic Circle

The Arctic Circle is the imaginary boundary of the north polar region. It runs parallel to the equator at 66° 30' north latitude. *See equator, latitude, and North Pole.*

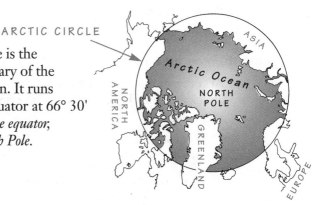

Arctic Ocean

The Arctic Ocean is the world's smallest ocean. It is located north of Asia, Europe, and North America. The North Pole is near the center of the Arctic Ocean.

are/our

▷ *Are* is a verb that forms the plural of *is*.

▷ *Our* is a possessive pronoun that shows ownership or belonging.

Example:

The movers are here to pick up our furniture.

See possessive pronoun and verb.

area

A number given in square units that indicates the size of the inside of a plane figure is called the *area*.

Example:

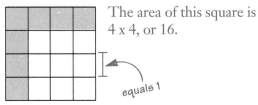

The area of this square is 4 x 4, or 16.

equals 1

argumentation

In writing, argumentation is the presentation of reasons and evidence in a logical way. Argumentative writing is meant to persuade the audience.

argumentum ad hominem

Argumentum ad hominem is a logical fallacy in which a person attacks the speaker or writer of an argument rather than the argument itself.

Example:

Suzie said that! Don't believe a word she says. Last month she told me what Dwayne said about me, and he said he didn't say it at all. And anyway, she's a Capricorn, and you know they can't be trusted.

See logical fallacy and poisoning the well.

aria

In opera, cantatas, and oratorios, the aria is a solo (usually of some length and requiring skilled singing) that expresses the feelings of the character in the developing story.

aristocracy

An aristocracy is a group of people who inherit or are awarded a high position in society. One reason for the French Revolution was that many people in France were poor and hungry, while the aristocracy led comfortable, privileged lives.

Aristotle

Aristotle (384–322 B.C.) was a Greek philosopher and teacher whose writings were concerned with logic, science, politics, ethics, metaphysics, and literary criticism. He studied with Plato in Athens and was later the teacher of Alexander the Great. *See Alexander the Great, Athens, and Plato.*

Armageddon

In the Bible, Armageddon is named as the place of the great and final battle between the forces of good and evil. The word is also used for any great and final conflict.

armistice

An armistice is a temporary peace or agreement by both sides in an argument, disagreement, or war to end fighting.

Armstrong, Neil

Neil Armstrong (b. 1930), one of the best-known American astronauts, was a member of the Apollo team that flew a spacecraft to the moon. On July 20, 1969, Neil Armstrong became the first person to set foot on the moon.

arraignment

At an arraignment, a criminal-court procedure, a person accused of a crime comes before a judge, hears the charges, and pleads guilty or not guilty.

artery

An artery is a blood vessel that carries blood away from the heart.

articles

The seven parts of the main body of the United States Constitution are the articles. Each of the articles gives rules for organizing the government and carrying out its business. For example, article 1 is about the legislative branch (law-making) and gives Congress the right (among many others) to print money.

artifact

Artifacts are objects made and used by people, especially clothing, tools, or weapons. Artifacts found from ancient times give us clues about how people lived long ago. *See archaeologist.*

arts and crafts

The term *arts and crafts* refers to the art of making handmade, often utilitarian, articles by weaving, woodworking, needlepoint, and the like. Most arts and crafts are hobbies, such as quilting. But at the highest levels, arts and crafts of any kinds—from basket weaving to metal work—are sometimes considered art.

Asia

Asia is the largest and most populated continent in the world. It is located between the Pacific Ocean to the east and Europe and Africa to the west. Almost three and a half billion people live in the forty-nine countries in Asia. The highest and lowest spots in the world are in Asia.

Asimov, Isaac

Isaac Asimov (1920-1992) wrote about 300 books and 1,000 magazine articles. He came to the United States from Russia when he was three years old, entered college at fifteen, and eventually received a doctorate in chemistry. He wrote primarily science fiction, including the *Foundation* series and a collection of short stories called *I, Robot*.

associative property

The associative property (sometimes called "the grouping property") states that the way in which numbers are grouped does not affect the sum or product.

Examples:

$$(7 + 2) + 5 = 7 + (2 + 5)$$
$$(7 \times 2) \times 5 = 7 \times (2 \times 5)$$

See product and sum.

assonance

Assonance is the repetition of similar vowel sounds followed by different consonant sounds in accented syllables.

Examples:

midnight ride

While in the wild wood I did lie,
A child—with a most knowing eye. (Edgar Allen Poe)

See rhyme.

asteroids

Asteroids are pieces of rock that orbit the sun. Most of them are found between the planets Mars and Jupiter. They may take up to five years to orbit the sun. Asteroids come in sizes as small as a finger to as large as 600 miles in diameter. Asteroids also are sometimes called "planetoids" or "minor planets."

astrolabe

An astrolabe is used to measure the angle
between planets and stars and the horizon.
Arabs used the astrolabe and passed it on to
the Europeans. The astrolabe helped sixteenth-century Europeans explore the New
World. The sextant later replaced the astrolabe.

astronomy

Astronomy is the study of space and the objects in it. Typically
astronomers study the origin of planets and the universe, the position and movement of planets, and composition of things in space.

asymmetry

The term *asymmetry* (the opposite of symmetry) means that
something—a figure or object—is not balanced or even.
It means that the sides are uneven or lopsided. *See
symmetry.*

atelier

An *atelier* is a French word for an artist's
workshop or studio.

Athena

In Greek mythology, Athena was the goddess of
wisdom, of household arts, and of war. Her
Roman name was Minerva.

Athens

Athens, the capital of Greece, is located in the southeastern part of
the country. In the 400s B.C., Athens was a powerful city-state and
the center of learning and culture for the ancient Western world.
Much of Western philosophy originated in Athens. Philosophers
such as Plato, Socrates, and Aristotle lived and worked there. *See
Aristotle, Greece, Plato, and Socrates.*

Atlantic Ocean

The Atlantic Ocean is the second largest ocean in the world. It is east of North and South America and west of Europe and Africa. It covers approximately 31.5 million square miles of the Earth's surface. *See ocean currents.*

atlas

An atlas is a reference book that features maps, tables, and charts. Atlases show the locations of cities and towns, rivers and lakes, and mountains and deserts. Atlases also present political boundaries. Historians credit Claudius Ptolemy, an Egyptian, with creating the first atlas in A.D. 1000. Flemish mapmaker Mercator was the first to call his set of maps an "atlas." *See reference.*

atmosphere

In writing, atmosphere is the mood the author creates. Atmosphere may be pleasant or unpleasant, funny or frightening. *See tone.*

atoll

An atoll is a ring-shaped coral island or group of islands partly enclosing a lagoon.

atom

An atom is the smallest particle of matter that cannot be divided chemically. Everything in the world is made up of atoms. Atoms themselves are composed of several different parts. The nucleus, or center of an atom, is made of particles called protons (which have positive electric charges) and neutrons (which have no electric charges). Electrons circle the nucleus and have negative electric charges. While most of an atom's mass is in its nucleus, most of any atom is empty space around the nucleus. *See electron, neutron, and proton.*

atom smasher

Atom smashers are used to discover new types of particles within atoms. To do that, scientists make some of the smaller parts within an atom move very fast. This is done within a large vacuum chamber that has a powerful electric field. The particles are made to spin rapidly inside the chamber and are then smashed into smaller particles within an atom. Scientists use large, powerful magnets that are able to focus the beams of particles.

atomic number

The atomic number is the number of protons in an atom. The periodic table of elements includes the atomic number for each element. *See periodic table.*

attorney general

The chief law officer of English-speaking countries is called the attorney general. In the President's cabinet, the Attorney General is head of the Department of Justice.

audience

In writing, the audience is those people who read a particular piece of writing. In a student newspaper, the audience would be other students. In a letter to a company about a product, the audience would be an adult who works for the company. A writer benefits from developing a clear sense of audience.

Audubon, John James

John Audubon (1785–1851) is known as one of the first nature conservationists. After being put in jail for bad debts, he traveled into the wilderness and began to paint pictures of birds. He completed more than 400 paintings, some of the most beautiful paintings of birds ever done.

Augustus

The first Roman emperor, Augustus (63 B.C.–A.D. 14) built new roads and encouraged development in towns and cities. Taking leadership in 27 B.C., he reigned at a time of peace and growth in the Roman empire. *See Ancient Rome.*

aurora

The glowing lights in the sky resulting from processes in the upper atmosphere is an aurora.

Auschwitz

Auschwitz, Poland, was the site of a Nazi concentration camp. During World War II, millions of Jews and other Europeans were forced into concentration camps where most died.

Austen, Jane

Jane Austen (1775–1817) was England's first great female novelist. Her stories, often set in small English towns, focused on women and their role in society. Her most famous novel is probably *Pride and Prejudice*.

Australia

Australia is both a continent and a country. It is the smallest continent and the sixth largest country in terms of area. Located between the South Pacific Ocean and the Indian Ocean, Australia lies entirely in the Southern Hemisphere. *See continent.*

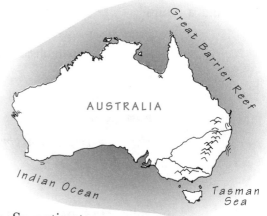

autobiography

An autobiography is a biography, a factual story about a person's life, written by that person. Benjamin Franklin, for instance, wrote a famous autobiography.

autumnal equinox

The first day of autumn is the autumnal equinox. On this day, both the Northern and the Southern Hemisphere have 12 hours of daylight and 12 hours of darkness.

avant-garde

A French term, *avant-garde* refers to a group of people, usually artists, who are ahead of their time in using or creating new ideas. Artists whose work is new or experimental are sometimes called "the avant-garde."

average

The number obtained by dividing the sum of two or more addends by the number of addends is the average.

Example:

If three people are aged 4, 6, and 11, their average age is

$(4 + 6 + 11) \div 3 = 7.$

See addend.

awhile/a while

▷ *Awhile* is an adverb.

▷ *A while* is a noun phrase most often used as an object of a preposition.

Example:

Burt pleaded awhile for Kim to stay for a while.

See adverb and prepositional phrase.

axes

In mathematics, axes are two intersecting perpendicular lines that are used for graphing.

axes

axis

An axis is an imaginary or real line that passes through an object and about which an object turns. An axis is often used to describe the way planets orbit and objects move. The axis of the Earth, for example, is an imaginary line running through the earth around which it rotates.

Aztec Empire

The Aztec Empire lasted from the 1400s through the early 1500s. Aztecs built temples and pyramids. They perfected the art of working with metal and were skilled in the use of herbs and plants for medicines. Mexico City now stands on the site of their capital city, Tenochtitlán.

B.C.

B.C. refers to before the time when Jesus is believed to have been born. To date an event in the time B.C., count backward from 1. The bigger the number is, the earlier in history the event happened.

Example:

Aristotle, the Greek philosopher, lived from 384 to 322 B.C.

See A.D.

Babbage, Charles

An English inventor and mathematician, Charles Babbage (1791–1871) first thought of the basic principles behind computers. His analytical engine, designed in the 1830s, was to complete complicated calculations to a series of instructions. Never built, the machine used a hand-powered series of toothed wheels hooked together by rods and links to make calculations. It would have been crude by today's standards, but it was designed to store bits of information that could be used later.

Babylon

Babylon was an ancient Mesopotamian city. Emperor Hammurabi made his capital here in the sixteenth century B.C. The Hanging Gardens of Babylon was one of the Seven Wonders of the Ancient World.

Bach, Johann Sebastian

Today, Bach is considered the outstanding composer of his time; but during his lifetime (1685–1750), he was acclaimed as the finest organist. His hundreds of compositions were largely ignored until rediscovered in the 1800s. His greatest compositions include *St. Matthew Passion, Mass in B minor,* the six *Brandenburg Concertos,* and a number of works for organ.

background

In art, the background is the section of a painting that appears to be farthest away. By contrast, the section of a painting that appears closest is called the foreground.

Bacon, Francis

Francis Bacon (1561–1626), a famous philosopher, is credited with helping establish the practice of experimenting. By writing about the value of "tinkering," he developed the idea of doing experiments to help someone learn more about a subject.

bacteria

Bacteria is a group of microscopic organisms that are classified as either monerans, having one cell without a nucleus, or protists, having characteristics of both plants and animals.

Bahama Islands

The Bahamas are a chain of about 3,000 islands in the West Indies that make up the independent country of the Bahamas. The Bahamas are located off the eastern coast of Florida. Only a few of the islands are inhabited, and about three-quarters of the people live on New Providence Island and Grand Bahama.

bail

When someone is accused of a crime and goes to jail, he or she usually has a chance to "post bail." That is, he or she can put up money or property in return for being let out of jail until the court hearing.

bait and switch

The term *bait and switch* refers to offering people a great deal at a low price, but then trying to sell them something much higher priced.

Example:

The offer "buy any book for 5 cents" sounds very good. But, if to get that deal, a person has to buy a set of 20 volumes of an encyclopedia for $100, then it is not a good deal.

balance of trade

The difference between the value of a country's imports and the value of its exports is its balance of trade. Countries try to have greater exports than imports to keep their economies healthy.

Balboa, Vasco Núñez de

Vasco Núñez de Balboa (1475?-1519) was a famous Spanish conquistador and explorer. In 1510 Balboa established the first Spanish settlement on the American mainland. Three years later, he explored west and was the first European to see the western shore of what is now the United States.

Baldwin, James

James Baldwin (1924-1987) wrote primarily about the role of black men in American life. His first novel, *Go Tell It on the Mountain*, was about growing up in Harlem, New York. His nonfiction included *Notes of a Native Son* and *The Fire Next Time*, both about race relations in the United States.

ballad

A ballad is a poem or song that tells a story in simple verse. *See verse.*

ballet

A ballet is a performance like a play with scenery and costumes, but it is performed with dancers and music. It began in French

royal courts in the fifteenth century. More recently, Russian, English, and American ballet companies have become famous for their performances.

ballot

The piece of paper, ticket, or object used in secret voting is a ballot. Registered voters go to polls (official places to vote), and make their choices known by marking a ballot. A ballot is also the name for a list of candidates for public office.

band

A band is an orchestra composed mainly of wind instruments. Types of bands include military bands, jazz bands, brass bands, or symphonic bands, which include a cello or a string bass.

bandwagon

The expression "to jump on the bandwagon" means to show support for something that is obviously popular. In the South during an election, a band occasionally went through the streets on a wagon to attract a crowd. Local leaders would jump on the wagon of the candidate of their choice.

banjo

A banjo is a stringed instrument used in popular music. It has a long neck and five or more strings that are plucked with the fingers. It was brought by slaves to America from west Africa.

barbiturate

A barbiturate is a depressant that promotes sleep and relaxation. A barbiturate calms a person down, but it can also become addictive so that he or she cannot stop using the barbiturate. A barbiturate produces an effect opposite to that of an amphetamine.

baritone

The term *baritone* describes a male voice of middle range.

barometer

A barometer is a weather instrument that measures air pressure. If a barometer indicates that the air pressure is dropping in a particular area, it usually means that a storm is approaching. Rising pressure, on the other hand, usually indicates that fine weather is ahead. *See air pressure.*

baroque

Baroque is a style of art and music common in Europe from the late 1500s to about 1750, following the Renaissance. This period featured elaborate ornamentation on a grand scale. Often people use the word *baroque* to mean "flowery" or "showy." *See Renaissance.*

barter

To barter is to trade by exchanging one kind of goods for another. When people barter, no money is exchanged. A farmer might barter with extra potatoes he or she has grown for shoes made by the shoemaker.

Barton, Clara

An American teacher and social reformer, Clara Barton (1821-1912) was known as the "Angel of the Battlefield." She worked as a nurse during the Civil War and eventually founded the American branch of the Red Cross in 1881.

base

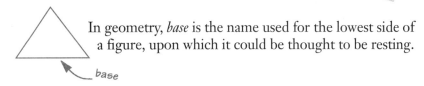

In geometry, *base* is the name used for the lowest side of a figure, upon which it could be thought to be resting.

base

base

In chemistry, a base is a compound that yields hydroxides when dissolved in water. Things like soaps and cleaning detergents contain bases. They all feel slick or slightly slippery. Bases are more or less opposites of acids. *See acid.*

bass

In music, a bass voice is the lowest male voice. It is the lowest part of a four-part quartet or choral work.

bass drum

A bass drum is a large drum that gives off a deep, low tone of no fixed pitch. Most bass drums are about three feet in diameter. This drum is usually held vertically and is played with a mallet with a wood, felt, or wool head.

basset horn

A basset horn is a musical instrument that looks like a long clarinet with an upturned end. *See clarinet.*

bassoon

The bassoon is the bass "voice" of the oboe (or double-reed) family of woodwind orchestral instruments. Its long tube

MORE NOTES →

holds a doubled pipe, and a small curved metal tube connects to the mouthpiece, which holds the double reed through which the player blows.

Bastille

The Bastille, a prison-fortress, used to stand in the heart of Paris. On July 14, 1789, angry French citizens started the French Revolution by storming the Bastille. Today Bastille Day, July 14, is an important French holiday.

Battle of Britain

The Battle of Britain (1940) is the name for the World War II air attack by the Nazis on England. Germany tried to weaken British air defenses before an invasion by bombing southern England continuously for 112 days. The outnumbered British air force saved Britain.

bazaar

The word *bazaar* comes from the Persian word for market. A bazaar is a marketplace, usually in the Middle East. A bazaar often has small, colorful, open shops and booths along a street.

Bede

Bede (673?–735) was an English scholar who is known as both "the father of English history" and "the Venerable Bede." It was Bede who introduced the custom of dating events from the birth of Christ. He also suggested that the calendar be revised because of his observations of the vernal equinox.

Beethoven, Ludwig van

Ludwig van Beethoven (1770–1827), a German, is one of the most famous composers of all time. He brought the classical style developed by Haydn and Mozart to its height. He wrote nine symphonies, five piano concertos, and many other compositions for both voice and instruments.

begging the question

Begging the question is a logical fallacy in which a person provides as evidence an assumption that needs to be proved.

Example:

Why do I think that Rick is a cheater? Because Rick is a cheater.

See logical fallacy.

Beijing

Beijing (also called Peking) is the capital of China. Located near the northeastern coast of the country, Beijing has been the center of government in China for most of the last thousand years. It is the transportation, financial, and political hub of China. *See China.*

Bell, Alexander Graham

Alexander Graham Bell (1847-1922), a Scottish-born American scientist, was a teacher of the deaf. He was especially interested in the way electricity could be used to transmit sound. After two years of experimentation, Bell and his assistant, Thomas Watson, successfully transmitted the human voice on March 10, 1876. While working on an instrument, Bell spilled something and cried out. Watson, who was upstairs, heard him at the other end of the phone line. Bell also experimented with sonar, a type of underwater radar.

bending light

Light bends when it moves from one material to another. Light, for example, travels faster through air than water.

Berlin

Berlin is the capital and largest city in Germany. Berlin was divided into East and West sectors in 1949 by communist forces occupying what became East Berlin. The city was reunited in December 1989 when the Berlin Wall was torn down. *See Berlin Wall and Germany.*

Berlin Airlift

After World War II, the Soviets disagreed with other Allied nations about national boundaries. As a part of their protest, in 1948 they cut off all supplies to Berlin in communist East Germany. Between June 1948 and May 1949, Allied airplanes saved the city by flying in food and other goods. This is commonly referred to as the Berlin Airlift. *See Berlin.*

Berlin Wall

The Berlin Wall was a fortified barrier that divided east and west Berlin. The communist government of East Germany built it in 1961 to keep its citizens from leaving for West Berlin, where people were free. Berlin was reunited in late 1989 when the Berlin Wall was torn down. Germany was reunited in 1990. *See Berlin.*

Bernoulli's principle

Daniel Bernoulli (1700–1782), a Swiss mathematician, discovered that the faster a fluid flows, the less pressure it exerts. Likewise, as the speed that a fluid flows slows down, the more pressure it exerts.

Bible

The Bible is a collection of writings viewed as sacred by believers. The Old Testament is sacred to the Jewish religion. This and the New Testament, a group of later writings, are revered by Christians. Muslims also respect the Bible.

bibliography

A bibliography is a list of writings and other materials related to a particular subject, historical period, or person. Bibliographies may also include notes about the subject, period, or person. An annotated bibliography summarizes the contents of the materials listed. Bibliographies are often required in research papers.

Big Bang Theory

The Big Bang Theory suggests that, between 10 billion and 20 billion years ago, the universe began in an enormous explosion—a "big bang"—and has continued to expand since. Scientists believe that the universe will either continue to expand indefinitely or will, at some point, begin to contract inward, which would ultimately result in another "big bang" and a whole new universe.

bilingual

The prefix *bi-* means "two." Someone who is bilingual can speak two languages. People who move to another country or live very near another country often become bilingual.

bill

A proposed law presented to a law-making body is a bill. The U.S. Constitution states the steps by which a bill can be made into a law. Most bills must pass a majority vote of both houses of Congress and be approved by the President.

Bill of Rights

The Bill of Rights is another name for amendments to the U. S. Constitution. Added when the Constitution was written, the Bill of Rights guarantees Americans basic liberties, such as freedom of speech and of religion. *See Constitution.*

The Constitution

binary code

A computer does not understand words and sentences. It only understands two numbers, 0 and 1. Here is the way some numbers look in binary code:

MORE ↗

number	binary code
1	0001
4	0100
6	0110

See computer.

biographer

A biographer is a writer of books about individual people. Biographers use many sources, such as letters, interviews, and diaries, to research their subjects. Carl Sandburg is a well-known biographer of Abraham Lincoln.

biography

A biography is a factual story about a person's life written by another author. *See biographer.*

biology

Biology is the scientific study of living things.

biosphere

The region on and surrounding the Earth—land, water, and atmosphere—that can support life is the biosphere.

bisect

In geometry, to bisect something is to divide it into two congruent, or equal, parts.

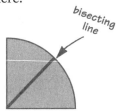

bisecting line

Bismark, Otto von

Otto von Bismark (1815–1898) was a German politician and head of the government. As the "Iron Chancellor," Bismark transformed a group of small German states into the unified empire of Germany in 1871.

bit

In computer jargon, a bit is one digit of information. Bit comes from the term "binary digit." *See binary code and byte.*

black codes

After the Civil War, many local southern governments were able to bypass state governments by enforcing numerous laws restricting the civil rights of blacks. These were referred to as "the black codes." These laws were used to govern the conduct of blacks by restricting what they did and where they did it.

Black Death

The Black Death was another name for the bubonic plague, which raged throughout Europe between 1347 and 1351. Living conditions were crowded and unclean. As much as one-fourth of the population died from the disease during this time.

black hole

Scientists believe that in some regions of space so much mass is concentrated exerting so much gravity that nothing—absolutely nothing, not even light—can escape. These "black holes" occur, some scientists believe, when a star collapses inward from its own weight.

bladder

The balloonlike sac at the base of the pelvis that holds urine is the bladder.

Blake, William

William Blake (1757–1827) was an English poet and artist. His most famous books, *Songs of Innocence* and *Songs of Experience*, include his watercolor illustrations as well as his poems.

blank verse

Blank verse is an unrhymed form of poetry that usually is written in iambic pentameter.

Example:

In Shakespeare's *Macbeth*, one of Malcom's speeches begins:

I speak not in absolute fear of you.

I think our country sinks beneath the yoke;

It weeps, it bleeds, and each new day a gash is added to her wounds.

See foot, free verse, poetry, and verse.

blew/blue

▷ *Blew* is a verb that forms the past tense of blow.
▷ *Blue* is a color.

Example:

The wind blew the blue awning from the window.

blitzkrieg

The word *blitzkrieg* is German for "lightning war." A blitzkrieg is a rapid, violent attack in war employing airplanes and tanks. The Nazis of Germany invented this technique during World War II.

bloc

A bloc is a group of people or nations that combine for a specific purpose. In the United Nations, a bloc of countries might unite to pass a resolution that meets their common needs—say, sending emergency aid to a country that suffered a disaster. Blocs change as interests and loyalties shift.

blood

Blood is made up of red and white blood cells and platelets located in plasma, a liquid that is about nine-tenths water. Arteries carry blood from the heart to provide oxygen to the body's cells. Veins remove carbon dioxide and other wastes and then return the blood to the heart. Scientists who study blood have noticed that these passages for carrying blood have valves, or gates, that only open one way, so the blood cannot flow backward. *See blood cells.*

blood cells

There are two types of blood cells: red cells and white cells.

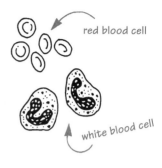

red blood cell

1. Red blood cells carry oxygen to all parts of the body. One microliter of human blood contains four to six million red blood cells.
2. White blood cells fight disease and infection.

white blood cell

See blood and cell.

blood pressure

Blood pressure is the force with which blood pushes against artery walls. *See artery and diastolic blood pressure.*

Blue and Grey

The Blue and the Grey were symbols for the opposing armies in the Civil War. The Union Army from the northern states wore blue uniforms. The Confederate Army from the southern states wore grey.

blues

"Blues" is a style of popular music, first heard about 1910 in New Orleans, with roots in spirituals and work songs. The blues are melodic and expressive and allow the singer or instrumentalist freedom to improvise.

boat people

People who take to the sea to escape harm or poverty in their own country are referred to as "boat people." In the 1970s, many

MORE ➔

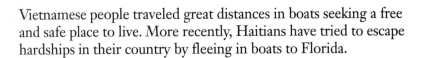

Vietnamese people traveled great distances in boats seeking a free and safe place to live. More recently, Haitians have tried to escape hardships in their country by fleeing in boats to Florida.

body

In a piece of writing, the body consists of the paragraphs between the introduction and conclusion. The body paragraphs present information to explain and support the central idea.

boiling points

When a liquid is heated, the molecules in that liquid move faster and faster. At a certain temperature (it varies depending upon the type of liquid and atmospheric pressure) bubbles of vapor or gas form and rise to the surface of the liquid. This process is known as boiling. These bubbles are the release of molecules from the liquid.

Bolívar, Simon

Simon Bolívar (1783–1830) was a South American revolutionary leader called "the Liberator." He led the early nineteenth-century fight that drove the Spanish out of South America. The country of Bolivia is named in his honor.

bones

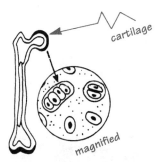

cartilage

magnified

When a baby is born, most of his or her bones are not hard yet. They are made of a soft, bendable tissue called *cartilage*. Bone cells within the cartilage use minerals to change the cartilage into hard bone tissue. Bones can grow longer because most of the change from cartilage to bone takes place at the tips, or ends, of the bones. A human's bones will continue to grow until a person reaches the ages of 16 to 22 years old.

boogie-woogie

Boogie-woogie is a style of instrument playing in which the left hand repeats a pattern of notes at different levels in a fast, rhythmic manner. It became popular in the 1930s.

boom town

A boom town is a community that grows very quickly because of sudden wealth. In the 1800s and early 1900s, people rushed to the American West when gold was discovered. The surge of people created boom towns that did not always survive when the wealth ran out.

Borges, Jorge Luis

Jorge Luis Borges (1899–1986) was an Argentine essayist and short story writer. Following the loss of his health and eyesight, Borges began writing narrative fantasies and fables, for which he is best remembered.

Borman, Frank

Frank Borman (b. 1928) commanded the *Apollo 8* flight that circled the moon on Christmas Day in 1968. In 1965 Borman, orbiting Earth in *Gemini 6*, made the first rendezvous in space.

Borneo

Borneo, the third largest island in the world, is located in Southeast Asia. It includes the country of Brunei and parts of Malaysia and Indonesia.

borrowed word

In English a borrowed word is a word adopted from another language and used widely. *Polka*, for example, is a borrowed word, as are *taco* and *typhoon*.

Boston

Boston is the capital city of Massachusetts and the chief seaport in the northeastern United States. The largest city in New England, it is the area's leading business and educational center. Because it was the birthplace of the American Revolutionary War, Boston is sometimes called the "Cradle of Liberty."

Boston Tea Party

The Boston Tea Party (1773) was one of the most famous colonial protests against English taxation. American colonists objected to England's taxes, especially a tax on tea. Dressed as Indians, they dumped a cargo of tea from an English ship into Boston Harbor. *See Boston.*

Botany Bay

The Australian bay where Captain James Cook landed in 1770 is Botany Bay. Cook, the first European to find Australia, claimed the east coast of Australia for England.

boundary

The border between states, countries, or other regions is a boundary. Sometimes boundaries are decided by surveyors who measure the land. Throughout history, disagreements between countries over boundaries have often been the cause of wars.

bourgeoisie

The group of people in any society who are neither very wealthy or very poor are known as *middle class* or the *bourgeoisie.* Towns-people in France during the Middle Ages enjoyed increased trade, made more money, and moved from the lower class up to the bourgeoisie.

bow

A bow is a thin, wooden stick used to play the violin, viola, cello, and other stringed instruments. It has a band of horsehair stretched its entire length, and this band is drawn back and forth across the strings of the instruments to produce the musical sound.

Boxer Rebellion

The Boxer Rebellion was the Chinese rebellion against foreigners in 1900. Chinese people felt that outside nations had placed unreasonable controls on their government. The Boxers, a secret society, killed many foreigners.

boycott

Refusal to buy or use goods in order to force others to take some action is a boycott. Before the Revolutionary War, American colonists boycotted English products to force England to change tax laws.

brackets

Brackets ([ ]) are punctuation marks most often used to enclose explanatory information within parentheses. Brackets are also used to enclose explanations within parenthetical material.

Example:

The awards ceremony was incredibly exciting (Natoia [an eighth grader] won the most valuable player award).

Bradbury, Ray

Ray Bradbury (b. 1920) is among the best-known writers of American science fiction. As a high school student, he founded and edited *Futuria Fantasia*, a magazine of science fantasy. His most famous novel is *Fahrenheit 451*. His collections of short stories include *The Martian Chronicles* and *The Illustrated Man*.

Brahms, Johannes

The compositions of Johannes Brahms (1833-1897) combined classic form with the spirit of Romanticism. He continued and further developed the symphonic form. He is best known for his four symphonies, *A German Requiem*, and many works for solo voice, chorus, and orchestra.

Braille, Louis

T U R N →

Louis Braille (1809-1852) was a French teacher and inventor.

An accident blinded Braille at the age of three. By the time he was fifteen, he developed a set of raised dots that blind people could read by touch. The Braille system is still in use today to help blind people read.

brain

The human brain controls all of the functions of the human body. It can handle thousands of sensory, regulatory, and thought processes per second. It is connected to the rest of the body through the spinal cord. Even though the brain is the most complex part of the body, it feels no pain at all. If a person's brain is cut, that person feels absolutely nothing.

brainstorming

In writing, brainstorming is the act of gathering and connecting ideas by thinking freely about the subject. Brainstorming with other people is often fruitful.

Brazil

Brazil is the largest country in South America in both population and area. Located on the Atlantic Ocean, it has the world's largest rain forest. The Amazon River flows eastward through Brazil. *See Amazon River and South America.*

breeder reactors

A breeder reactor is a nuclear reactor that produces at least as much fissionable material to use as energy as it burns up as energy.

brief

In legal matters, a brief is a written document that explains one side's position in a legal case.

bring/take

▷ *Bring* is a verb used when the motion is toward the speaker.
Example:
Bring that paper here, please.

▷ *Take* is a verb used when the motion is away from the speaker.
Example:
Take that garbage out to the curb, please.

Bronte, Emily

Emily Bronte (1818–1848), an English novelist and poet, wrote *Wuthering Heights.* She was the middle of three sisters, all of whom published novels in 1847.

bronze

Bronze is a metal alloy made up primarily of the elements copper and tin. It is used in statues and metal working because it is a harder substance than brass.

Bronze Age

The Bronze Age is a prehistoric period, following the Stone Age, during which people made and used bronze tools and weapons. Different civilizations went through a Bronze Age at different times. The earliest known Bronze Age began around 3000 B.C. in what is known as Thailand.

Brooks, Gwendolyn

Gwendolyn Brooks (b. 1917), the poet laureate of Illinois, published her first poem in her early teens. In 1950 she won the Pulitzer Prize for poetry. Her collections of poetry include *A Street in Bronzeville, Annie Allen,* and *The Bean Eaters.*

Browning, Elizabeth Barrett

Elizabeth Barrett Browning (1806–1861) was an English poet best remembered for her *Sonnets from the Portuguese.* She was married to Robert Browning, another English poet.

brush

Artists paint with a tool called a *brush*, which can be made of synthetic bristles or animal hairs. Brush tips can be pointed, flat, or rounded, and each type produces a different visual effect. Often the kind of brush that an artist uses is determined by the kind of paint he or she is using.

Buck, Pearl S.

Pearl S. Buck (1892–1973) was the first American woman to receive the Nobel Prize for Literature. Although she was born in the United States, she grew up in China where her parents were missionaries. Her most famous novel, *The Good Earth*, received the Pulitzer Prize for its portrayal of the lives of Chinese peasants.

Buddha

Buddha (563?–483 B.C.?) is the founder of Buddhism. The Indian prince Gautama gave up a life of luxury to become Buddha, "the enlightened one." Buddha preached self-discipline and universal brotherhood. *See Buddhism.*

Buddhism

Buddhism is a religion based on the teachings of Buddha. Beginning about 500 B.C., Buddha traveled through India preaching his belief about peace and brotherhood. Today many people in eastern Asia, as well as in other parts of the world, practice Buddhism. *See Buddha.*

bugle

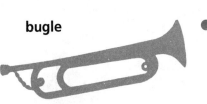

A bugle is a trumpet-shaped brass horn used mostly for signaling, as it can play only a limited number of notes.

bulimia

Bulimia is an eating disorder in which a person overeats and then forces vomiting or uses laxatives to rid the body of food. *See anorexia nervosa.*

Bull Run

The First Battle of Bull Run (1861) was the first real battle of the American Civil War. The South surprised the Union Army by winning this fight at Manassas, Virginia. The North realized then that the war would be longer and more difficult than expected.

Bunker Hill

Bunker Hill (1775) refers to the first major battle of the American Revolution, which actually took place on nearby Breed's Hill. In 1775, Colonial troops stopped the British near Boston. The Americans lost when their ammunition ran out, but they had proven themselves to be strong fighters against the better-armed British soldiers.

Burbank, Luther

Luther Burbank (1849–1926) was a botanist. He loved gardening and growing things. He studied the ways different types of plants could be bred so as to produce a completely new kind of plant (known as a "hybrid"). Some of the unusual plants he "invented" include the plumcot (a cross between a plum and an apricot) and the pomato (a cross between a potato and a tomato).

bureaucracy

A bureaucracy is an organization that involves many levels of workers. Authority is spread out over a number of people. Bureaucracy has come to mean inefficiency and "red tape," or too much petty detail, especially in government.

Burke, Robert O'Hara

An Irish soldier and police officer, Robert O'Hara Burke (1820–1861) emigrated to Australia. His 1860 expedition was the first by Europeans to cross the Australian continent. The difficulties of the trip, however, cost him his life.

Burns, Robert

Robert Burns (1759–1796) was a Scottish poet best known for his observations of and insight into the natural world and the life of the people of Scotland. He wrote or rewrote over two hundred songs in the Scots dialect.

Burton, Sir Francis

Sir Francis Burton (1821–1890) is remembered as a writer, translator, archaeologist, and explorer. Burton explored Arabia and Africa and wrote books about his adventures. While searching for the source of the Nile in 1858, he was the first European to see Lake Tanganyika.

bylaws

Clubs, companies, and other groups often write a constitution to describe their purpose and reason for existence. These laws or rules are an organization's bylaws.

Byrd, Richard Evelyn

Richard Evelyn Byrd (1888-1957) was a polar explorer and aviator. Byrd was the commander and navigator of the first flight over the North Pole in 1926. He also took part in several expeditions to Antarctica.

Byron, Lord

George Gordon Noel, Lord Byron (1788–1824), was an English Romantic poet. His most famous works are *Childe Harold's Pilgrimage* and *Don Juan*. He died at age thirty-six while attempting to help the Greeks in their war of independence against Turkey. *See romanticism.*

byte

In computer jargon, a byte is a unit of information that is eight bits long. *See bit.*

cabinet

A group of advisors chosen by a leader of a country is a cabinet. In the United States, cabinet members head departments of government. In a nation headed by a parliament, such as Great Britain, members of the cabinet have seats in Parliament.

Cabot, John

John Cabot (1450–1498?) was an Italian sailor and explorer who led an expedition for England to the eastern coast of what is now Nova Scotia. In his search for Asia, Cabot explored the eastern coast of North America. His 1497 findings established England's claims to land in the New World. *See Jacques Cartier.*

cactus

A cactus is a plant that has adapted to the harsh conditions of its environment, usually a desert. A desert receives no more than ten inches of rainfall each year. Some cacti shed leaves so they do not lose water. Others grow very wide or very deep roots to tap any available water. Mainly, however, cacti have adapted to living without much water.

cadence

A cadence is a series of notes or chords that ends either a melodic phrase, a section of music, or an entire composition. *See melody.*

cadenza

A cadenza is a challenging section of the soloist's part (usually just before the end of a vocal or orchestral work) during which the accompanying instruments are quiet, giving the soloist freedom to display his or her expressive and technical skill.

Caesar, Julius

A Roman general and statesman, Julius Caesar (100?–44 B.C.) greatly extended the Roman empire. He became dictator for life when he successfully concluded the 49–45 B.C. civil war. Fearing his power, enemies killed him on the "Ides of March" (the 15th).

Cairo

Cairo is the capital city of Egypt and the largest city in Africa. It is located on the Nile River in the northeastern part of Egypt. The Pyramids and the Sphinx, which were built by ancient Egyptians, are nearby. *See Africa, Egypt, and Nile River.*

calendar

Any system for keeping track of days, weeks, and months of the year is a calendar. Sometime between A.D. 250 and 900, the ancient Mayans had an accurate calendar. Today we use the Gregorian calendar, adopted in 1582 by Pope Gregory.

calisthenics

Calisthenics are exercises done using one's own body weight as resistance. Push-ups and sit-ups are examples of calisthenics. *See isometric exercise.*

call number

A call number is combination of numbers and letters given to every item of material a library owns. The materials in any library are organized according to call numbers so that the materials can be easily located. The two most common systems used to classify materials in libraries are the Dewey Decimal System and the Library of Congress System. *See catalog, Dewey Decimal System, and Library of Congress System.*

calligraphy

Calligraphy is very beautiful handwriting. People paint letters or symbols with brushes or pens to produce calligraphy. Muslims believe that since calligraphy displays the word of God, it is the highest art.

Calligraphy

Calligraphy   Calligraphy

calorie

A Calorie is a measure of the amount of energy in foods. In science, a calorie is the amount of energy needed to raise the temperature of one gram of water 1° Celsius.

calypso

Calypso is a type of singing that originated in the Caribbean islands. In calypso singing, the accent falls on weak syllables; for instance, you would sing "hel-lo" with the accent on the first syllable, not the last.

Canada

Canada is the second largest country in the world. Located north of the United States, it extends across North America from the Atlantic Ocean to the Pacific Ocean. Although it is larger than the United States, Canada has a population only about one-tenth as large. *See North America.*

canvas

In art, canvas is the fabric stretched across the frame on which an artist paints. Most canvas is a woven linen or cotton fabric. Painters use a canvas surface especially for oil and acrylic paints—that is, heavy paints.

canvass

Canvassing is calling on people in an area according to an organized plan, especially to ask for votes. Supporters of a political candidate often canvass a district to get an idea of how well their candidate will do in the upcoming election.

Cape Horn

The southernmost part of South America is Cape Horn. Before the Panama Canal was completed in 1914, ships traveling from one United States coast to the other had to sail thousands of miles around Cape Horn.

capillaries

Capillaries are very tiny blood vessels with thin walls. Capillaries are so small that red blood cells can go through them one at a time. When the red blood cells pass through a capillary, they release oxygen. The oxygen then enters the other cells outside the capillary walls. So many capillaries exist inside a person that almost every cell in the body is near a capillary.

capital/capitol

▷ *Capital* refers to a city, an upper-case letter, or money.
▷ *Capitol* refers to a building.

Example:

The Capitol is located in Washington, D.C., the capital of the United States.

capitalism

Capitalism is the economic system generally followed in the United States. In this system, buyers and sellers are free to decide upon the best price for goods and services. The government tries to stay out of business between two individuals or businesses. Capitalism encourages private—rather than government—ownership of land and businesses. In a noncapitalist system, the government tries to control prices and determine who gets certain goods and services.

capitalization

Capitalization is the use of capital letters. Although there are dozens of rules for capitalization, the general rules are:

1. Capitalize all proper nouns, abbreviations of proper nouns, proper adjectives, and any words used as proper nouns.
2. A capital letter begins every sentence.

See proper noun.

capital

carbohydrate

A carbohydrate is a nutrient that cells use for energy. The scientist who described the way food is broken down in the body and turned into energy is Hans Adolf Krebs. He won the Nobel prize for discovering "the Krebs cycle." It explained how tissues use carbohydrates to create acids and liberate energy.

carbonation

To create a carbonated beverage (soda pop, seltzer water, and so forth), carbon dioxide is pumped under pressure into the beverage. This causes the gas to dissolve in the liquid. When a can or bottle of liquid is opened, a fizzing sound occurs. This happens because the pressure on the liquid is lowered, thus allowing the gas to escape from the liquid.

cardiovascular fitness

Cardiovascular fitness is the ability to exercise for long periods of time because one has a strong heart, healthy lungs, and clear blood vessels. *See physical fitness and total fitness.*

cardiovascular system

The cardiovascular system consists of the heart and blood vessels. Ths system moves oxygen and nutrients to body cells and removes cell wastes.

caret

A caret (^) is a mark in a line of writing used to show that some word or phrase should be inserted at that point in the text.

caricature

A caricature is a drawing, something like a cartoon, that exaggerates and pokes fun at its subject.

Example:

An artist might draw extra-large ears on a subject known to have somewhat large ears.

Carnegie, Andrew

A Scottish-born American industrialist and philanthropist, Andrew Carnegie (1835-1919) achieved great success in business. In 1901 he sold his vast steel company and gave large amounts of money to educational and cultural organizations, such as libraries.

carnivores, herbivores, omnivores

Animals may be classified according to what they eat.

▷ *Carnivores:* Some animals, such as owls, lions, and sharks, only eat other animals. Thus, they are known as *carnivores.*

▷ *Herbivores:* Other animals, such as cows, chipmunks, and grasshoppers, only eat plants. These animals are known as *herbivores.*

▷ *Omnivores:* A third group of animals, known as *omnivores,* eats both plants and animals. Most humans are omnivores.

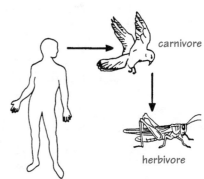

carnivore

herbivore

omnivore

carpetbagger

In the years after the American Civil War, a Northerner who went to the South for political or economic gain or to implement social change was a carpetbagger, so-called because of the type of suitcase he often carried.

Carson, Rachel

One of the most important science books of recent time, *Silent Spring* (1962), was written by scientist Rachel Carson (1907–1964). Carson described what would happen if humans kept poisoning the planet with pesticides such as DDT (used to kill insects). As a result of her book, people have encouraged lawmakers to pass legislation to outlaw dangerous chemicals and preserve plants and animal life.

For her book *The Sea Around Us*, Rachel Carson won the National Book Award. In it, she wrote, "The sea surrounds all humans. Ships cross it. Winds are born on the sea and return to their place of birth. The continents dissolve in the seas and the rains rise from those seas and return the grains back to where they came."

Carthage

Carthage was an ancient city-state of North Africa. Between 264 and 146 B.C., Rome and Carthage fought over control of the Mediterranean Sea. Rome destroyed Carthage in the last of three long and bloody wars.

Cartier, Jacques

Jacques Cartier (1491?–1557), French navigator and explorer, claimed eastern Canada for France in 1534. This duplicated John Cabot's 1497 claim for England and would later cause conflict between England and France. *See John Cabot.*

cartilage

The tough, elastic, flexible material that covers bones in joints to prevent friction and absorb vibrations is cartilage. *See bones.*

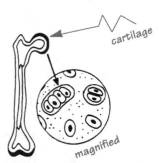

cartilage

magnified

Carver, George Washington

Born into slavery, George Washington Carver (1864–1943) was orphaned soon after his birth. He was raised by his "owner," Moses Carver, who saw to it that George Washington Carver received an education. Eventually Carver began teaching at the Tuskegee Institute in Alabama and became director of Agricultural Research. He devoted himself to finding ways to conserve and enrich land so that it would be suitable for farming. He also became well known for finding a wider variety of uses for common crops. He found, for example, more than two hundred ways to use peanuts, a common crop in the South.

case

Case is the term used for the change in the form of English nouns and pronouns depending upon how the word is used in relation to other words in a sentence. There are three cases of pronouns:

> Nominative case: I, she, they
> Objective case: me, her, them
> Possessive case: my, hers, their

Examples:
I asked her to give them his number.
She asked me to tell her their addresses.

cash crop

A crop that is grown in quantity to be sold for a profit rather than for use on a farm is a cash crop. Soybeans, for example, are often grown for the cash they bring when sold rather than for use on the farm where they're grown.

caste system

The caste system is one in which people are ranked and separated by means of livelihood and birth. A person born to a family of priests and scholars would enjoy that status—as would his or her children. This system developed most clearly in India. By tradition, a Hindu is born into a caste and cannot change his or her position.

catalog

In a library, a catalog is a list of materials that the library owns. Titles, subjects, and authors are listed alphabetically in the catalog. The catalog may be on cards located in drawers (a card catalog) or on a computer.

cathedral

The church of a Roman Catholic, Eastern Orthodox, or Episcopal bishop is a cathedral. In the Middle Ages, whole European communities worked for years to build grand cathedrals. Romanesque-style churches have rounded arches. Gothic-style cathedrals use pointed arches.

Cather, Willa

Willa Cather (1873–1796) was an American writer whose novels often grew out of her memories of her childhood spent on a ranch in Nebraska. Her novel, *One of Ours*, a story of World War I, won a Pulitzer Prize in 1923. *Death Comes to the Archbishop* (1927), a story about the Catholic Church in New Mexico, is often considered her masterpiece.

Catherine the Great

The Empress of Russia from 1762 until her death in 1796, Catherine the Great increased the boundaries of Russia. She encouraged European influence on Russian arts and culture.

caucus

A caucus occurs when members of a political party meet to make plans, choose candidates, or decide how to vote.

Cavendish, Henry

Henry Cavendish (1731-1810), an English physicist, became famous for discovering composition of water, properties of hydrogen, and many fundamental laws of electricity. He also determined the gravitational constant and density of Earth. His personal life, however, was almost as interesting as his scientific discoveries. He rarely spoke to anyone because he was so shy and usually communicated with people through notes. Even though he was well-off financially, he devoted himself solely and completely to science. For his devotion, Cavendish is remembered as one of the great scientists of all time.

cede

To cede means "to give something up to someone else."

Example:

In 1819 John Quincy Adams, then James Monroe's secretary of state, convinced Spain to cede part of Florida to the United States.

cell

A cell is the smallest living part of an organism. The word cell comes from the Latin word cella, meaning "small room." An English scientist by the name of Robert Hooke used the word to describe the structure of cork. Later the word cell was picked up to describe the small structures of all living things. Groups of cells that work together to do a special job in the body are known as tissues.

cell membrane

The cell membrane is a thin structure, usually two-layered, that regulates substances moving into and out of the cell. *See cell.*

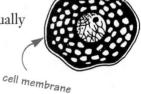

cell membrane

cell theory

Cell theory states that all living organisms are made up of cells, that the cell is the basic unit of structure, and all cells are formed from other living cells. *See cell.*

cell tissue

Millions and millions of cells make up the human body. Groups of cells that work together to do a special job in the body are known as tissues. For example, bone and muscles are tissues. Each of these tissues has a special function in the body. *See cell.*

cell waste

As cells work, they create wastes. It is important for the body to get rid of these wastes so that it can function properly. The part of the body that helps get rid of waste is the excretory system. The lungs are part of this system. They help get rid of carbon dioxide from the air an organism breathes. The skin gets rid of water and salt, and the kidneys help get rid of nitrogen wastes.

cello

The full name for the cello is *violoncello.* It is the baritone voice in the five-voice violin family in an orchestra, and is played with a bow. It is about twice the length of a violin and rests on the floor.

cellulose

Cellulose is a carbonate substance—made up of carbon, hydrogen, and oxygen—that makes up the major part of the cell walls of most plants. *See cell and plant cell.*

Celsius

Anders Celsius (1701–1744), an astronomer, devised the Celsius thermometer and temperature scale of one hundred degrees between the boiling point and the freezing point of water. This is now the scale used by scientists everywhere.

census

An official count of people in a country or a region is a census. The United States government takes a census every ten years. The first U.S. census in 1790 counted almost 4 million people. In 1890

MORE

the population had grown to about 63 million, and today the United States has about 249 million people.

centimeter

A centimeter is a unit of length in the metric system. A person's little finger is about one centimeter wide.

 centimeter

Central America

Central America is the narrow strip of land at the southern end of South America that connects North America and South America. Central America runs from Mexico in the north to Colombia in the south. It includes the countries of Guatemala, Belize, El Salvador, Honduras, Nicaragua, Costa Rica, and Panama.

central idea

The central idea is the main point of a piece of writing. Although the central idea may be implied, it is generally presented clearly in a thesis statement or topic sentence. See thesis statement and topic sentence.

Central Intelligence Agency (CIA)

The Central Intelligence Agency (CIA) is a federal agency that gathers and evaluates information for various parts of the government, including the President of the United States. The information helps the President make decisions involving other countries.

centrifugal force

Centrifugal force is a force that makes something moving around a center to move away from the center.

Example:

If a marble is put on a table, a glass jar is placed over the marble, and the glass is moved in a circle and then lifted, the marble will not fall out immediately. This is because of centrifugal force.

ceramics

Ceramics is the art of making clay or similar objects by baking them at very high temperatures in a kiln, a type of oven. Any clay or porcelain works are also called ceramics.

cerebellum

The cerebellum is the part of the brain that controls muscle coordination and balance. *See cerebrum.*

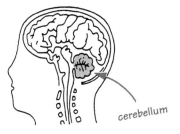

cerebellum

cerebrum

The cerebrum, like the cerebellum, is a part of the brain. In fact, the cerebrum is the largest part of the human brain. It receives and interprets nerve impulses from sense organs, directs movements, and controls thinking, imagining, and decision-making.

chanson

The term *chanson* is the French word for song. In several forms, it has been popular since the eleventh century.

character

A character is a person in a story or play.

Example:
Scout is a character in *To Kill a Mockingbird*.

See characterization.

characterization

A writer's characterization is his or her development of a character's personality in a play or story. Characterization may be shown through dialogue and action, through the character's words and deeds. *See character.*

charcoal

Artists will often sketch their drawings first with charcoal, a black crayon made of charred wood. Use of charcoal dates back to Roman times. Because the black charcoal easily comes off, artists began to use it as a first step in making drawings or sketches. Now artists use soft pencils for the same purpose.

Charlemagne

Charlemagne (742–814), king of the Franks, ruled most of Christian Europe at one time. In 800, Pope Leo III crowned him the Emperor of the Romans, which eventually led to the title Holy Roman Emperor. Charlemagne made many educational and political reforms in western Europe.

Chaucer, Geoffrey

Geoffrey Chaucer (1340?–1400) was the first great English poet. His most famous work is *The Canterbury Tales*. When he died, he was buried in Westminster Abbey in the area that later became known as Poets' Corner.

checks and balances

A system of checks and balances lets each branch of a government check, or limit, the actions of the other branches. The United States has a government with a system of checks and balances. The authors of the Constitution planned this so that no one branch would become too powerful.

chiaroscuro

In art, the Italian word *chiaroscuro*, an Italian word meaning "clear/dark," refers to a technique used in drawing or painting. The artist uses light and shade to achieve a three-dimensional effect. This effect was made famous by the Italian painter Leonardo da Vinci.

Chicago

Chicago is the third largest city in the United States. Located on Lake Michigan in northeastern Illinois, Chicago is one of the nation's leading industrial and transportation centers. See Great Lakes.

Chichen Itza

Chichen Itza is one of many ancient Mayan cities in Central America. About A.D. 950, Chichen Itza was attacked and taken over by the toltec, people from the central highlands of Mexico. Toltec rule collapsed around A.D. 1200. Today, a huge ceremonial pyramid remains in Chichen Itza from the Mayan period. Descendants of the Maya still farm in the area.

China

China is the world's most populous country. It is located in East Asia. About one-fifth of all the people in the world live in China. See East Asia and Beijing.

chip

A chip is an integrated circuit in a computer. It is called a chip because it is made from a tiny fragment of silicon.

chisel

In sculpture, a chisel is used to carve or chip away the material to shape the finished work of art. Most chisels are made of tempered (hardened) steel. Artists hit the chisel with a hammerlike mallet, cutting away a part of the material to make a sculpture.

chivalry

Chivalry is the name for rules of behavior for knights in the Middle Ages. Among the ideal qualities of chivalry were bravery, courtesy, and helpfulness. Young men were trained in the code of chivalry before they could become knights.

chlorophyll

The green material in plants that absorbs energy from the sun is chlorophyll. In addition to absorbing light, the chlorophyll is responsible for changing light energy into chemical energy. *See cell and plant cell.*

chlorophyll is contained in chloroplast

chloroplast

chloroplast

The small body in a green plant cell that contains chlorophyll and where photosynthesis occurs is chloroplast. *See cell and plant cell.*

cholesterol

Cholesterol is a fatty substance found in all animal cells and, therefore, in such foods as dairy products and egg yolks. *See fats.*

choose/chose

▷ *Choose* is a verb that means to select.

▷ *Chose* is a verb that forms the past tense of choose.

Example:

I chose the first time so now it is your turn to choose.

chorale

A chorale is a hymn in the tradition of the German Protestant church, founded by Martin Luther (1843–1546). To encourage congregational participation, Luther wrote many chorales whose texts were in the language of the people, with tunes often drawn from folk melodies, though some were his own compositions.

chord

In geometry, a chord is a line segment with both endpoints on a curve. A diameter is a special kind of chord. *See diameter.*

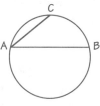

$\overline{AB}$ and $\overline{AC}$ are chords

chord

In music, a chord is a group of two or more notes sounded at the same time.

chorus

A chorus is a group of singers, typically with more than one singer to each vocal part: soprano, alto, tenor, bass.

Christianity

Christianity is religion based on the teaching of Jesus of Nazareth. The Bible, both the Old and the New Testaments, is the sacred book of Christianity. Today Christianity is practiced widely, especially in Europe and the Americas. *See Bible.*

chromatic

A term based on the Greek word *chroma* (color), *chromatic* describes a scale of twelve semitones, or a musical work that uses tones in addition to the seven that make up the diatonic scale.

chromosome

A chromosome is a structure made up of DNA (a molecule that carries genetic code) and proteins. The chromosomes are found in the nucleus of a cell. A chromosome, for example, determines hereditary characteristics including whether a person is male or female.

chronology

Chronology is the placement of events in the order of time—the order in which the events occurred. In narrative writing, events are usually presented in chronological order.

Churchill, Winston

British statesman, prime minister, and Nobel Prize-winning author, Winston Churchill led the British during most of World War II. He inspired the British with his eloquent speeches and his determination to resist Nazi Germany. He was not only a highly respected political leader but also an outstanding writer and speaker.

cilia

Cilia are hairlike projections on some cells that help some organisms move. They also line the inside of the lungs. As the cilia move, they help clean foreign particles out of the respiratory system.

circle

A circle is a closed, curved line on which all points are the same distance from a given point called the *center*.

circumference

The distance around a circle is the circumference. The formula for finding the circumference of a circle is c=2πr or c=πd (where r is the radius and d is the diameter). *See diameter and radius.*

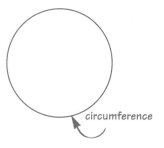

circumference

cirrus clouds

Cirrus clouds are thin, feathery clouds made of ice crystals. Another common type of cloud is cumulus, which are rounded on the top and flat on the bottom.

citizen

A citizen is a person who is by birth or by choice a member of a particular nation. For example, a person born in America becomes an American citizen. Citizenship means that the person owes the nation loyalty, and the nation guarantees certain rights.

city planner

A city planner is hired by a community to help solve such problems as housing, land use, traffic, and transportation. Understanding the past helps city planners propose solutions for the future.

city-state

A city-state is an independent state that is made up of a city and the nearby territories that depend on it. Ancient civilizations often formed themselves into city-states. Athens and Sparta were two famous city-states in ancient Greece. *See Athens.*

civics

Civics is the study of the duties, rights, privileges, and responsibilities of citizenship.

civil disobedience

Refusal to obey a law that one thinks is unjust is civil disobedience. It can often take the form of nonviolent public protest. In the 1950s, for example, black civil rights workers sat in places that were closed to them because of segregation laws. Henry David Thoreau, the author of *Walden*, went to jail in the 1840s for refusing to pay a tax to support the Mexican War. Mahatma Ghandi used it very effectively to help India gain its independence from Great Britain in 1945, and Martin Luther King, Jr., used civil disobedience to protest discrimination against blacks in America in the 1950s and 1960s.

civil liberty

Civil liberties are the freedoms that people are entitled to under a country's laws. People are entitled to these rights without restriction. For example, in America a person's race or sex in no way disqualifies him or her from the right to vote.

civil rights

Rights granted to citizens of the United States by the Constitution are civil rights. In the 1950s, black

CONTINUED

Americans and their supporters started the civil rights movement, because these rights were being denied to them.

civil service

Civil service refers to occupations not in the military services but in the government by appointment. A person whose career is in government—for example, someone who collects taxes—is called a civil servant.

civil war

In a civil war, opposing groups within one nation wage war against each other. The American Civil War (1861–1865) was the war between the northern and southern states. The issues that led to the war were an individual's right to be free of slavery and a state's right to secede from the Union.

civilization

The term *civilization* refers to the advanced stage of human life in which people have cities and organized governments. Usually historians talk about how advanced or primitive a civilization is. Stone-Age civilization was quite primitive—no cities, little culture, and so forth. Our current civilization is quite advanced; it has many complex organizations, cities, governments, and arts.

clarinet

The clarinet, a member of the woodwind group of orchestral and band instruments, comes in several sizes. All are tube-shaped with a single-reed mouthpiece and holes along the front that the player opens and closes with keys to create the melody.

classicism

Classicism is the term used to refer to architecture and art created during ancient Greek and Roman times, or more recent art that harkens back to that time. Balance, simplicity, elegance, and harmony are key elements in any classical art.

clause

A clause is a group of words that has a subject and predicate and is used as part of a compound or complex sentence. A clause may be independent or subordinate (dependent). Noun clauses, adjective clauses, and adverb clauses are types of subordinate clauses.

Example:

independent clause

When Cori opened the window, the bee flew into the room.

subordinate
clause

clay

Clay is a natural substance from the Earth that is soft and moist but also plastic—that is, it can be shaped but does not fall apart in one's hands. Potters use clay to create objects that can be fired to a hardened state using a kiln.

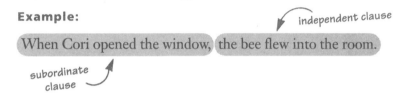

G-clef, circles
around the G

F-clef, circles
around the F

clef

A clef is a sign at the beginning of a musical staff. It indicates the pitch of the notes for that staff. Most common today is the G-clef for the upper staff, and the F-clef for the lower.

Clemens, Samuel Langhorne (Mark Twain)

Samuel Langhorne Clemens (1835–1910) was the author of *The Adventures of Huckleberry Finn*, often considered the finest novel ever written by an American. Among his other books are *The Adventures of Tom Sawyer* and a memoir, *Life on the Mississippi*. His tales about the Middle West and the American frontier and his humor and wit gained him worldwide fame.

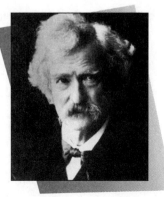

cliché

Any word or phrase that has been overused is a cliché. Avoid cliches because they tend to have lost their original meanings.

Example:
It rained cats and dogs.

climate

Climate is the characteristic weather in a region over a period of years. On the Earth, there are twelve major kinds of climates:

- tropical wet
- highlands
- steppe
- subtropical moist
- continental moist
- polar

- tropical wet and dry
- desert
- subtropical dry summer
- oceanic moist
- subarctic
- icecap

The United States mostly has areas with temperate and dry climates. In Antarctica, a polar climate, temperatures plunge to -94° Fahrenheit or lower.

climax

The climax is the turning point or highest emotional point in a story. Everything in a story builds toward the climax. The turning point is sometimes called a technical climax. The highest emotional point is sometimes called a dramatic climax. *See plot.*

clustering

In writing, clustering is the grouping of ideas and details during prewriting. Ideas are connected by circles and lines so that the relationship among the ideas and details becomes clear.

Example:

See prewriting.

clustering

In mathematics, clustering is an estimation method used when all of the numbers are close to the same number.

Example:

To estimate 28 + 32 + 26, one might decide all of the numbers cluster around 30, and 3 x 30 is about 90. (The actual sum is 86.)

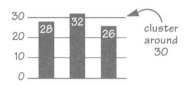

coalition

When two or more interest groups join together to work for a common goal, the combined group is a coalition.

Example:

The interests of farmers and of another group, for example, Hispanics, may be in common on one issue. When the two groups join together, they are called a coalition.

cocaine

Cocaine is a stimulant that can cause anxiety or aggressiveness, followed by feelings of depression or confusion. It is highly addictive, meaning that once a person starts taking cocaine, his or her body begins to depend on it. Cocaine causes a number of physical problems, including a deterioration of the lining of the nasal passages.

Code of Hammurabi

About 1800 B.C., Emperor Hammurabi put together one of the earliest known systems of written law, which came to be known as the Code of Hammurabi. Hammurabi's Code was an important step forward for civilization.

coherence

In writing, coherence is the clear, logical arrangement of ideas and evidence, which enables the audience to follow easily from one point to the next.

cold war

An undeclared conflict is referred to as a "cold war."

Example:

Distrust grew between the Soviet Union and the United States after World War II. The United States and Great Britain disagreed strongly with the aggressive Soviet actions in Europe after the war, such as controlling all of Berlin. The result was a long "cold war" in the 1950s marked by distrust and suspicion on both sides.

Coleridge, Samuel Taylor

Samuel Taylor Coleridge (1772–1834) was an English poet and literary critic. His poems "The Rime of the Ancient Mariner" and "Kubla Khan" are considered masterpieces of romantic poetry.

collective noun

A collective noun is a noun that names a group.

Examples:

- team
- troop
- Congress
- club
- band

Even though a collective noun refers to more than one person, it is treated as singular.

Example:

The band plays quite nicely.

colloquialism

A colloquialism is a word or phrase used primarily in conversation rather than in writing. Colloquial expressions are appropriate in speech and informal writing but not usually in formal writing. *See idiom and slang*.

colon

A colon (:) is a punctuation mark most often used before a list or a long quotation or statement. A colon often means "note what follows." Colons are also used to separate independent clauses when the second clause explains the first. Other uses of the colon include separating the hour and minute in the writing of the time (2:30), and after the salutation of a business letter (Dear Sir:).

colony

A colony is a group of people who have emigrated from their own country to another land but remain citizens of their original country.

Example:

The people who emigrated to the New World from England in the 1700s formed colonies here, but they remained citizens of England.

color

Light travels in wavelengths, and any light contains wavelengths of all colors. In fact, when light is broken apart by a prism, it looks like a rainbow. Even the color white, when broken apart, looks like a rainbow. Colors are produced because any surface absorbs some wavelengths of light and reflects back others. In a color, then, we see the part of the light that is reflected back, not the part of the light that is absorbed.

The primary colors are red, blue, and yellow. Other colors are produced by mixing two or more of the primary colors. The chart below shows some of the main colors that can be made by mixing two primary colors.

- green (blue and yellow)
- purple (blue and red)
- orange (red and yellow)

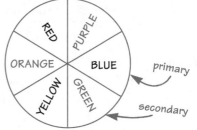

Green, purple, and orange, the colors produced by mixing two primary colors, are secondary colors.

color spectrum

A spectrum is a rainbow-colored band of light. The colors of the spectrum are arranged according to their wavelengths or frequencies. Colors in a spectrum appear in the following order:

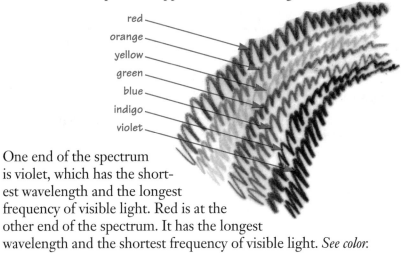

red
orange
yellow
green
blue
indigo
violet

One end of the spectrum is violet, which has the shortest wavelength and the longest frequency of visible light. Red is at the other end of the spectrum. It has the longest wavelength and the shortest frequency of visible light. *See color.*

Colorado River

The Colorado River is a large North American river flowing from northern Colorado into the Gulf of California. The Grand Canyon is located on the Colorado River in Arizona.

Colosseum

The Colosseum was a Roman arena completed in A.D. 80. Gladiators, men who fought for sport in ancient times, battled each other or with wild animals for the entertainment of the people who came to the Colosseum to watch. Today the ruins of the Colosseum can still be seen in Rome.

Columbus, Christopher

Christopher Columbus (1451–1506), an Italian navigator who led an expedition for Spain, landed in the Bahamas in 1492 while searching for a sea route to India. He is credited with being the first European to return home with descriptions of the new land.

comedy

A comedy is a piece of writing, especially a play, that points out the absurd in human behavior and usually ends happily. Although a play does not have to be funny to be considered a comedy, most comedies use humor to amuse and entertain the audience. Shakespeare's *A Midsummer's Night's Dream* is a comedy, as is Neil Simon's *The Odd Couple*.

comets

Comets are balls of frozen gases, ice, and dust that race through space. The tail of a comet can extend more than 100 million miles—the distance between the Earth and the sun.

comma

A comma (,) is the most frequently used punctuation mark. It generally groups words that are related and separates them from words that are not related. Commas are used in a variety of ways.

1. separating words or phrases in a series (Minda enjoys sailing, hiking, and jogging.)
2. setting off long introductory phrases (Wondering what to do about the problem, Judy asked Mary for advice.)
3. separating independent clauses joined by a conjunction (David went to the game, but he was too upset to enjoy it.)
4. separating two or more adjectives preceding a noun or pronoun (The large, dark mansion frightened the children.)
5. setting off unessential phrases in a sentence (Tom, an avid photographer, took pictures of the Grand Canyon.)
6. separating items in addresses (Miami, Florida) and dates (October 1, 1949)

commerce

Commerce is another term for buying and selling merchandise.

common denominator

A common multiple of two or more denominators is called a *common denominator.*

Example:

The common denominator of 1/2 and 1/5 is 10 (1/2 x 1/5 = 1/10).

Common Market

The Common Market is a group of European countries, organized in 1958, for the purpose of trading freely across borders. By 1962, the Common Market (now called the European Community, or EC) had become the largest trading bloc in the world.

common noun

A common noun is a noun that does not name a particular person, place, thing, or idea.

Examples:

- woman
- town
- door

See noun and proper noun.

communications

The means of sending information—whether by computer, fax machine, radio, television, newspaper, magazine, telephone, book, or talking—from one place to another is called *communications.*

communism

Communism, like capitalism, is an economic system. In communism, most or all property is owned by the government and shared by all. The former Soviet Union and China are among the countries in this century that have practiced some form of communism.

The Communist Manifesto

The Communist Manifesto is the name of a book written in 1848 by Karl Marx. He described a society in which government owns everything and all people share the wealth equally. After the Russian Revolution of 1917, founders of what became the USSR based their government on his ideas.

commutative property

The commutative property (or order property) states that the order in which numbers are added or multiplied does not affect the sum or product.

Examples:

$$4 + 6 = 6 + 4$$
$$4 \times 6 = 6 \times 4$$

compare/contrast

The word *compare* is used to show similarities. The word *contrast* to show differences.

Examples:

We compared the color of the leaves.

Today we will contrast the sizes and shapes of the two animals.

compass

A compass shows direction—north, south, east, and west. The first compass was a magnetized needle floating on cork in water. Because the needle always pointed north, it could guide early explorers and traders on land or sea.

compass

In mathematics, a compass is an instrument used for drawing circles. It has two legs: one with a sharp point and one that holds a pencil. When a person places the sharp point on a piece of paper, and then moves the end with the pencil around in a circle, a perfect circle appears on the paper.

compensation

Compensation is a term for adding or subtracting from a number so that it is easier to use when computing. It also assumes that the answer is then altered to make up for the earlier changes.

> **Example:**
>
> 113 + 107 can be compensated for as 110 + 100, which is 210. Then, the additional adjustment for the compensation involves adding back the 3 + 7, making the total 220.

complement/compliment

A *complement* is something that completes or serves as a counterpart. A *compliment* is a statement of praise.

> **Examples:**
>
> Because Greg works fast and Ella is careful, they complement each other in their work.
>
> They received a compliment for their work.

complex sentence

A complex sentence is a sentence that has one independent clause and one or more subordinate (dependent) clauses.

> **Example:**
>
> dependent clause
>
> The catcher, who has a strong arm, threw the ball to second base.

See clause, independent clause, and subordinate clause.

composition

A composition is a unified piece of writing that presents ideas and evidence.

compound noun

A compound noun is a noun of more than one word.

Examples:
Chicago Bulls
best-seller
junior high school

compound sentence

A compound sentence is a sentence with two or more independent clauses but no subordinate (dependent) clauses.

Example:
The catcher threw the ball to second base, but the base runner slid under the tag.

See clause, independent clause, and subordinate clause.

compound subject

A compound subject is made up of two or more subjects that have the same verb and are joined by a conjunction.

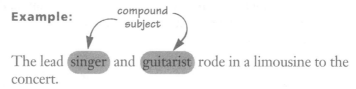

The lead singer and guitarist rode in a limousine to the concert.

See conjunction and subject.

compound verb

A compound verb is made up of two or more verbs that have the same subject and are joined by a conjunction.

Example:
The police surrounded the house and telephoned the people inside.

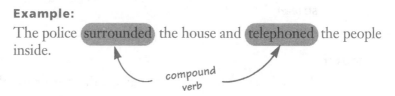

See conjunction and verb.

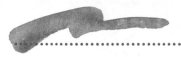

compound-complex sentence

A compound-complex sentence is a sentence that has more than one independent clause and one or more subordinate (dependent) clauses.

Example:

The catcher, who has a strong arm, threw the ball to second base, but the runner, who was exceptionally fast, slid under the tag.

See clause, independent clause, and subordinate clause.

compression

To compress something is to reduce its volume.

Example:

When someone takes a handful of snow and packs it together in the form of a snowball, he or she compresses it.

compromise

In a compromise, two sides settle an argument by each giving in a little. If each person gives up part of what is wanted, the two parties can reach an agreement sooner. The "giving in a little" is called *compromise*.

Compromise of 1850

The Compromise of 1850 was a series of acts passed by Congress that tried to please both proslavery and antislavery groups: California became a free (nonslave) state; the Utah and New Mexico territories were allowed to decide for themselves to become free or slave states; the slave trade was banned from the District of Columbia; and the Fugitive Slave Laws were made stricter.

computer

A computer is an electronic machine that performs calculations and processes, stores, retrieves, and produces information. The first working computer filled an entire room and weighed as much as thirty tons. No single person invented the computer. Charles

Babbage, a mathematician, developed the idea of a computer, and because of this he is sometimes referred to as "the grandfather of computers." *See Charles Babbage.*

computer science

Computer science is the study of computers and computer programming. *See computer and program.*

concerto

A concerto is a composition (usually of three sections or movements) for a solo instrument and an orchestra. The soloist and orchestra take turns in being featured, but there is always a place for the soloist to display outstanding skills in the "cadenza." See cadenza.

conclusion

A conclusion is the ending of a piece of writing. The conclusion, often a paragraph, ties together different parts of the composition or summarizes the information presented or brings the composition to a close—or does all three at once.

concrete noun

A concrete noun is a noun that names something that can be seen, heard, touched, smelled, or tasted.

Examples:
- television
- table
- pizza

See noun.

condensation

The process in which a gas changes into a liquid is condensation. The moisture that appears during this process is also called condensation.

Example:

Moisture in the air condenses into water droplets, or dew, under the right temperatures.

conduction

The movement of heat from one molecule to the next is conduction.

Example:

A gas stove, when turned on, heats gas that burns. A pot or pan that touches the flame heats the molecules in the pan, and these in turn heat the molecules of the food in the pan.

conductor

A conductor is the leader of an orchestra, band, or chorus. He or she guides the music's speed (tempo), rhythm, and loudness or softness, by facial expressions and motions of hands or a baton. *See orchestra.*

cone

A cone is a solid figure formed by connecting a circle to a point not in the plane of the circle.

Example:

A funnel is cone-shaped.

cone bearers

Trees that have seeds enclosed in cones are called *conifers*, a Latin word for "cone-bearing." These "cone bearers" are often simply called pine trees or evergreens. They live a long time and are quite hardy. Some conifers are the largest plants on the Earth. This kind of tree is especially useful as lumber and for making paper.

Confederacy

In 1861, the southern states seceded from the United States. They formed a separate country called the Confederate States of America, or the Confederacy, with Jefferson Davis as president. After the Civil War, the Confederate states rejoined the United States.

conflict

The struggle between characters or opposing forces in a story is called the *conflict*. The problems and complications in a story present the central conflict. The conflict can be internal or external. An internal conflict is a problem within a character. An external conflict is a problem caused by outside forces.

Confucius

A Chinese philosopher and teacher, Confucius (551?–479 B.C.) stressed the need to develop moral character and responsibility toward oneself and society. Today, more than 2000 years later, many Chinese people still honor his ideas. His thought had a profound and lasting effect on all China.

Congo (Zaire) River

The Congo River is a large river in western Africa that flows from southeastern Zaire into the Atlantic Ocean. The fifth largest river in the world, the Congo carries more water than any other river except the Amazon. *See Africa.*

congruent figures

In geometry, two figures with the same size and shape are called *congruent figures.*

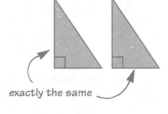

exactly the same

conjunction

A conjunction is a word used to connect words, phrases, clauses, or sentences.

Examples:

- and
- but
- yet
- because

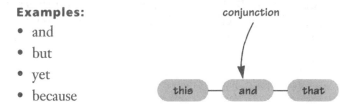

connotation

The connotation is a word's implied or suggested meaning.

Examples:

The word *soldier* connotes a contemporary person who fights in a war.

Warrior connotes a person from the past who fought in wars.

The word *freedom* has a number of connotations.

See denotation.

conquistador

A *conquistador* is the name for a Spanish conqueror from the 1500s. Spanish explorers conquered many parts of the Americas. Exploiting and enslaving the natives, they sent vast Native American treasures back to Spain.

Conrad, Joseph

Joseph Conrad (1857–1924) was a British novelist who wrote *Lord Jim* and *Nostromo,* and the short stories "Heart of Darkness" and "The Secret Sharer." Born in Poland, he went to sea at twenty, and, over a sixteen-year career became a British citizen and worked his way up to being a ship's captain. Many of his novels and stories were based on his youthful adventures.

conservation

Conservation means "protection, management, and wise use of natural resources." The United States and other countries are passing conservation laws to try to conserve, or save, the Earth's natural resources. In its scientific sense, the word means saving energy, using less energy, or using energy wisely.

Constantine the Great

The first Christian emperor of Rome, Constantine the Great (275?–337) became emperor in 324. He worked throughout his reign to reunite the empire that had been torn apart by war. He moved the capital from Rome east to Byzantium and renamed it Constantinople.

constellation

A constellation is a group of stars that form a pattern. When ancient stargazers looked into the sky, they saw patterns of stars— for example, the seven stars that make up the Big Dipper. Now 88 constellations are defined. They include the Big and the Small Dipper, Orion, and Gemini.

Little Dipper

North Star

Big Dipper

constituent

Lawmakers represent a particular area or district. The voters in the lawmaker's district are his or her constituents.

Constitution of the U.S.

The Constitution is the foundation for all government in the United States. Delegates to the 1787 Constitutional Convention in Philadelphia had a huge task. After disagreement and compromise, they created a set of laws for the new United States, and that was what we now call the Constitution.

We the People of the U
mestic Tranquility, provide for the common Defence, promote the general Welf
and establish this CONSTITUTION for the United States of America.

consul/council/counsel

▷ A *consul* is a public official, usually the representative of a foreign government (the Spanish consul).

▷ *Council* usually means a group of people working together (the student council).

▷ To *counsel* usually means to give advice, and a counsel, like a counselor, is a person who gives advice (the counsel made the recommendation).

consumer

Any person who uses food, clothing, or anything grown or made by producers is a consumer. A consumer can be anyone who buys something. *See consumerism.*

consumerism

Consumerism is a move to protect people from unsafe products or misleading advertising. *See consumer.*

continent

Each of the large dry-land masses of the world is a continent. A continent usually has large plateaus or plains, at least one mountain range, and is totally or nearly surrounded by water. The seven continents are Asia, Africa, North America, South America, Antarctica, Europe, and Australia.

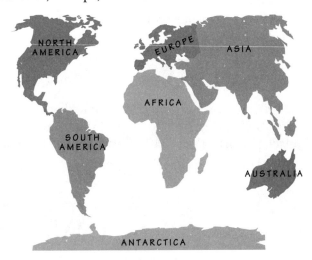

continental drift

Some scientists believe that, at one time in the Earth's history, all of the continents of the world were touching and only gradually over 200 million years drifted apart. This theory is called continental drift.

continental shelf

Most of the living organisms in the ocean live in areas known as the continental shelf. This part of the ocean is the shallow part of the seabed that slopes out from a continent to a depth of about 600 feet. In some places, the continental shelf may be half a mile wide. In other places, it may be as much as 480 miles wide.

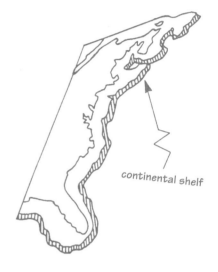

continental shelf

contract

A contract is a formal agreement between two parties. What makes a contract special is that it can be enforced by law.

Example:

If a person who has a contract to purchase wood for $50 a ton is charged $60 a ton, he or she can take the matter to a court of law.

contraction

In English, a contraction is a shortening of a word through the omission of a letter or letters and the use of an apostrophe. For example, *we're* is a contraction for we are, and *doesn't* is a contraction for does not.

contradictory premises

Contradictory premises is a logical fallacy in which a person presents premises that contradict each other.

Example:

Example:

Despite the current crises with the budget and the huge deficit, American government is as efficient as it could possibly be.

See logical fallacy.

controlled experiment

In a controlled experiment, a scientist sets up two experiments that are identical except for one variable.

Example:

To see if taking vitamin C prevents colds, one group of people take vitamin C and another group does not take it. Taking vitamin C is then the only variable between the two groups of people. That way, a scientist can be sure that the variable—in this case, vitamin C—created any difference observed between the two groups of people.

convection

Most homes are heated through a process known as convection. When a heat source (such as an electric heater or radiator) gives off heat, the heat rises upward. The cooler, heavier air moves down to replace the heated air that rises. That cool air is then heated, and it eventually rises. This causes a stream of constantly moving air that can heat up an entire room.

convention

A convention is a meeting or gathering of people. In a political convention, representatives from across the country meet to select a candidate for the election. In a business convention, businesses interested in a certain idea, for example, toys, all meet to show and sell products to one another.

Cook, James

James Cook (1728–1779) was the first European to explore the eastern coast of Australia. He established England's claim for later settlement there.

coordinates

Coordinates give the location of a point in a coordinate plane.

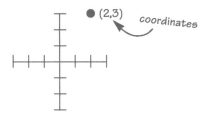

coordinating conjunction

A coordinating conjunction is a conjunction that connects similar words to words, phrases to phrases, or clauses to clauses.

Examples:
and
but
for
nor
or
yet

See conjunction.

Copernicus, Nicolaus

Nicolaus Copernicus (1473–1543), a Polish astronomer, was the first modern scientist to claim that the planets revolved around the sun. Up until then, it was thought the planets revolved around the Earth. His idea was known as the "heliocentric theory."

Copperhead

During the American Civil War, a person who lived in the North but sympathized with the South was called a *Copperhead*. Copperheads wanted to have peace at almost any price, so they were named after the deadly snake—a copperhead.

Coriolis forces

Why is there wind? One reason is because the Earth spins, or rotates. Also, water and air move faster in the middle of the Earth at the Equator than they do farther north, say, in Canada. Water and air coming from the Equator (moving fast) goes east, and water and air moving toward the equator (moving slower) moves westward. That is called the Coriolis force, after Gaspard de Coriolis, who discovered it.

cornea

The cornea is the eye's transparent covering that helps it focus light rays.

cornet

The cornet is a brass instrument shaped like a shortened trumpet, with a trumpetlike but darker sound. It is used mostly in jazz and military bands. *See band.*

corona

The faint, outermost region of the sun's atmosphere is the corona.

corporation

A corporation is a business owned by stockholders. Those who own stock in a corporation elect a board of directors who choose the top management people to run the business.

correlative conjunction

Correlative conjunctions are conjunctions that are always used in pairs.

Examples:
- both   and
- either   or
- neither   nor
- not only   but also

See conjunction.

Cortés, Hernando

A Spanish adventurer and conquistador, Hernando Cortés (1485–1547) captured the Aztec emperor Montezuma. With the help of neighboring Indian tribes, Cortés completely subdued the warlike Aztecs in August 1521.

could have/could of

The phrase *could have* suggests a possibility. *Could of* is never correct.

Example:
You could have gotten a perfect score on the exam if you had not used *could of* incorrectly.

counterpoint

Counterpoint is a style of music writing in which each part has a melody. When played or sung together, the melodies move toward or away from each other to create harmony.
Outstanding examples of counterpoint are found in the music of J. S. Bach.
See Johann Sebastian Bach.

Cousteau, Jacques

Jacques Cousteau (b. 1910) has become famous for his work in exploring and discovering the world under the

MORE

sea. In 1943, he helped invent the aqualung®, which supplied air to divers under water and allowed them mobility. This invention led to today's sport scuba diving. Cousteau and his crew explored the oceans in the ship *Calypso*, which is a name of a nymph in Homer's *Odyssey*. The nymph ruled over an island and gave shelter to Ulysses during the journey.

CPU

The CPU, or central processing unit, controls the basic functions of a computer. It allows a computer to add, subtract, multiply, and divide. It locates where vital information is stored, and it tells the computer what to do first, second, and so forth. Nowadays, the CPU is all put on a thin chip of material about 1/4" square. *See computer.*

Crane, Stephen

Stephen Crane (1871–1900) was an American poet, short-story writer, and novelist. *The Red Badge of Courage*, his realistic novel about the Civil War, is often considered the best war story ever written by an American. His other novel, *Maggie: A Girl of the Streets*, was the first realistic American novel.

Creole

A Creole was a white settler born in the Americas of French or Spanish parents. Creoles were often educated and lived well on ranches, but they were barred from high government positions. These positions went instead to peninsulares, or people born in Spain.

Creole language

A Creole language is a European language that has been greatly influenced by another (usually African) language. In nineteenth-century America, for example, slaves often used Creole language, mixing their native African language with English.

Crete

Crete is a Mediterranean island and the site of the Minoan civilization. About 5,000 years ago, Crete was a power in the ancient world. Its culture is named for King Minos, a legendary ruler of Crete.

crevasse

A deep crack in an earthen embankment or a glacier is a crevasse. *See glacier.*

Cromwell, Oliver

An English political leader, Oliver Cromwell (1599–1658) led the army of the Parliament that defeated King Charles I during the English Civil War of the 1640s. Cromwell ruled England, first under the Commonwealth and then as Lord Protector, from 1653 until his death.

Cronos

In Greek mythology, Cronos was the father of the king of the gods of Olympus, Zeus. *See Olympus.*

cross section

A cross section is a view of a solid object that shows what it would look like if it had been cut in half and the inside shown.

Example:

A cross section of a grapefruit would show the pink inside sections, as if it were cut in half.

Crusades

The Crusades (1096–1291) were a series of battles between the Christians and the Muslims for possession of the Holy Land. Christian forces won the first Crusade. In fighting over the next 200 years, however, the Muslims regained control of the Holy Land.

crustaceans

Crustaceans usually are marine animals such as lobsters, crayfish, and crabs. Crustaceans belong to a larger group of animals known as *arthropods* (animals with external skeletons and jointed legs). A crustacean has eyes, six to fourteen legs, and antennae.

cube

A cube is a regular solid figure with six square faces.

Cubism

Cubism is a style of art begun in the early 1900s. It features shapes such as squares, triangles, and straight lines. Some cubist sculptures look almost like stick figures. Other paintings show only sides or angles. Still others might show fractured objects from different angles at the same time. Pablo Picasso was one of the best-known cubists.

Picasso, Pablo. *Ma Jolie* (Woman with a xither or guitar), 1911–12.

culture

A culture is the whole way of life for a group of people. Language, religion, arts, and government are all part of culture. Each Native American Indian group, for example, developed a culture of its own.

Cummings, E. E.

Edward Estlin Cummings (1894–1962) was an American poet known for his bold experiments with language. He broke words apart, ran words together, and altered punctuation and capitalization to make the form of his poems fit the ideas and feelings he wanted to express.

cumulus clouds

Large, round-topped, flat-bottomed clouds are called cumulus clouds. By contrast, thin, feathery clouds are called cirrus clouds.

cuneiform

Cuneiform is an ancient system of writing. About 3,000 B.C., the Sumerians invented cuneiform writing. Writers, called scribes, made wedge-shaped marks, usually in soft clay. The baked clay tablets were used for financial records and letters.

Curie, Marie

Together with her husband Pierre, Marie Curie, or Madame Curie (1867-1934), won the Nobel Prize for their work in discovering two new elements, radium and polonium.

currency

The money used in a country is its currency. Coins and paper money are currency in the United States. Some early American Indian societies used shells as currency.

custody

When someone is "in custody," the person is in someone's care. Custody can also mean that someone is in the care of the police because he or she is accused of committing a crime.

custom

A custom is a way of doing something that has been handed down from generation to generation. An example of a custom is the serving of special food on certain holidays—for example, corned beef and cabbage on St. Patrick's Day or turkey on Thanksgiving.

customary units of measure

The customary units of measure are a system for measuring length

in inches, feet, yards, and miles; capacity in cups, pints, quarts, and gallons; weight in ounces, pounds, and tons; and temperature in degrees Fahrenheit.

cyan

The word *cyan* comes from Greek and means "dark blue." The color blue is often referred to as cyan, especially in the fields in printing and photography.

Cyclops

In Greek mythology, the Cyclops were a race of giants. Each cyclops had only one eye in the center of its forehead.

cylinder

A solid figure with two circular bases that are parallel and congruent is a cylinder.

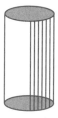

Example:
The hollow cardboard inside a roll of paper towels is a cylinder.

cymbals

Cymbals are a pair of thin brass plates with handles in the center. They come in many sizes but usually range from twelve to twenty-two inches in diameter. To play them, the percussionist rubs or strikes the two together or strikes one with a drumstick or metal brush.

czar

The term *czar*, also spelled tsar, comes from the Latin word for caesar, a title used by Roman emperors. The emperor in pre-revolutionary Russia was called the czar. Ivan the Great, the first Russian czar, expanded Russia into Siberia in the mid-1500s. Nicolas II, the last czar, was was overthrown in 1917 and executed in 1918.

da Gama, Vasco

Vasco da Gama (1469?–1524) was the first European to sail around the southern tip of Africa. He left from Portugal, his native country. This trip opened up a profitable trade route to the East for the Portuguese.

da Vinci, Leonardo

Leonardo da Vinci (1452-1519), an Italian artist and inventor, was one of the world's greatest painters. He is best known for his painting *Mona Lisa*. Da Vinci was also an inventor. He sketched plans for flying machines, submarines, and many other inventions centuries before they were actually built. *See Renaissance.*

Daedalus

In Greek mythology, Daedalus was a skilled craftsman who designed the labyrinth in Crete. With his son Icarus, he escaped imprisonment by creating wings of feathers fastened with wax. *See Icarus.*

Daguerre, Louis

Louis J. M. Daguerre (1789–1851) was a French painter and inventor who in 1839 produced the first practical means of photography. His method, the daguerreotype, was used until the twentieth century, when improvements led to photos that could be copied.

daguerreotype

A daguerreotype is an early type of photograph invented by Frenchman Louis J. M. Daguerre. Such photographs were popular during the 1800s. *See Louis Daguerre.*

Daimler, Gottlieb

Gottlieb Daimler (1834–1900), a German engineer, patented the internal combustion engine in 1885. This was the engine that made the automobile possible. He went on to found, in 1890, an automobile company that eventually produced the Mercedes-Benz.

dark horse

A little-known candidate for public office is often referred to as a *dark horse*. If groups at a political convention cannot agree on a presidential candidate, they may compromise on a dark horse. In 1940, for example, Wendell Willkie was nominated for President this way, but he later lost the election.

Darwin, Charles

Charles Robert Darwin (1809–1882) was an English naturalist. After thinking about becoming a doctor or a priest, he settled upon natural history. He landed a job as naturalist on the ship the *Beagle* and set off on a trip around the world. The voyage allowed him to examine species of plants and animals. Eventually in 1859 he published his observations in his book *On the Origin of Species*, in which he first explained his theory of evolution.

dash

A dash (—) is a punctuation mark most often used to show an abrupt change in a sentence. Dashes are also used to present an explanation or to emphasize a word or phrase.

Example:

. . . .

Example:

Amy is the best basketball player in the league—the absolute best.

data

Data, the plural form of the word *datum*, are facts or information from which a conclusion can be drawn. Computers are capable of storing and retrieving a great deal of data. *See database.*

database

A database is a large amount of information stored in a computer's memory and available to the computer's user. *See data.*

daylight-savings time

Daylight-savings time is one hour ahead of standard time. It is put into effect in spring and summer so that there is an additional hour of daylight in the evening.

de La Salle, Sieur

The Sieur de La Salle, born René Robert Cavelier (1643–1687), was one of the greatest explorers of the New World. In 1679 La Salle and his men set out from Canada and explored lands along the Mississippi River. He claimed a large part of inland North America for France.

de Soto, Hernando

Hernando de Soto (1500?–1542) explored the southeastern part of the present-day United States between 1539 and 1542. He may have been the first European to see the Mississippi River.

Dead Sea Scrolls

The Dead Sea Scrolls are ancient Hebrew manuscripts of the Old Testament—the earliest written documents of the Bible ever discovered. In 1947, shepherds discovered

MORE →

some fragile parchment scrolls sealed in jars. They had remained hidden in caves near the Dead Sea for about 1900 years. This led to further discoveries of manuscripts by archaeologists in the 1950s and 1960s.

decibel

A bel is a unit of measurement to express the intensity of a sound. A decibel is one-tenth of a bel. When a sound increases by ten decibels, it means that the intensity of that sound is multiplied by 10. The human ear can hear decibels of 0-85 loudness without sustaining any damage. However, when sound reaches a decibel level of more than 115 for an extended period of time, permanent hearing loss can result. *See ear.*

deciduous tree

A deciduous tree sheds its leaves annually, usually in the fall, and later grows new ones.

Examples:

| oak tree | walnut tree | maple tree |

decimal

A decimal is a number containing a decimal fraction, that is, a fraction whose denominator is 10 or a multiple of 10. It is expressed by placing a decimal point to the left of the whole number.

Examples:

2.5   two and a half, or two and five tenths

4.25   four and a quarter, or four and twenty-five hundredths

See denominator.

decimeter

A unit of length in the metric system, a decimeter is one-tenth of a meter.

Declaration of Independence

The Declaration of Independence is a document in which the American colonists declared their independence from Great Britain. In 1776, Thomas Jefferson drafted a public letter from the Continental Congress to King George III of England. It explained the colonists' reasons for proclaiming their freedom. *See American Revolution.*

Declaration of Rights of Man and of the Citizen

Issued in 1789 during the French Revolution, the Declaration of the Rights of Man and of the Citizen abolished feudal society. It declared that the French government must be based on liberty and equality for all citizens. *See French Revolution.*

declarative sentence

A declarative sentence is a sentence that makes a statement. A declarative sentence tells something about the subject of the sentence.

Example:

Megan went to the cafe.

See sentence.

deduction

Deduction is reasoning that begins with a general idea and moves to specific points and a conclusion. *See induction.*

Deere, John

John Deere (1804–1886) was an Illinois blacksmith who invented a new and improved kind of plow for farming. Tired of hearing complaints from farmers that gluey prairie soil stuck to their wooden and iron plows, Deere made a self-cleaning plow out of a steel saw blade. His invention opened up great stretches of American prairie for farming.

defendant

In a legal trial, the defendant is a person who is accused of a crime or is being sued.

deficit

A deficit is a shortage. Usually this term refers to money—specifically, the difference between the income (money coming in) and the expenses (money going out) of a business, organization, or government.

delta

A delta is a deposit, usually fan-shaped, of sand, gravel, and so forth, at the mouth of a river. For example, the delta of the Mississippi River occurs where the river flows into the Gulf of Mexico.

delta

Demeter

In Greek mythology, Demeter was the goddess of Earth, agriculture, grain, and fertility. Her Roman name was Ceres.

democracy

A democracy is a government that is run directly by its citizens or indirectly through its elected representatives. Government managed by elected representatives and, usually, a president, as in the United States, is also called a *republic*. America is, therefore, a democratic republic.

demographer

A demographer is a person who studies human populations. By studying the rate of births, deaths, marriages, diseases, and so forth, demographers can provide information to help predict future trends.

demonstrative pronoun

A demonstrative pronoun is a pronoun used to point out people or objects. For example, *this, that, these,* and *those* are demonstrative pronouns when used to point out or call attention. *See pronoun.*

Denmark

Denmark is a Scandinavian country in Northern Europe. Located between the Baltic Sea and the North Sea, Denmark is almost completely surrounded by water. *See Scandinavia.*

denominator

The number below the line in a fraction is a denominator. It names the number of equal parts or objects.

Example:

3/4   *denominator*

See numerator.

denotation

Denotation is a word's exact, literal meaning. *See connotation.*

denouement

The denouement, often called the *resolution,* is the outcome or solution of the plot in a play or story. The denouement usually comes after the climax. *See climax, plot, and resolution.*

density

The density of something is its amount of mass for a standard volume. For example, water has a greater density than air. The given volume of water weighs more than the same volume of air. The density of solids or liquids is usually measured in grams per milliliter or in pounds per cubic foot. The density of gasses is usually measured in grams per liter or in pounds per cubic foot.

deregulate

To deregulate means "to remove regulations or restrictions that have been placed on a business or industry."

descant

A descant is an ornamental melody sung above the normal melody in a hymn or chorale. A descant is either written or improvised. *See chorale and hymn.*

description

In writing, a description creates a picture of someone, something, or some place. Description uses vivid details and sensory imagery. *See details.*

design

A design is the organized arrangement of elements—that is, the visual composition of a piece. Someone who designs decides on the overall "look" of a piece, its colors, lines, textures, and shapes. A designer of a book, for example, decides on the size of type, length, and height of the pages, and the way the art or photos are used. A clothing designer works with different fabrics, especially their colors and textures, and the manner in which the pieces of cloth are sewn together, to create a new piece of clothing.

despot

A ruler who has unlimited power is a despot. A tyrant is a despot who rules cruelly or unjustly. Historically, most despots have ruled as tyrants. *See dictator.*

details

In writing, details are images, facts, evidence, bits of observation, and so on. Details in description and narration give a reader a clear impression of what the writer has observed or experienced; details in explanation or persuasion help support or prove generalizations. *See central idea.*

deuterium

Deuterium is a stable isotope of hydrogen. The nucleus of a deuterium atom has a proton and a neutron. The nucleus of a regular hydrogen atom has only a proton.

electron

neutron

proton

H²

developing nation

A developing nation has a shortage of food, few sources of power, and a low gross national product compared to developed nations. Most developing countries, which typically gained independence during the last century, are experiencing an increase in population because birth rates remain high while death rates decrease due to the introduction of modern medicine. Many African states are considered developing countries.

dew

Condensed water vapor from the air that forms on cold surfaces is dew. Most often dew appears early in the morning and can be seen on grass, cars, and other surfaces. *See dew point.*

dew point

The dew point is the temperature at which moisture in the air begins to condense as dew. Similar droplets of moisture also form in clouds. Clouds are made up of millions of small droplets of moisture. At a specific temperature, the moisture will form into rain or snow or ice and fall from the sky. *See cirrus clouds, cumulus clouds, and dew.*

Dewey Decimal System

The Dewey Decimal System is used in many libraries to organize and classify books. In the Dewey Decimal System, all possible subjects are divided into ten main categories and assigned particular numbers (the arts, for example, are assigned the numbers 700–799). Each of the ten main categories is then subdivided into ten more specific categories (painting, for instance, is assigned 750–759). Subcategories—for example, types of paintings—are assigned decimals, such as 750.1 or 751.2.

dhow

A dhow is a single-masted ship with a triangular sail. More than 1,000 years ago, Arab traders carried goods in dhows between China, India, and Africa. Dhows are still used today along the coasts of Arabia and East Africa.

diagonal

diagonal

A diagonal is a line segment that connects a polygon's or polyhedron's corners that are not next to each other.

dialect

A dialect is a way of speaking characteristic of a certain geographical area or a certain group of people. Dialects differ from the standard language in pronunciation. A single language may have many different dialects. In Boston, for example, some people say *yahd* for yard and *idear* for idea. *See idiom.*

dialogue

A conversation between two or more characters in a play or story is called dialogue. For example, here is dialogue from Shakespeare's *Romeo and Juliet:*

JULIET: Good-night, good-night! parting is such sweet sorrow/That I shall say good-night till it be morrow.

ROMEO: Sleep dwell upon thine eyes, peace in thy breast!/ Would I were sleep and peace, so sweet to rest!

See monologue and soliloquy.

diameter

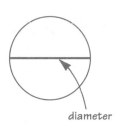

diameter

In a circle, a diameter is a line segment that passes through the center and has both endpoints on the circle. *See radius.*

diamonds

The hardest substance in the world is a diamond, a precious stone formed of pure carbon in crystals. Because of the hardness of diamonds, industries use them for cutting other hard substances. South Africa is the world's main source of diamonds. *See Mohs' scale.*

diastolic blood pressure

Diastolic blood pressure is the lowest blood pressure exerted against artery walls. *See artery and blood pressure.*

Dickens, Charles

Charles Dickens (1812–1870) was one of the greatest and most popular English novelists. Dickens's works drew attention to the dire social problems brought about by the Industrial Revolution. His most famous books include *Great Expectations, Oliver Twist, David Copperfield,* and *A Tale of Two Cities. A Christmas Carol* has been adapted many times for the stage, screen, and television.

Dickinson, Emily

Emily Dickinson (1830–1886) was an American poet who lived most of her life in seclusion in the house in which she was born in Amherst, Massachusetts. Almost none of her poetry was published during her lifetime, but after her death, more than 1,700 of her poems were made public.

dictator

A dictator has complete control over the government of a country. Adolph Hitler was dictator of Germany from 1933 to 1945. *See despot.*

diction

Diction is a writer's or speaker's choice of words or style of speaking or writing. Diction may be formal or informal, literal or figurative. A writer or speaker can change diction depending upon the subject and the audience.

dictionary

A dictionary is a reference book containing words, arranged alphabetically, and their definitions. Most dictionaries also include information about the forms, uses, pronunciations, and etymologies of the words. *See etymology and reference.*

dicto simpliciter

Dicto simpliciter is a logical fallacy in which a person presents an argument based on an unqualified generalization.

Example:

All high school freshmen chatter constantly in the hallways.

See generalization and logical fallacy.

difference

The number found by subtracting one number from another is the difference.

Example:

$$95 - 68 = 27$$

difference

digestive system

In humans, food is broken down into usable fuel for the body by the digestive system. A person's digestive system begins with the mouth, which is used to chew and break up food into parts. The esophagus carries the food to the stomach, where food is broken up more. Then the food passes into the small and the large intestines, where it becomes usable for the body. The small intestine is about one and a half times as long as a person is tall.

digit

In mathematics, a digit is one of the symbols used for writing numbers.

Examples:

0　　1　　2　　3

digital recording

A digital recording uses computer technology to translate musical sounds into a series of binary digits (0s and 1s). Sounds converted into a series of numbers are more clear and pure and truer to the original sounds. A CD (compact disk) is a digital recording. *See binary code.*

pteranodon

dinosaurs

Dinosaurs were the largest animals that ever lived. They dominated the Earth for millions of years but became extinct about 65 million years ago. Some dinosaurs were plant eaters, and others were meat eaters. Our information about dinosaurs comes from fossils. Some scientists believe that the closest living relatives of dinosaurs are birds. They even think that bird feathers may have evolved from dinosaur scales. Some dinosaurs, such as the pterodactyl, or flying lizard, were quite like birds.
See fossil.

diplomat

A diplomat is skilled in managing the day-to-day relations between two nations. He or she usually lives in another country. An American diplomat, for example, might live in Germany and help manage the relations between Germany and the United States. *See foreign policy.*

direct object

In a sentence, the word that receives the action of a transitive verb is the direct object. A direct object answers *Whom?* or *What?* after an action verb.

Example:

Example:

The second baseman dropped the grounder.

direct object

See verb.

disinterested/uninterested

▷ *Uninterested* means "bored or lacking interest."

▷ *Disinterested* never means bored; it means "fair or impartial."

Example:

A judge should always be disinterested, never uninterested, during a trial.

disk

In data processing, a disk is a plate made of or coated with magnetic material used to store computer data. A floppy disk is made of flexible Mylar. Disks are loaded into a disk drive of a computer, where they can be "read" for information or have information loaded onto them. Some disks are 5 1/4" across, others 3 1/2" across. The size of the disk depends on the kind of computer being used. Information for a computer can also be stored on a CD-ROM disk. *See data.*

distillation

The process by which a substance is separated from a solution by evaporation is distillation. At the simplest level, if a glass is filled halfway with water and left on a hot radiator, the water will evaporate, leaving a chalky residue of salts and minerals.

distributive property

In mathematics, the distributive property states that when a multiplicand is a sum, multiplying each addend before adding does not change the product.

Example:

$5 \times (6 + 2) = (5 \times 6) + (5 \times 2)$

Both sides of the equation equal 40, so it does not matter if the addends are multiplied before or after they are added. *See addend.*

diving animals

Many sea animals dive deep under the surface of the ocean to locate food. The deeper they go, the more the pressure of the water presses against them. At a depth of one mile, the water pressure is more than one ton per square inch. Yet many marine creatures, such as whales, can survive these pressures because their tissues consist mainly of water. Water, unlike air, is very difficult to compress. Thus, the water pressure does not hurt the diving whale.

divisor

The divisor is the number by which another number is divided.

Example:

divisor

Dixieland

Dixieland, one of the earliest types of jazz, features a strong 4-4 beat and freestyle solo sections. It was developed in New Orleans early in this century by black jazz musicians and usually features clarinet, cornet, trumpet, trombone, and drums. *See jazz.*

DNA

The abbreviation DNA stands for "deoxyribonucleic acid." It is the substance in all living cells that carries genetic code. That is to say, it contains the "instructions" that tell any organism what it ought to look like and how it ought to grow. The DNA molecule has a shape called the "double helix," which looks like a spiral staircase.

DNA molecule

Dolby

Dolby is the name for a noise-reduction recording system invented by Ray Dolby. It reduces the hissing sound that audio tapes make when they are played.

Doppler effect

Christian Doppler (1803–1853) was a physicist from Austria who made an important discovery about sound, light, or radio waves. He figured out that waves coming from a moving source change. The most common example is a whistle on a train. As the train approaches, the sound waves from the whistle have a shorter distance to travel. The frequency of the sound waves increases, and the pitch is higher. This change is referred to as the Doppler effect. *See decibel and ear.*

double star

A double star is two stars so close together that they appear as one to the naked eye.

doublespeak

Doublespeak is a term used for vague and complicated language that hides the truth or otherwise misleads people. Politicians are sometimes accused by reporters of using doublespeak to conceal what is really happening in government.

Example:

The aforementioned refuse management system demonstrates salient inadequacies in both its retrieval and disposal modes.

This sentence simply means that the garbage is not being collected properly.

See gobbledygook and jargon.

Douglass, Frederick

Frederick Douglass (1817–1895) was an American writer and editor best known for his 1845 book *Narrative of the Life of Frederick Douglass.* Born a slave in Maryland, Douglass escaped in 1838. He later became an abolitionist and an advocate for the rights of blacks to vote. *See abolition.*

download

In computer jargon, downloading is moving a computer file from one computer program to another.

Drake, Sir Francis

An English sea captain and explorer, Sir Francis Drake (1540?–1596) became in 1580 the first Englishman to sail around the world. He also raided Spanish ships and helped destroy the Spanish Armada in 1588. *See Spanish Armada.*

drama

A drama is a play performed by actors for an audience. The word *drama* can also be used to describe a situation that presents an emotional conflict. Comedies and tragedies are types of drama. *See comedy and tragedy.*

Dred Scott Decision

In 1857, the U.S. Supreme Court decided a case about a slave named Dred Scott. He had sued for his freedom because he lived in a nonslave state and territory. In a setback for the abolitionists, the Court ruled that Scott was property, not a free citizen, and therefore, could not bring suit in a federal court. This decision was important because it negated the Missouri Compromise, making it unconstitutional for Congress to forbid slavery in U.S.-held territories. *See abolition.*

Drew, Charles

Dr. Charles Drew (1904–1950), an American physician born in Washington, D. C., did extensive research on blood plasma. Plasma is the watery part of blood. People need it during an operation or whenever they lose blood in an accident. Drew found that plasma could be stored far a longer period than whole blood and that it worked even better than whole blood in emergency situations. Drew set up the first blood banks. *See blood.*

drought

A drought is a long period of dry weather or a complete lack of rain. In the 1980s, for example, California experienced a long period when it did not rain as much as usual, which was a kind of drought.

dry cell

A dry cell is an electrical cell in which current is contained in a gelatin or paste so as not to spill.

dubbing

Dubbing is the mixing of two or more separately taped tracks of music or speech to create a complete performance.

due to

▷ In formal English, *due to* is only used as an adjective meaning "caused by."

Example:

We were late for the game due to an earlier dentist appointment.

▷ In informal English, *due to* can also be used as a preposition meaning "because of."

Example:

Due to his age, Juan was not able to see the movie.

See adjective and preposition.

dynasty

A ruling family that controls a country for a number of generations is a dynasty. China was ruled by a series of dynasties from the time of its earliest recorded history until the early twentieth century.

E-mail

E-mail is short for "electronic mail." In computer jargon, E-mail are messages sent between people on a computer network.

ear

In humans, the outer ear catches sound waves as they pass through the air. The sound waves are then sent through the external auditory canal to a thin tissue known as the eardrum. Sound waves cause the eardrum to vibrate, or move quickly back and forth. That causes three small bones in the middle of the ear to vibrate too. These bones pass the sound along to the inner ear, which is filled with liquid. Inside the liquid are tiny, hairlike endings. They transfer the vibrations to a nerve in the brain, where they are decoded as sounds. *See decibel.*

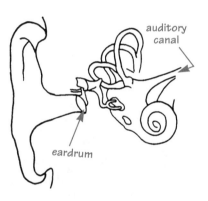

Earhart, Amelia

Amelia Earhart (1897–1937?) was the first woman to pilot an airplane alone across the Atlantic Ocean. Later, during her attempt to fly around the world, her plane vanished over the Pacific Ocean.

Earth

The Earth is an exceptional planet. Its surface is covered mostly by water, making it—along with Mercury—one of the densest planets. It orbits the sun once each year, averaging 66,641 miles per hour. And it spins completely around once every 24 hours.

Earth's layers

The Earth has four main layers. The outer layer, the crust, is about 25 miles thick under the continents and five miles thick under the oceans. The next layer, or mantle, lies immediately below the crust and consists of solid rock. Below the mantle is the outer

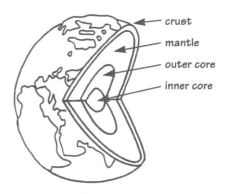

core, which scientists believe is made up of melted iron and nickel. The inner layer is called the inner core and consists, scientists believe, of solid iron and nickel. *See Earth.*

Earth's weight

Scientists have calculated that the Earth weighs 6,600,000,000,000,000,000,000 tons. That calculation was first performed by Henry Cavendish. He used a rod from which balls of lead were suspended by some wire. He measured the force of gravity on the balls of lead, and from this he calculated the weight of the Earth. *See Earth.*

earthquake

According to the plate tectonic theory, the crust of the Earth consists of plates of rock that move very slowly. Sometimes a break, or fault, forms in one of these plates. Often, because of extreme pressure, the rocks along a fault will move against each other from side to side or up and down. These movements cause the ground to shake, creating what we know as an earthquake. The study of earthquakes is seismology. Scientists now cannot always predict when an earthquake will occur, but they know around where it will

occur. No one was
surprised when an
earthquake hit near San
Francisco in October 1989 because
that area is very close to the San Andreas Fault
in California.

easel

An easel is a wood or metal structure used to hold a painting on
which an artist is working or to exhibit a completed work.

East Asia

The eastern region of Asia is East Asia. This area includes the
countries of China, Japan, North Korea, South Korea, and
Taiwan. *See Asia.*

ebony

Ebony is a kind of dark, durable hardwood that comes from tropical trees in Africa, Asia, and North and South America. Because of
its hardness, ebony is used frequently for black piano keys, furniture, or sculpture.

ecology

Ecology is the study of the relationships between living things and
their environment. The term is now often used to talk about the
interrelationship between people and the Earth. Every plant,
every animal, and every person on Earth affects others. A pond, for
example, is a small ecosystem where fish, insects, and plants all
depend upon one another for life. A person who studies ecology is
called an ecologist. *See ecosystem, environment, and environmental
movement.*

economy

An economy is the system by which goods and services are
made, sold, and distributed in a society. The United States
has an economy based on capitalism—a system in which
people own land, homes, factories, and so forth. In another

MORE
STUFF ON
ECONOMY

kind of economy, the government might own all land, all homes, and all factories.

ecosystem

An ecosystem is physical environment, such as a wetland, that consists of a community of plants and animals and the nonliving environment, such as climate, water, and soil. A wetland has one ecosystem, a desert another. *See ecology.*

Edison, Thomas

Thomas Edison (1847–1931) was a pioneer in the use of electricity. He succeeded by combining intelligence with a willingness to work hard. He once said, "Genius is ninety-nine percent perspiration and one percent inspiration." He patented more than 1,000 inventions, including moving pictures. Among his more spectacular feats was the creation of a practical electric lighting system. In 1879 he invented a bulb with a filament that lasted forty hours. He also built factories to produce his inventions, making sure that his ideas were brought into general use.

Egypt

Egypt is a country located in eastern North Africa. Although most of Egypt is desert, the area around the Nile River is densely populated. About five thousand years ago, Egyptians developed a highly sophisticated culture. *See Africa and Nile River.*

Einstein, Albert

Albert Einstein (1879–1955) was a scientist who is best known for his theory of relativity, which he formulated in 1905, when he was in his early twenties. This theory, which is often described by the equation $E = mc^2$, implied that enormous amounts of energy could be released from a relatively small

$E = mc^2$

amount of matter, establishing the basis of atomic power. Although he is now regarded as one of the most brilliant scientists ever, as a child he was a slow learner and not an especially good student.

Eisenhower, Dwight D.

Dwight D. Eisenhower (1890–1969) was the Allied commander in Europe during World War II. He led the Allied forces to victory over Nazi Germany. He was later head of NATO. In 1952, he was elected to the first of his two terms as President of the United States.

either-or argument

An either-or argument is a logical fallacy in which a person presents opposites or extremes as the only possible choices.

> **Example:**
>
> There's no doubt about it. Rich people either inherited their money or they got lucky in business.

See logical fallacy.

electoral college

The group of people chosen by the voters to elect the President and Vice-President of the United States is the electoral college. Originally they voted for the candidates that they felt were best. Today electors have made an implied pledge to vote as their political party directs.

electrical conductor

Metal and water are good conductors of electricity. That is, electricity flows through them quite easily. Other materials—for example, rubber, plastic, and wood—are poor conductors of electricity. As a result, they make good insulators. Because they do not let electricity flow easily through them, insulators are used around light plugs to prevent shocks. *See electricity.*

electricity

Electricity is a form of energy. In the 1800s, British scientists first discovered how to send electric current through wires. This discovery led to Edison's development of a practical electrical lighting system.

electromagnet

Whenever an electric current passes through a wire, it creates a magnetic field. If the wire is coiled or formed into loops, the magnetic field gets stronger. An electromagnet is usually a piece of iron that is wrapped with many coils of wire. When current runs through the wire, the iron and wire become magnetic.

electromagnetic waves

There are many kinds of electromagnetic waves. Light comes in waves. Sound from a radio comes in waves. A microwave oven uses waves. We can only see a very small range of waves—the visible light spectrum. Other waves, such as X-rays or radio waves, have wavelengths and frequencies that are too long or too short for humans to detect.

electron

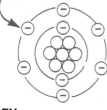

An electron is a negatively charged particle that moves around the nucleus of an atom. Joseph J. Thomson, a British physicist, is generally recognized as the discoverer of electrons. *See atom, neutron, and proton.*

elegy

An elegy is a somber poem, usually about death. Thomas Gray, for example, wrote "Elegy Written in a Country Churchyard," which begins:

> The curfew tolls the knell of parting day,
>
> The lowing herd wind slowly o'er the lea,
>
> The plowman homeward plods his weary way,
>
> And leaves the world to darkness and to me.

See poetry.

element

An element is a substance composed of atoms that have the same atomic number and that cannot be separated into simpler parts by chemical means. All matter is composed of either single elements or groups of elements. Gold, carbon, sulfur, iron, hydrogen, and oxygen are among the 106 known elements that make up the periodic table. *See periodic table.*

Eliot, T. S.

Thomas Stearns Eliot (1888–1965) was an American poet, playwright, and essayist who lived most of his adult life in England. *The Waste Land* is his most famous poem. *Murder in the Cathedral* is usually considered his best verse play. In 1948, Eliot was awarded the Nobel Prize for literature.

Elizabeth I

Elizabeth I (1533–1603), the second daughter of Henry VIII, was a powerful queen of England. During Elizabeth's 45-year reign, her navy gained control of the European seas, culminating with the defeat of the Spanish Armada in 1588. Thus England became a world power. The Elizabethan period also produced some of England's greatest literature— for example, the plays of William Shakespeare.

ellipse

An ellipse is an oval—a circle that is flattened a bit so that it is not quite round. Planets, for example, travel in an orbit that is an ellipse.

ellipsis

An ellipsis is the omission of one or more words in text. In the sentence "Bob is taller than I," the phrase "am tall" is an ellipsis omitted after "than I." Marks, such as three periods, used in a sentence to indicate an omission are also ellipses.

Ellis Island

Ellis Island is a small island in New York harbor. Many nineteenth- and early twentieth-century European immigrants stopped at Ellis Island to register before settling in the United States. Some immigrants often waited there weeks, sometimes months, before finally being able to come to the mainland. A museum now commemorates the immigrant experience.

Ellison, Ralph

Ralph Ellison (b. 1914) is an American novelist, essayist, and short-story writer. His novel *Invisible Man* won the National Book Award in 1952. Trained as a musician, Ellison turned to literature after being encouraged by Richard Wright and Langston Hughes.

Emancipation Proclamation

The Emancipation Proclamation was an executive order issued by Abraham Lincoln on January 1, 1863, that declared freedom for slaves in those states that remained in rebellion against the Union. It did not free slaves in slave states that had remained loyal to the Union, such as Maryland and Kentucky. The proclamation also announced that black men would be accepted into the Union Army. In all, approximately 200,000 black people served during the Civil War. The Emancipation Proclamation is considered important because Lincoln, for the first time, appeared to back the abolition of slavery as one of his aims for the war. It was also the first step toward the Thirteenth Amendment, which abolished slavery in the United States.

embargo

An embargo is an order by a government to keep people and goods from entering or leaving a place, usually a seaport. An embargo is often used by one country to make another country follow the wishes of the first. The embargo of Boston by the British in 1774 was one of the causes of the American Revolution. An embargo often precedes harsher measures, such as war.

embryo

An organism in the early state of development is an embryo. For example, in the early stages of a baby's development, it is referred to as an embryo. The tiny part of a seed that can grow into a plant or animal is an embryo. Usually the embryo has a protective covering. The purpose of the protective shell is to keep the embryo from harm and to feed it. A lima bean, for example, is mostly food for the embryo it encloses.

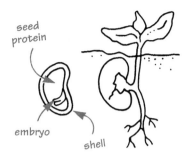

Emerson, Ralph Waldo

Ralph Waldo Emerson (1803–1882) was an American lecturer and essayist known for his philosophy that stressed the importance of individualism. His most famous essays include "The American Scholar" and "Self-Reliance."

emigrant/immigrant

▷ An *emigrant* is a person who leaves a country and settles somewhere else.

▷ An *immigrant* is a person from somewhere else who settles in a particular country. A person emigrates *from* a country and immigrates to a country.

Example:

An emigrant from Korea can become an immigrant to the United States.

emolument

An emolument is a salary paid to someone for doing a job. The payment may not always be in the form of money. A car given to someone for business is an emolument.

empire

An empire is a group of different states or nations under one ruler or government. One of the first known emperors was Sargon, who

MORE ➡

conquered and established the Sumerian empire about 2300 B.C. One of the largest empires in history was the Roman Empire. *See Ancient Rome.*

enamel

Enamel is a glassy, hard substance (glaze) fused to the surface of pottery or metal to form a strong, protective coating.

encore

An encore is an extra selection, or repetition of a piece, given by a performer in response to the audience's applause.

encyclopedia

An encyclopedia is a reference book that contains information about all branches of knowledge, usually arranged alphabetically. An encyclopedia may also contain in-depth information about a particular branch of knowledge. Many encyclopedias are published in multiple volumes. *See reference.*

endangered species

An endangered species is a species that is in danger of completely dying out. The California condor, for example, is an endangered species. Extinct species are organisms that have already died out. The passenger pigeon and dodo bird are two extinct species. *See passenger pigeon.*

endosperm

The food stored in a seed for the early nourishment of an embryo is the endosperm. *See embryo.*

endpoint

In mathematics, the point at the end of a line segment or a ray is the endpoint. *See ray.*

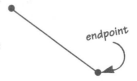

endpoint

energy

Energy is the capacity to do work. Energy cannot be created or destroyed. However, it can change its form. Chemical energy can be changed into electrical energy (a battery filled with chemicals, for instance, powers a flashlight). A match, too, is a form of chemical energy that can change into light energy. Even though energy changes form, there is never any more or less of it. The major sources of energy are oil, coal, gas, water, and nuclear power. By far the most important resource now is oil. It accounts for more than 40 percent of all of the world's energy.

energy of motion

The energy of motion is kinetic energy. When something is standing still, it has potential energy. That is to say, it has energy that is stored and that can be changed into kinetic energy. A person standing perfectly still, for example, has potential energy while a person running uses kinetic energy. *See energy and kinetic energy.*

England

England is one of the countries, along with Scotland, Wales, and Northern Ireland, that make up Great Britain. It is the largest, more southern part of Great Britain.

English Bill of Rights

The English Bill of Rights is a declaration presented by Parliament to the monarchy that assured certain rights of the people and limited the monarchy's power to tax and keep a standing army.

English Channel

The English Channel is the body of water that separates England and France. It is the busiest sea passage in the world. *See England and France.*

English horn

The English horn (which is neither English nor a horn) is a double-reed woodwind instrument, pitched to sound a fifth lower than its cousin, the oboe. It is similar to the oboe in shape, but longer, and has a ball-shaped opening. *See oboe.*

Enlightenment

The Enlightenment was an intellectual movement in Europe during the 1700s that stressed clear thinking and intellectual freedom. During the Enlightenment people believed that the world operated according to natural laws—that is, an orderly set of rules. Benjamin Franklin, who spent time in Europe during this period, was one of the great figures of the Enlightenment.

ensemble

An ensemble is a musical group in which each member plays a different instrument or sings a different part. As in sports, a good ensemble is made up of good "team players."

entrepreneur

A person who organizes and operates a new business is an entrepreneur. An entrepreneurial business is often risky because it is not yet fully established.

environment

The environment is the land, air, and water of the Earth. People need to become aware that the Earth is a living planet. When one part is changed or destroyed, it affects other parts. If parts of the Amazon jungle, for example, are cut down, thousands of species of plants and animals that live in the jungle are affected. Often, the term *environment* is used broadly to mean one's surroundings. An ant's environment is the sidewalk and dirt and surrounding grass. For people, the environment is all surrounding conditions, including family, society, and the world at large. *See ecology.*

environmental movement

The environmental movement is the collective efforts of people to improve the land, air, and water of the Earth. Environmentalists seek to educate people about using the Earth's resources wisely. *See ecology and environment.*

epic

An epic is a long, narrative poem that often tells a story about the heroic deeds of divine beings and people. In epics, the fate of an entire nation often depends on the actions of the hero. Homer's *Odyssey* is an example of an epic. The word *epic* may also apply to any story that has the scope and qualities of an epic poem. *See Homer.*

epicenter

The point on the surface of the Earth that is directly above the focus of an earthquake is the epicenter. *See earthquake.*

epidermis

The epidermis is the outer, protective layer of skin that covers the dermis layer of skin in vertebrate animals.

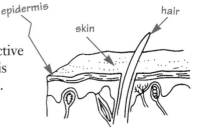

epigram

An epigram is a brief, witty poem or saying. Epigrams are often ironic and sometimes satirical. Samuel Taylor Coleridge, for example, wrote:

> What is an epigram? A dwarfish whole,
> Its body brevity, and wit its soul.

See irony and satire.

epoch

In geology, an epoch is a unit of geologic time that is a division of a larger period—for example, the Recent epoch of the Quarternary period. In nonscientific conversation, *epoch* is also used to mean a very long period of time, as in "the epochs of long ago."

equal opportunity

The United States Constitution assures equality, or equal opportunity, for all. Differences in race, gender, or religion do not change the equal chance to which everyone has a right.

equal time

Equal time was a Federal Communications Commission rule stating that each candidate for a public office must be allowed the same amount of time on radio and television. (If one candidate, for instance, is on TV for five seconds, all candidates must receive five seconds of air time.) This rule has now been revoked.

equation

In mathematics, an equation is a linear arrangement of mathematical symbols expressing the equality of two quantities.

Examples:

$2 + 2 = 4$

$3 \times 5 = 15$

equator

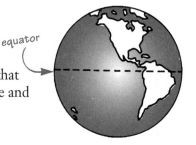

equator

The equator is an imaginary circle that lies halfway between the North Pole and the South Pole.

equilateral triangle

An equilateral triangle has three congruent sides—that is, the three sides are the same length, and thus, each of the three angles is the same.

all sides are equal

equilibrium

In a state of equilibrium, the forces acting on an object cancel each other out. The force from one side balances the force from the opposite side.

equinox

An equinox occurs when the center of the sun crosses the celestial equator, and both day and night are of equal length in all parts of the Earth. This occurs twice a year on about March 21 (vernal) and September 22 (autumnal).

Eriksson, Leif

Leif Eriksson was a Norse explorer who lived in the late tenth and early eleventh centuries. Eriksson sailed from his home in Greenland to explore lands to the west. Old stories and archaeological discoveries indicate that he reached the coast of Canada.

Eros

In Greek mythology, Eros was the son of Aphrodite and the messenger of love. He is often depicted as a winged boy holding a bow and arrow. His Roman name was Cupid. *See Aphrodite.*

erosion

The process by which land is worn down is erosion. The soil can be blown away by wind or washed away by rain or flood. Erosion is a problem for farming, which requires topsoil to grow good crops.

essay

An essay is a brief composition that attempts to explain a subject, discuss a topic, or persuade an audience about a thesis. Most essays present the writer's personal views.

estimate

In mathematics, an estimate is a judgment or opinion of the approximate number of something. For example, if 99 jelly beans were in a jar, a good estimate would be 100.

estuary

An estuary is the broad mouth of a river into which the sea flows. A marsh that is washed part of the time by salt water and part of the time by fresh water is also called an estuary.

ethnic group

A group of people with a common culture or a common country are from the same ethnic group. Examples include the Irish, Philippino, and Jewish ethnic groups.

étude

The French word *étude* means "study." An étude is based on one type of musical difficulty to help the musician improve and polish the skill needed to perform the selection well.

etymology

Etymology is the study of the origins and development of words.

euphemism

A euphemism is an indirect or inoffensive word or phrase substituted for a harsh or offensive word or phrase. The phrases "passed on" or "passed away," for instance, are euphemisms for "dead."

Euphrates River

The Euphrates River is a river in southwestern Asia that flows from Turkey through Syria and Iraq into the Persian Gulf. The area between the Euphrates River and the Tigris River is often called the cradle of civilization because it was there that the world's first culture developed. The ruins of the ancient city of Babylon lie by the Euphrates. *See Fertile Crescent and Tigris River.*

Euripides

Euripides (480–406 B.C.) was a Greek playwright who, along with Aeschylus and Sophocles, is considered one of the three great tragic dramatists of ancient times. He has in modern times been the most highly imitated and influential of the ancient Greek play-wrights. His plays were known for their social criticism. *See Aeschylus and Sophocles.*

Europe

Europe is the continent west of Asia and north of Africa. Although Europe is the second smallest continent, its people have had the strongest influence on world history. Western civilization developed first in ancient Greece and then in the Roman Empire. *See Ancient Greece, Ancient Rome, Athens, and continent.*

evaporate

Evaporation occurs when a liquid changes from a liquid to a gas. This happens when a puddle disappears after a rainstorm. The sun heats the water in the puddle until it is warm enough to evaporate. The same process occurs when water is boiled and becomes steam.

evolution

Evolution is a theory that organisms began from simpler forms of other organisms. Gradually, over time, organisms adapted and changed to suit their environment. This led to a better chance of survival and the evolution of the species. For example, an animal may develop a coloring that hides it better among the trees in which it lives. The animal will probably live longer because it can hide better than others like it. It will have offspring with this same coloring, and they will live longer too. And, after many generations, a new species will have evolved. *See Charles Darwin.*

exclamation point

▷ An exclamation point (!) is a punctuation mark used after a word, phrase, or sentence to express strong emotion. An exclamation point is most often used to end an exclamatory sentence.

Example:

Example:

Kevin's shot was incredible!

▷ An exclamation point is also sometimes used to end an imperative sentence that is meant to be very forceful.

Example:

Shut that door!

See exclamatory sentence and imperative sentence.

exclamatory sentence

An exclamatory sentence is a sentence that expresses strong emotion or surprise. An exclamatory sentence ends with an exclamation point.

Example:

What a great game that was!

See exclamation point and sentence.

executive branch

The executive branch of government enforces, or executes, laws.
The President is the leader of the executive branch in the United
States. The President and the people under him or her have the
power to carry out the laws passed by Congress.

exile

A person forced to leave his or her country is an exile. Often exile,
or banishment, is used as a punishment. Napoleon, for example,
was exiled from France first to the island of Elba and then to St.
Helena to keep him from waging war in Europe. *See Napoleon I.*

expatriate

When someone leaves one country and goes to live permanently in
another, he or she expatriates. That is to say the person gives up
citizenship in one country and becomes a citizen of another country. During World War II, many German Jews were persecuted in
their own country so they expatriated to other countries.

Explorer I

On January 31, 1958, the United States made its first space launch, *Explorer I*. This space voyage discovered radiation belts around the Earth called Van Allen belts. No astronauts flew aboard *Explorer I*, but just eleven years later humans set foot on the surface of the moon.

exponent

In mathematics, an exponent is a number that tells how many times the base is to be used as a factor.

Example:

In the expression 4^3, 3 is the exponent. It means $4 \times 4 \times 4$ and is read as "4 to the third power."

exports

Goods sent out for sale or use in another country are exports. Goods brought into a country are imports. The difference between the value of imports and exports makes up a nation's balance of trade.

exposition

In writing, an exposition explains a topic in a clear, organized way. Some exposition is also used in many novels, stories, and other forms of literature.

extended family

A group of people who are related and live together or near one another are an extended family. That is, a person who lives with his or her grandparents, aunts or uncles, and brothers and sisters lives in an extended family. Today some people—single parents, for example—miss the support of an extended family.

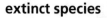

extinct species

A species becomes extinct when its last member dies. Many people are becoming concerned about the number of plant and animal species that are in danger of permanently disappearing from the Earth. *See endangered species.*

extinct

extradition

When someone accused of a crime is removed from one state to another to stand trial, that movement is called *extradition*. For example, suppose someone robbed a bank in New York and fled to New Mexico and was caught. The New York police would ask the New Mexico authorities to extradite the prisoner.

eye

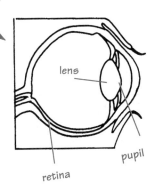

lens

retina

pupil

The human eye is actually a convex lens. That is, it is thicker in the middle than it is at the sides. When light enters the eye, the shape of the eye causes the light to be focused on the retina, the small part of the back of the eye. The retina transforms the light into electrical signals, which the brain interprets as visual images.

fable

A fable is a brief tale told in order to present a moral truth. The characters are often animals. Aesop, for instance, created many fables in ancient Greece. *See Aesop, folklore, legend, parable, tale, and tall tale.*

face

In geometry, a face is a flat surface that is part of a solid figure. It is the flat side, top, or bottom of the figure. A cube, for example, has six faces.

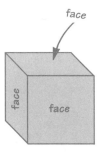

fad diet

A fad diet is a nutritionally unbalanced diet that falsely promises a quick weight loss. *See nutrition.*

fallacy of oversimplification

Fallacy of oversimplification is a logical fallacy in which a person looking at a complex problem comes up with an overly simple and easy solution.

Example:

In order to solve the world's environmental problems, all we have to do is recycle our garbage every week.

See logical fallacy.

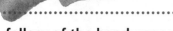

fallacy of the bandwagon

Fallacy of the bandwagon is a logical fallacy in which a person states that because everyone else is doing something, it is the correct thing to do.

Example:

You have to let me go to that concert, Mom, because everyone is going.

See bandwagon and logical fallacy.

false analogy

False analogy is a logical fallacy in which a person draws a conclusion based on an analogy with premises that are not similar.

Example:

Just as a car will not run unless it has gas, you will not be able to function unless you eat your vegetables.

See analogy and logical fallacy.

famine

A famine is a period of starving. When people cannot get enough food because of drought or disaster, it is called a famine.

fantasy

Imaginative writing that takes the reader into an unrealistic or supernatural world is fantasy.

Examples:

The Black Cauldron by Lloyd Alexander

The Crystal Cave by Mary Stewart

See science fiction.

Faraday, Michael

Michael Faraday (1791–1867) was an English scientist who studied how electricity could be produced. He discovered that moving a magnet through a coil of copper

wire caused electrical current to flow through the wire. His discovery (called "the principle of electromagnetic induction") formed the basis of electrical motors and generators.

farther/further

▷ *Farther* is usually used with distances in space.

Example:

Kim can run farther than I.

▷ *Further* is generally used with degrees or quantities.

Example:

Their careful planning has moved them further toward their goal.

fascism

Fascism is a form of government that favors dictatorial rule, limited individual freedom, strong central control of industry and labor, and extreme nationalism and militarism. Benito Mussolini was the leader of the Fascist Party and dictator of Italy from 1922 to 1943. *See dictator.*

fats

Fats provide energy, help growth, repair cells, and dissolve and carry certain vitamins to cells. *See nutrients.*

Faulkner, William

William Faulkner (1897–1962) was an American novelist who won the Nobel Prize for literature in 1949. His writing often focused on the traditions and history of the South, with many of his stories set in a mythical county in Mississippi. Among his best-known novels are *The Sound and the Fury* and *Light in August.*

fault

A fault is a break in the Earth's crust along which rocks move or slide. These cracks in the Earth are "read" by scientists called geologists. From faults, geologists can tell what minerals—such as lead, zinc, and copper—may or may not be present in the Earth below.

Federalist

The Federalist is a series of eighty-five letters published in New York newspapers in 1787 and 1788. Written by Alexander Hamilton, James Madison, and John Jay, the essays urged ratification of the new constitution by showing how it would provide for an effective, strong national government that still conformed to republican ideals.

felony

A felony is a serious crime. Armed robbery, for example, is a felony. Lesser crimes are misdemeanors.

feminism

Feminism is the movement to gain fair and equal treatment for women. Feminists are people who work for equal social, economic, and political rights for women.

Ferdinand and Isabella

Ferdinand (1452–1516) and Isabella (1451–1504) were Spanish rulers. They financed Columbus's voyage to America in 1492 and encouraged Spanish expansion in the New World. They expelled the Jews from Spain, fought the Muslims, and supported the Spanish Inquisition.

Fertile Crescent

The land between the Tigris and the Euphrates rivers extending from the Persian Gulf to the Mediterranean Sea is the Fertile Crescent. An ancient civilization first emerged there about 3500 B.C. *See Euphrates River and Tigris River.*

Fertile Crescent

fertilization

Fertilization is the act of a sperm cell joining with an egg cell. Most plants and animals rely on fertilization in order to produce new offspring. Certain organisms do not reproduce this way (algae, for example, are single-cell organisms, each of which divides itself in two). In many common plants and flowers, a yellow powder called pollen fertilizes the organism so it will reproduce.

fetus

Before it is born, a developing baby is called a *fetus*. Specifically, a fetus is a baby from eight weeks after conception until its birth.

feudalism

Feudalism is a social, political, and economic system without a strong central government. In feudal societies, vassals give service to a lord in return for protection. Japan, China, and western Europe have had feudal societies in the past.

fewer/less

▷ *Fewer* is used with plural words that could be replaced by specific numbers (dollars, hours, actions).

▷ *Less* is used with singular words showing quantity or amount (money, time, work).

Example:
Because there was less money to pay them, the laborers worked fewer hours.

fiction

Fiction is any prose literature with imaginary characters and events. Short stories and novels are the most common forms of fiction. "The Most Dangerous Game" is fiction, as is *To Kill a Mockingbird.*

figurative language

Language that says one thing and means something more is figurative. Figures of speech often compare things that are alike in an important way. By using figures of speech, a writer or speaker can make a point more clearly and quickly. Similes and metaphors are the most common figures of speech. Personification, paradox, and hyperbole are other examples of figurative language. Robert Burns's poem "A Red, Red Rose" uses figurative language:

O my luve is like a red, red rose
Tha'st newly sprung in June:
O my luve is like the melodie
That's sweetly played in tune.

file

In computer jargon, a file is an electronic entity that stores under a single name related information on a computer or a computer disk.

filibuster

A filibuster is a deliberate action, such as a very long speech, used by members of the minority to delay or stop passage of a bill into law. The only way to stop a filibuster in the U.S. Senate, for example, is by a special legislative vote called a *cloture*.

fin de siècle

The French phrase *fin de siècle* means "end of the century." It refers especially to the last two decades of the nineteenth century (1880–1900). The period gave rise to specific movements in art and literature.

fiord

A long, narrow bay of the sea bordered by steep cliffs is a fiord. Norway, for instance, is known for its fiords.

firing

Firing is the process of baking clay or fusing glaze or enamel by exposing the objects to intense heat in a special oven called a kiln. Such a process often changes the color of the objects.

First Amendment freedoms

The First Amendment to the U.S. Constitution is part of the Bill of Rights. It was added to the Constitution in 1791. The rights of people to freedom of speech and religion, to a free press, and to hold peaceful meetings are First Amendment freedoms. *See Bill of Rights.*

fish

Fish are animals with backbones that live their entire lives in water. Fish breathe through gills rather than with lungs. The gills are thin pieces of tissue filled with many very tiny blood vessels. Water passes through the mouth of a fish over a series of gills. Oxygen in the water passes into the blood vessels. Then the oxygen is absorbed into the fish's body.

Fish fins are used for many purposes—balance, steering, the power to move. The tail fins propel fish, and the others help them steer.

There are also a number of unusual species of fish. If a starfish, for instance, is cut up into several chunks, each piece will eventually grow into a completely whole starfish. The seahorse has a tail that allows it to grab and cling to seaweed. It is also unusual because the male looks after the eggs and carries them in a pouch in his belly.

fissure

A fissure is a crack in the ground where lava can reach the surface. *See lava.*

Fitzgerald, F. Scott

Francis Scott Key Fitzgerald (1896–1940) was an American novelist and short-story writer who often wrote about the temptations

MORE

of wealth and fame in the period called "the Roaring Twenties" (the 1920s). *The Great Gatsby* is considered his best novel.

flamenco

Flamenco is a style of music and dancing created by Spanish gypsies. The music, usually by guitar and castanets, is fast, with dramatic rhythms, emphasized by the stamping and clapping of the dancers.

flashback

A flashback is an interruption in the action of a narrative or other piece of writing to show an episode that occurred at an earlier time. *See foreshadowing and plot.*

flashlight

A flashlight is a portable electric light in a metal or plastic case, usually cylindrical. Batteries in a flashlight contain stored energy. To make a flashlight work, an electrical current has to flow through the flashlight. That happens because of a circuit. Current begins to move from the batteries to the bulb when the flashlight is switched on. The switch makes a circuit between the batteries and the bottom of the light bulb in the flashlight. The electricity only flows when this circuit is complete. The two pieces of metal touch at the circuit, and the light goes on. *See electricity and energy.*

flat

flat

In music, the symbol for a "flat" indicates a pitch lowered by a half-step. It is placed in front of the note being lowered or is written at the beginning of each staff of the score to indicate the key signature. Singing or playing "flat" indicates performing at pitches slightly lower than the correct ones. *See score and sharp.*

flood plain

A plain bordering a river is a flood plain. When the river overflows its banks after a heavy rain, it leaves mud and sand on the flood plain. This land is generally very fertile because of the sediment deposited by the water.

flowering plants

Of the more than 350,000 species of plants that have been identified, more than 250,000 are flowering plants. All of these plants produce seeds. These plants range from grass to much less common plants such as orchids.

fluorescence

Fluorescence is a special quality of an object that produces light or glows in the dark when exposed to X-rays, ultraviolet rays, or certain other kinds of rays.

flute

A flute is the soprano of the orchestra's woodwind family. It has the shape of a long, slim tube, usually made of silver, and is played by blowing across an opening near one end of the instrument. Flutes, among the oldest instruments known, were played in ancient Egypt and ancient China.

focus

The focus is the continual concentration on the specific topic of a piece of writing, art, or photography.

foil

A foil is a character in a story or a play who serves as a contrast to another character. In Mark Twain's *The Adventures of Huckleberry Finn*, for example, Jim serves as a foil for Huck.

folklore

Folklore includes the customs, legends, songs, and stories passed from generation to generation of an ethnic group or nationality. *See ethnic group and tale.*

food chain

A food chain is the path that energy and materials take in a community. For example, when a snake eats a mouse, it is completing one part of a food chain. The next link in the chain may occur when a hawk captures the snake. Eventually, the snake's remains may serve as fertilizer for the soil. Plants will grow in the soil, and these will serve as food for the insects and animals on which mice feed. The chain, in other words, eventually makes a full circle.

food groups

The four basic food groups include the meat-poultry-fish-bean group, the bread-cereal group, the fruit-vegetable group, and the milk group.

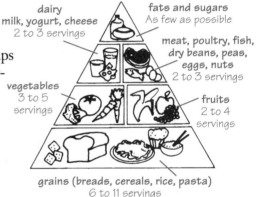

dairy
milk, yogurt, cheese
2 to 3 servings

fats and sugars
As few as possible

meat, poultry, fish, dry beans, peas, eggs, nuts
2 to 3 servings

vegetables
3 to 5 servings

fruits
2 to 4 servings

grains (breads, cereals, rice, pasta)
6 to 11 servings

foot

In poetry, a foot is a unit of meter that presents a combination of stressed and unstressed syllables. A line of verse has a particular number of feet. A line written in iambic pentameter, for example, has five feet of an unstressed syllable followed by a stressed syllable. *See meter, poetry, rhythm, scansion, and verse.*

Forbidden City

A walled section of Beijing, the capital of China, is called the Forbidden City. Behind the walls are palaces and other buildings of the Chinese Empire. Built in the fifteenth, sixteenth, and seventeenth centuries for the imperial family, the Forbidden City is today open to tourists. *See Beijing.*

Ford, Henry

Henry Ford (1863–1947) was an American engineer and industrialist who, in 1896, built his first gasoline-driven automobile. By using assembly lines in his factory, Ford made cars inexpensive enough for large numbers of people and helped bring them into general use.

foreground

In art, the foreground is the part of an artwork that appears closest to the viewer. The part of the painting that appears farthest away is called the background.

foreground

foreign policy

Plans by a government about how to act toward other nations and groups are the nation's foreign policy. Usually, each American President has his own foreign policy.

foreshadowing

Foreshadowing is a writer's hints or clues suggesting events what will happen later in a story. In John Steinbeck's *Of Mice and Men*, for example, Lenny's accidental killing of a puppy foreshadows the tragedy at the end of the story. *See flashback and plot.*

forgery

A forgery is a work that is an imitation or counterfeit work which is created to fool or deceive someone. Usually a forger creates a false document in order to sell the forgery for a lot of money. Experts in art spend a part of their time making sure that works in museums are, indeed, fine works of art rather than forgeries.

forte

The term *forte* is Italian. When written in music, this direction appears as a symbol, the letter *f.* It tells a performer to play or sing moderately strongly.

forth/fourth

▷ *Forth* means forward.

▷ *Fourth*, formed from the number four, means next after third.

Example:

The knight went forth and searched until he found the fourth sword.

fossil

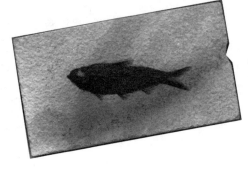

A fossil is the remains of an ancient animal or plant that has hardened into rock. Fossils are usually pre-served in the Earth's crust or rock. *See dinosaurs.*

fossil fuel

A fuel created over millions of years from the remains of plants and animals is a fossil fuel. Coal and oil, for example, are kinds of fossil fuel. Oil is found in many parts of the United States such as Alaska, Texas, Pennsylvania, and California. Scientists believe that the remains of plants and animals millions and millions of years ago collected at the bottom of seas and lakes. As they became cov-ered with sand and dirt, the pressure on them increased tremen-dously so that they eventually liquified and became oil.

Founding Fathers

The Founding Fathers are the American statesmen who signed the Declaration of Independence and wrote the Constitution. These Revolutionary War leaders are thought of as the "fathers" of the United States.

fracture

A fracture is a break. When a bone is fractured, for example, it is broken. Scientists also use the this term to describe the way miner-als break.

France

France is the largest nation in Western Europe. It has coastlines on both the Atlantic Ocean and the Mediterranean Sea. Although France has a long history of agriculture, most French people now live in cities. *See Europe and Paris.*

Frank, Anne

Anne Frank (1929–1945) was the young German woman whose diary captured the plight of Jewish people during the Nazi persecution in World War II. Frank's *The Diary of a Young Girl* serves as a strong testament to the vitality of the human spirit in the face of horror. The diary was written during Frank's two years in hiding from the Nazis. From 1942 to 1944, an Amsterdam family kept the Franks hidden in a secret attic in an office building. At the end of that time, an informer revealed their hiding place. Later, Anne, her mother, and her sister died in a concentration camp.

Franklin, Benjamin

One of America's great statesmen, authors, and inventors, Benjamin Franklin (1706–1790) helped write the Declaration of Independence and attended the Constitutional Convention of 1787. He invented the lightning rod, bifocal glasses, and the Franklin stove. Franklin also earned fame as a writer. His short sayings such as, "A penny saved is a penny earned," are still remembered today.

free verse

Poetry without regular meter or rhyme scheme is free verse. For instance, many of Walt Whitman's poems in *Leaves of Grass* are written in free verse. *See meter and rhyme.*

free writing

Free writing is writing openly and freely about any topic. Free writing often involves stream of consciousness—the free associations that pour from the writer's mind.

freedom of the press

The First Amendment of the Constitution guarantees the right to freely publish books, newspapers, magazines, and other written materials. This is one of the fundamental rights of citizens. *See Bill of Rights and First Amendment freedoms.*

freezing

The temperature at which a liquid is turned into a solid is its freezing point. Bodies of water freeze from the top down rather than from the bottom up because the surface water above is cooled by the air above it, while the water below stays warmer longer. This explains why lakes and rivers freeze over on top, while water flows beneath the surface. *See irradiation.*

French and Indian War

The French and Indian War (1754–1763) was a series of battles in North America between the French and their Indian allies and the British forces. The winner, Britain, gained all of Canada.

French horn

A French horn is a brass orchestral instrument whose tube is wound in a circular pattern, opening in a wide bell. It is played by means of valves and has a rich, mellow tone.

French Revolution

The French Revolution (1789–1799) began when a Parisian mob, on July 14, 1789, stormed the Bastille, a royal fortress that was a hated symbol of oppression. The beheading of Louis XVI in 1793 ended 800 years of French monarchy. The ten-year revolution finally ended when Napoleon became France's ruler in 1799.

frequency

The number of times a certain item occurs in a set of data is that item's frequency.

Example: ➚

Example:

During four games a basketball player scores 10 points, 12 points, 13 points, and 10 points. The frequency of 10 is 2. The frequency of 12 and of 13 is one.

fresco

Fresco is the art or technique of painting on a moist plaster surface. The colors of a fresco are ground up in water and applied to the plaster. During the Renaissance, painters made some of their greatest accomplishments with frescoes in Italian churches and at the Vatican in Rome. *See Renaissance.*

fresh water

Fresh water—unlike the salt water of oceans—contains little or no salt and is drinkable. Rivers, lakes, and streams contain fresh water. As water shortages become more common, society is looking for sources of fresh water. More than 99 percent of all the fresh water on Earth is trapped in icecaps and glaciers. *See glacier.*

fret

Frets are raised pieces of wood or metal at intervals across the neck of stringed instruments such as a lute, guitar, banjo, and ukelele. Frets separate one pitch on a string from another.

friction

Friction is a force that slows down the motion of moving objects. According to Newton's law objects in motion tend to stay in motion, but friction is what slows them down and eventually stops them—friction with the air, of parts rubbing together, and so forth. Sandpaper rubbed against wood, for example, causes friction that smooths the wood. *See Isaac Newton.*

WAIT, THERE'S MORE!

frontier

The border between two countries or between two types of settlements is a frontier. *Frontier* can also mean "a new

area or far-off place." For example, the American West was a frontier for settlers in the East, and space is a frontier for the people of Earth.

Frost, Robert

Robert Frost (1874–1963) was among the most honored of American poets. He won the Pulitzer Prize for Poetry four times and was awarded numerous honorary degrees. Frost most often used New England for the settings of his poems about nature and the nature of humankind.

frostbite

Frostbite is damage to body tissue caused by cold. *See hypothermia.*

frozen food

Freezing is an important method of preserving food. The Inuit people of Canada taught Clarence Birdseye, a fur trader, how to freeze food. On his return to the United States, he perfected the method and started a frozen food business.

fulcrum

A fulcrum is the support on which a lever rests in moving or lifting something. *See lever.*

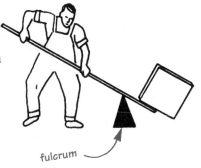

fulcrum

fundamental counting property

The fundamental counting property states that: If there are M possible outcomes for one event, N possible outcomes for a second event, and P possible outcomes for a third event, then the total number of possible outcomes is M x N x P.

fundamentalist

A fundamentalist is a person who believes that the words of the Bible were inspired by God and should be taken literally and followed exactly.

fungi

Fungi are simple plants without leaves, flowers, or the green coloring matter chlorophyll. Mushrooms and toadstools are examples of large fungi. What makes fungi distinct is the way they get their food. Fungi live with other living things in a beneficial relationship; off other living things in a parasitic relationship; or off dead, decaying things, such as old tree stumps.

fuse

A fuse is a safety device that protects an electrical circuit from damage due to excess current. Electrical energy flows through fuses, which have pieces of soft metal in them. When the wire becomes too hot, the metal melts, breaking the circuit, and the electricity stops flowing.

Gagarin, Yuri

Yuri Gagarin (1934–1968) was a Soviet pilot and cosmonaut. On April 12, 1961, Gagarin became the first man in space. His ship, *Vostok 1*, made a complete trip around the Earth. The entire flight lasted 1 hour and 48 minutes. He proved that man could travel to space and return safely. He later died in a plane crash in 1968.

Galapagos Islands

The Galapagos Islands are an archipelago, or cluster of islands, 600 miles off the coast of Ecuador in South America. The islands were named for the large, nearly extinct tortoises (turtles) that live there and grow to weigh as much as five hundred pounds. Charles Darwin, who made the island famous, was most interested in finches, a species of bird. By studying the varieties of finches on the Galapagos, Darwin formed some of his most important observations about evolution. *See Charles Darwin and evolution.*

galaxy

A group of stars, dust, and gases held together by gravity is a galaxy. The Milky Way galaxy is the one in which the Earth is located. It is so large that, travelling at the speed of light, it would take hundreds of years to go from one end to the other. Scientists

have learned, however, that not all galaxies have the same shape. Some appear to be spiral, with a center with several arms coming out from it. Others, though, are elliptical (shaped like a football). Edwin P. Hubble began the system of classifying galaxies in 1925. All of the galaxies together are the universe.

Galilei, Galileo

Galileo Galilei (1564–1642), born in Pisa, Italy, has been called the father of modern, experimental science. He discovered the law of falling bodies, that is, that objects fall at the same rate. A marble falls as fast as a baseball if the resistance of the air is taken into account. Legend has it that he demonstrated this idea by dropping two cannonballs of different sizes from the Tower of Pisa. In 1607 he invented a thermometer and improved on the design of the telescope, which enabled him to make important discoveries about the moon, the moons of Jupiter, and about the Milky Way.

gallon

A gallon is a unit for measuring liquids. *See customary units of measure.*

Gandhi, Mohandas K.

Known as the "Mahatma," or "great soul," Mohandas K. Gandhi (1869–1948) helped gain independence for India in 1947 after years of struggle. His method of nonviolent resistance was later used by Martin Luther King, Jr., during the American civil rights movement. *See Martin Luther King, Jr.*

gastric juice

The stomach produces a substance called *gastric juice* to aid in the digestion of food. The gastric juices contain hydrochloric acid, digestive enzymes, and water. They help break down meat, eggs, and milk into nutrients that the body can use. *See digestive system.*

Geiger counter

A Geiger counter is an instrument used to detect ionizing radiation from a radioactive material. Hans Geiger (1882–1945), a German physicist, developed a way to locate radioactive material, which cannot be seen but can be harmful.

gender

Gender is the term used to classify words according to whether they are masculine (he), feminine (she), or neuter (it). In many languages, nouns, pronouns, and their modifiers have special endings to show gender, but in English most nouns show gender only through their definition.

Examples:
- aunt/uncle
- niece/nephew
- hen/rooster

genealogist

A genealogist charts the history of a family. Genealogists record information about family members as far back in time as there are records. Author Alex Haley, for instance, wrote the book *Roots* about his genealogy.

general welfare

The term *general welfare* means good living conditions for all. The health and happiness of people and the relative degree of comfort of their lives are their general welfare.

generalization

In writing, a generalization is a statement of the general idea rather than the specific details of a topic.

generator

A generator is a machine that changes mechanical energy into electrical energy. That is, a generator powered by gasoline can change that energy into electricity. *See electricity and energy.*

genetics

Genetics is the study of how parents pass characteristics onto off-spring. Through a study of genetics, plants can be bred to provide higher yields. For example, farmers who grow peas and corn often use special seeds that grow pea pods with exactly six pods or rows of corn that are perfectly straight. This can be done through cross-breeding, which is an important part of genetics.

genre

Genre is a term used to classify a particular kind of literature. The murder mystery and Gothic romance, for example, are genres of modern fiction.

geographer

A geographer studies the Earth's surface, climate, continents, countries, people, industries, and products.

geology

Geology is the study of the Earth and the processes that act on the Earth. The Earth's crust, its volcanoes and mountain ranges, and its minerals and their composition are all the subjects of geology.

Germany

Germany is a country located in central Europe. It is bordered by nine other countries. Between 1949 and 1990, it was divided into West Germany and communist East Germany. *See Berlin and Europe.*

gerrymander

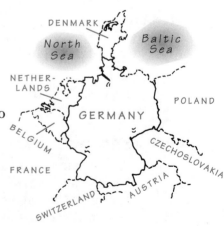

To arrange the political divisions of an area to give one political party an advantage is gerrymandering. The term comes from Elbridge Gerry. In 1812, Governor Gerry's party changed the voting boundaries of Massachusetts so that the shape of one district looked like a salamander, which was highly unusual except that those boundaries gave his party an advantage. The word gerrymander comes from Gerry and salamander.

Gershwin, George

Well-known American composer George Gershwin (1898–1937) blended popular musical styles with classic forms as in *Rhapsody in Blue, An American in Paris,* and his folk opera *Porgy and Bess.* He also wrote many popular songs to the lyrics written by his brother Ira.

gerund

A gerund is an *-ing* verb used as a noun. Gerunds are often used in gerund phrases.

Example:

Reading books is a good idea.

See noun and verb.

Gettysburg

The battle of Gettysburg (1863) marked the turning point of the American Civil War. Union forces defeated General Lee's army in southern Pennsylvania. Lee had planned to invade the North, but his weakened army had to retreat south instead. *See civil war.*

Gettysburg Address

Abraham Lincoln's speech at Gettysburg, Pennsylvania, in 1863 became famous as "The Gettysburg Address." In that speech, Lincoln dedicated the battlefield as a cemetery and eloquently explained that the Civil War was being fought to preserve the Union. *See Emancipation Proclamation and Gettysburg.*

Four score and seven years ago . . .

Gilbert and Sullivan

Sir William S. Gilbert (1836–1911) wrote the words and Sir Arthur S. Sullivan (1842–1900) composed the music for thirteen light or "comic" operas in the late nineteenth century. They have enjoyed lasting popularity both in their native England and in other English-speaking countries. Best known are *The Mikado, The Pirates of Penzance*, and *H.M.S. Pinafore*.

glacier

A glacier is a large mass of ice that moves, usually across land. Glaciers move at different speeds. Most glaciers plod along at very slow speeds, sometimes only a few hundred feet per year. Other glaciers, though, move more than fifty feet per day. Long ago, glaciers covered large parts of North America.

gladiator

A gladiator was a captive or paid fighter of ancient Rome, who entertained the public by fighting animals or other fighters. The contests were held in arenas, which were open circular theaters. *See Ancient Rome.*

glass

Glass is composed primarily of sand, lime, and soda. These substances are ground up into very small particles and then heated in very hot fires. Eventually the sand and soda ash melt together and form a liquid. This liquid is poured into molds and allowed to cool. Then, the glass is clear enough to see through.

glaze

A glaze is a thin, glassy coating that is fused to the surface of a clay object by baking it in a kiln. A glaze can be applied in a variety of ways, including brushing and spraying.

glee club

A glee club is a male singing group of three or more sections, developed in England, and now also common in America. The music is usually of a lighthearted nature.

global meltdown

The fuel we burn to keep warm releases carbon dioxide. As more carbon dioxide is released, we have what scientists call the greenhouse effect. That is, the Earth is kept warm because radiation (heat) is prevented from escaping into space. Thus, the temperature on Earth is gradually becoming higher. Eventually, the ice caps at the North and South Poles may melt, raising the level of the seas. *See greenhouse effect.*

glossary

A glossary is a list of specialized words and their meanings. A glossary is often placed near the end of a textbook.

glucose

Glucose is a sugar occurring in plant and animal tissue. Plants make glucose during the process of photosynthesis. The cells in the human body get their energy from foods people eat. The body breaks foods down into different parts, one of which is glucose. The blood stream then carries glucose to all of the cells in the body.

GNP (gross national product)

The GNP, or gross national product, is the value of all goods and services produced by a nation in a given period. The value of all the products and services—food, clothing, automobiles, everything—in a country, added together, produces the country's GNP. The GNP of the United States, for example, is billions of dollars.

gobbledygook

Gobbledygook is speech or writing that is difficult to understand because it includes too many technical terms and other complicated words. *See doublespeak and jargon.*

Goddard, Robert

The "father" of American rocketry is Robert Goddard (1892–1945). He launched his first rocket in 1926—a rocket only four feet tall and six inches in diameter. Goddard first suggested that rockets could be used for research and developed the first liquid fuels to propel them. *See rocket.*

Golden Age of Greece

As with the Renaissance or Enlightenment, historians mark the period between 477–431 B.C. as one of the great periods in history. It was a time of great learning in classical Greece. A great statesman, Pericles encouraged democracy and supported the arts, architecture, and science. Athenian achievements influenced other cultures, and the time came to be known as the Golden Age of Greece. *See Ancient Greece, Athens, Enlightenment, and Renaissance.*

Pericles

Golding, William

William Golding (b. 1911) is an English writer whose most famous novel is *Lord of the Flies*. Golding won the Nobel Prize for Literature in 1983.

good/well

▷ *Good* is an adjective.
  Example:
  Scottie is a good player.

▷ *Well* is most often used as an adverb.
  Example:
  Scottie plays well.

See adjective and adverb.

Goodall, Jane

Jane Goodall (b. 1934) studies chimpanzees in Africa. Her research involves long, careful observations. Her discoveries are about how chimpanzees use tools to eat, how they travel through forests, and how they protect themselves. Her work is important because it gives us a better understanding of how animals learn and behave.

gospel music

The term *gospel music* refers to religious songs whose words present Christian teachings as found in the four Gospels of The New Testament of the Bible. The rhymed lines are set to lively, singable tunes with simple harmonies.

Gothic

Gothic is a style of art and architecture developed in Western Europe between the twelfth and fifteenth centuries. Gothic cathedrals are known for their pointed arches and ribbed vaults. The word *gothic* is also used to describe styles in painting and calligraphy, characterized by elaborate decoration and the bright colors and architectural detail of stained glass windows.

governor

The governor of a state is the leader of the executive branch of the state government. He or she makes sure that the laws are carried out. *See executive branch.*

graffito

Graffito is a scratched drawing or inscription. This artistic style began in ancient Rome and appeared on buildings, walls, and pillars. The Italian word *graffito* is usually given as the plural *graffiti*.

grafting

Grafting is a method of uniting parts of two plants to form a single plant with characteristics of both. It is primarily done to propagate certain plants. It is done by putting a bud or shoot from one plant into a slit in another so that it will grow there permanently. *See genetics.*

gram

A gram is a unit for measuring weight in the metric system. A raisin weighs about one gram.

grammar

Grammar is the study of the structure of language. Grammar provides the rules for the correct usage of language. One easy way to think about grammar is to think of it as a description of how language works. *See usage.*

graph

A drawing used to show the relative sizes of numerical quantities is a graph.

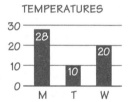

graphics

In computer jargon, graphics are visual representations on a computer screen.

graphite

Graphite is a soft, lustrous black carbon material used in lead pencils and as a lubricant.

grass roots

Grass roots is an idiom that means at the neighborhood or local level. Used this way, grass roots means ordinary citizens.

gravity

Gravity is the natural force that causes objects to tend to move toward the center of the Earth. The strength of gravity depends on the masses of the bodies and the distance between the bodies—for example, how far it is between the Earth and the sun. The gravity of the moon is much less than the Earth's gravity because it has less mass. That is the reason astronauts can jump higher on the moon than they can on the Earth. The theory of universal gravitation was formulated by Isaac Newton in 1665. This law states that the gravitational force between two objects is proportional to the size of their masses; that is, the larger the two masses are, the greater the force is between them. He discovered this as he watched an apple fall from a tree. *See Isaac Newton.*

Great Barrier Reef

The Great Barrier Reef is the longest coral reef in the world. It is located near the northeast coast of Australia. *See Australia and reef.*

Great Depression

A severe slowdown in business in the United States and many other countries occurred in 1929. Banks closed, companies failed, and people were out of work. The period was called the Great Depression. In the United States, the Great Depression continued until 1942.

Great Lakes

The group of five lakes between Canada and the United States is the Great Lakes: Lake Ontario, Lake Erie, Lake Huron, Lake Michigan, and Lake Superior. Together the Great Lakes contain almost one-fifth of all the fresh water in the world. *See Canada, North America, and the United States.*

Great Wall of China

The Great Wall of China is a wall more than 4,000 miles long in north and northwest China. Begun in the 400s B.C. and completed in the A.D. 1600s, the

Great Wall is the longest structure ever built in the world. *See China.*

greater than

The symbol for greater than (>) shows a relation between two numbers. In 8 > 5, the symbol shows that 8 is larger than 5.

Greece

Greece is a country in southeastern Europe on the Mediterranean Sea. Ancient Greece provided the birthplace for western culture in the 500s B.C. *See Ancient Greece, Athens, and Europe.*

greenbacks

In 1862, the Union created paper money that did not have gold or silver to back it up. This money was called *greenbacks* because it was printed with green ink on one side. Its value rose or fell with the successes of the North in the Civil War, so that it might be worth 60 cents one day and 80 cents a month later.

greenhouse effect

"The greenhouse effect" is the name scientists have given to the trapping of extra heat in the air surrounding the Earth. When fuels such as coal and oil (called fossil fuels) are burned, they release carbon dioxide into the air. Since carbon dioxide tends to hold hot air, the more fuel that is burned the warmer parts of the Earth become. Many scientists worry that the greenhouse effect might eventually cause severe problems in our ability to grow crops. *See fossil fuel and global meltdown.*

Greenland

Arctic Ocean

NORTH AMERICA

GREENLAND

Arctic Circle

Greenland, most of which lies north of the Arctic Circle off the Northeast Coast of North America, is the largest island in the world. Although it is located in North America, Greenland is a province of Denmark. *See Denmark and North America.*

Gregorian chant

A Gregorian chant is vocal music used in the liturgy, or ritual, of the Roman Catholic Church. It is melodic and follows the rhythm of the words. During the reign of Pope Gregory (590–604), earlier chant forms were set into this form, which is still used today.

Guatemala

Guatemala is a country in northwest Central America. It is the most heavily populated country in Central America. Guatemala City, its largest city, is the capital. *See Central America.*

guild system

The guild system refers to groups of workers who organized to keep the quality of work high and to protect their interests. In Europe during the Middle Ages, guilds controlled many occupations—for example, printing.

guitar

A guitar is a six-stringed instrument with a long, narrow, fretted neck. The acoustic guitar has a flat, hollow body with an opening over which the strings are stretched. Strings are plucked or strummed. The electric guitar has a flat, solid body, with the sound amplified through speakers.

gulf

A gulf is a large body of salt water partially enclosed by land.

Gulf Coast

The southeastern region of the United States bordering on the Gulf of Mexico is the Gulf Coast. It extends from Florida to Texas. *See United States.*

Gulf Stream

The Gulf Stream is a warm current in the Atlantic Ocean that flows from the Caribbean Sea into the Gulf of Mexico along the Eastern United States to Cape Hatteras, then out into the North Atlantic. It influences both climate and sea travel.

gunpowder

Gunpowder, which explodes when fired, was first invented in China about A.D. 1,000. The knowledge of gunpowder moved west into Muslim nations and then on to Europe in the 1200s, where it changed medieval life. Neither castle walls nor mounted knights in armor could stand up against cannons and guns.

Gutenberg, Johannes

Johannes Gutenberg (1395?-1468) was a German who invented the type mold, making movable type practical for the first time. In 1456, he printed the first European book in movable type—the *Gutenberg Bible.* Before movable type, books had to be copied by hand, and so very few books were available to people.

habitat

A habitat is a place where an organism naturally lives. The habitat of a gopher, for example, may be a hole in the ground; the habitat of a squirrel is a nest high in a tree. Clearing land for farming and filling in swampland for building are examples of ways humans destroy habitats of animals. Birds and animals depend on the forests and grasslands to make their homes. By destroying their habitats, humans begin the process that will destroy these species. *See ecosystem.*

hacker

In computer jargon, a hacker is a person who understands computers and computer software exceptionally well. The word is also used to describe a person who breaks into a computer system connected to a telephone network.

Hades

In Greek mythology, Hades was the god of the underworld. Hades was also the name of the underworld that he ruled. In Roman mythology, Hades's name was Pluto.

haiku

Haiku is a form of poetry that has three lines. The first line has five syllables, the second seven syllables, and the third five syllables. Traditional Japanese haiku were about nature. Here is an example of a haiku:

The moon in the trees
Caught by skeletal branches
Loneliness rising

See poetry.

hail

Hail consists of balls of ice. When water vapor in a cloud freezes, it is sometimes pushed higher into the air by strong winds. Each time that hail is pushed higher, it adds another layer of ice. Eventually, when the hail becomes too heavy for the winds to keep it up, it falls to the Earth.

half-life

The time it takes for half of the nuclei in a quantity of radioactive material to decay is its half-life. The term is often used when scientists try to fix the date of something.

Halley's comet

In 1705, Edmund Halley, an English astronomer, correctly predicted the return of a comet previously seen in 1531, 1607, and 1682. Halley said the comet would return to view in 1758. Unfortunately, Halley did not live long enough to see the return of the comet, which was subsequently named for him.

hallucinogen

A hallucinogen is a drug that distorts the user's understanding of himself or herself or his or her surroundings. The drug LSD is a hallucinogen. It causes people who use it to see, hear, and feel things that don't exist or that exist only in their imagination, which is part of the reason the drug is so dangerous.

Hannibal

THERE'S MORE

A Carthaginian general, Hannibal (247–183 B.C.) led Carthage against the Romans in the Second Punic Wars. In one daring

attack, he crossed the Alps—a nearly impossible feat—with 60,000 soldiers and a train of elephants.

Hansberry, Lorraine

Lorraine Hansberry (1930–1965) was an American playwright. In 1959 she became the youngest playwright and first black writer to win the New York Drama Critics Circle Award for her play, *A Raisin in the Sun*. *To Be Young, Gifted and Black* is a compilation of her journals, letters, and other autobiographical writings.

Hardy, Thomas

Thomas Hardy (1840–1928) was a British poet and novelist. His most famous novels include *Far From the Madding Crowd*, *The Return of the Native*, *Tess of the D'Urbervilles*, and *Jude the Obscure*.

harmonica

A harmonica, also called a "mouth organ," is a small rectangular instrument with openings for the pitches, arranged in a row along one side. As the harmonica is moved from side to side, the player blows through the openings to activate the metal reed within.

harmony

Harmony refers to a combination of chords (notes arranged vertically) whose relationship creates a musical phrase. *See melody.*

harp

One of the earliest stringed instruments known, the harp continues to be popular. It ranges in size from a small hand-held instrument, through a larger floor-standing model such as the Irish harp, to the large double-pedal harp used in symphony orchestras. *See symphony.*

harpsichord

A harpsichord is a musical instrument with a keyboard similar to that of a piano. Unlike a piano, whose strings are struck with small hammers, the harpsichord's strings are plucked to make a bright, tinkling sound. A harpsichord may have one to three keyboards.

Harvey, William

William Harvey (1578–1657) was a physician for kings in England. He studied the way blood traveled through the body. He believed that the heart was a muscle and acted like a pump, pushing blood throughout the body. By measuring what the heart could do, he discovered that more blood passes through the heart in one hour than is contained in the entire body. He had discovered the workings of the circulatory system, or how blood travels through the veins, arteries, and capillaries.

hasty generalization

Hasty generalization is a logical fallacy in which a person draws a conclusion even though there are too few examples to support that conclusion.

Example:

Two policemen were convicted of taking bribes last week. Last year, three policeman were also convicted. It's too bad that the police department is so corrupt.

See generalization and logical fallacy.

Hawthorne, Nathaniel

Nathaniel Hawthorne (1804–1864) was an American novelist and short-story writer. His stories, usually set in New England, often dealt with evil and its effects on people. His most famous novels are *The Scarlet Letter* and *The House of Seven Gables.*

hazardous waste

Hazardous waste is material that is sometimes dumped into landfills, rivers, and other sites and can be harmful to people and the

MORE

environment. Solid, liquid, or gaseous wastes that might be toxic, explosive, infectious, or radioactive are all hazardous wastes.

heart

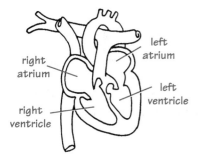

The heart is the muscle in the body that pumps blood throughout the circulatory system. The heart has four chambers. Blood flows through veins into the right atrium of the heart. Then it is pumped to the right ventricle. From there, the blood is pumped to the lungs, where the blood receives oxygen. The blood then moves to the left atrium and then the left ventricle. Finally the blood leaves the left ventricle and flows throughout the body through arteries.

heart operation

One night in 1893, a black surgeon named Dr. Daniel Hale Williams performed the first operation on the human heart. A man came into the hospital after being stabbed in the chest with a knife. As the man's condition worsened, Dr. Williams opened the man's chest and closed the wound to the heart—the first heart operation in medical history. The patient went on to live for more than twenty years thanks to Dr. Williams. *See heart.*

heart rate

The heart rate is the number of times a person's heart beats per minute. In one year, the human heart beats about 36 million times. In one day, the heart pumps more than 7,000 quarts of blood through it. More than 85 average-size refrigerators would be needed to hold all of that blood. *See heart.*

heart transplant

The first human heart transplant was performed by Dr. Christian Barnard on December 3, 1967. The heart was taken out of a woman who had died when she was hit by a car. Dr. Barnard put her heart into the chest of a man. The operation took about four hours to perform. The patient lived for eighteen days with his new heart. *See heart.*

heat exhaustion

Heat exhaustion is a condition caused by an excessive exposure to heat. It is characterized by cold, clammy skin and symptoms of shock. *See heat stroke.*

heat stroke

Heat stroke, also called "sunstroke," is a condition caused by exposure to excessive heat. It is characterized by high fever and hot, dry skin. *See heat exhaustion.*

heath

An open wasteland with heather or low bushes is a heath. The terms *heath* and *moor* are synonyms.

Helios

In Greek mythology, Helios was the god of the sun, usually depicted driving a chariot through the heavens. He was also called Apollo. *See Apollo.*

Hellenic Period

The Hellenic Period is the period between 776 B.C. to the death of Alexander in 323 B.C. This period saw many great leaders—for example, Alexander the Great—and advances. Poets, dramatists, and philosophers tried to describe the ideals of truth and beauty.

Hemingway, Ernest

Ernest Hemingway (1899–1961) was an American novelist and short-story writer who won the Nobel Prize for Literature in 1954. His novel *The Old Man and the Sea* won the Pulitzer Prize in 1953. Three of his other novels are *For Whom the Bell Tolls*, *A Farewell to Arms*, and *The Sun Also Rises*.

hemisphere

A hemisphere is one-half of the Earth's surface. The equator divides the Earth into the Northern and Southern hemispheres. The prime meridian and the 180th meridian divide the Earth into the Eastern and Western hemispheres. *See meridian.*

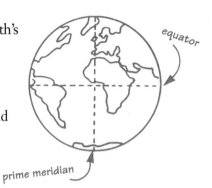

hemoglobin

The color of red blood cells comes from a protein molecule called *hemoglobin*. Hemoglobin contains iron. Since iron attaches easily to oxygen, the red blood cells are able to carry molecules of oxygen. An individual red blood cell will live for about four months.

Henry VIII

Henry VIII (1491–1547), the King of England, founded the Church of England when he broke with the Catholic Church in 1534 over his divorce from his first wife, Catherine of Aragon. Henry went on to marry five more times.

Hera

In Greek mythology, Hera was the wife of Zeus and the queen of the gods. Her Roman name was Juno.

heredity

The passing of genetic traits from parents to their offspring is heredity. If both parents are tall, for instance, a study of heredity would show that the child's chances of growing tall are also very good. *See genetics.*

heritage

Culture and customs handed down from one generation to the next are one's heritage. People in the United States have fought in wars to protect their heritage of freedom. People often speak of their religious heritage—a Jewish heritage, for example. This means their background and the beliefs they developed during their upbringing.

Hermes

In Greek mythology, Hermes was the messenger of the gods and the guide of dead souls to the underworld. He was also the god of travel, business, and cleverness. His Roman name was Mercury.

Herodotus

Herodotus (484?–425? B.C.), an ancient Greek historian, is believed to be the first person to use the word *history* to tell about past events. He wrote a nine-volume history of the Persian invasion of Greece in the fifth century B.C.

hertz

In physics, hertz is a unit of measurement to describe a wave's frequency. One cycle per second is a hertz.

hexagon

A six-sided polygon is a hexagon.

regular hexagon

irregular hexagon

hibernation

Many animals hibernate, or go into a deep sleep, during the winter months. During the fall months, these animals store lots of fat in their bodies. They may crawl into a log or cave and fall asleep for several months. Bears, squirrels, and chipmunks are animals that hibernate in the winter months.

hieroglyphic

A hieroglyphic is a picture or symbol standing for an idea, object, or sound. Ancient Egyptians developed hieroglyphic writing between 4000 and 3000 B.C. They wrote on scrolls of papyrus, a paper made from reeds. *See Egypt, Nile River, and papyrus.*

Hillary, Sir Edmund

Sir Edmund Hillary (1919–1993) was a New Zealand mountaineer and explorer. In 1953, Hillary and his Sherpa guide, Tenzing Norgay, became the first men to climb to the summit of Mount Everest. Hillary also explored the Antarctic.

Himalayas

The Himalayas are mountains in Central Asia that form the northern border of India. The highest mountain range on Earth, the Himalayas include the three tallest peaks in the world. *See India.*

Hinduism

Hinduism is an ancient religion, still widely practiced today in India and other countries. Hindus believe that by living their lives correctly they can be reborn or reincarnated into another and better life.

Hinton, S. E.

Susan Eloise Hinton (b. 1948) is an American writer of novels for young adults. She wrote her best known book, *The Outsiders*, when she was sixteen years old. Her other novels include *That Was Then, This Is Now*, and *Rumble Fish*.

Hiroshima

An industrial city in Japan, Hiroshima was destroyed by the United States in World War II when the American forces dropped the first atomic bomb on it. This act led to the surrender of Japan and the end of World War II. A monument to peace now marks the site.

Hispaniola

Hispaniola is an island in the West Indies. Christopher Columbus landed there and on San Salvador in 1492. He later returned to set up a colony for Spain. Today the island is divided into the countries of Haiti and the Dominican Republic.

historian

A person who researches and writes about history is a historian. Historians read everything they can find about a subject before writing about it. The world's oldest known history was written in China before 1,000 B.C.

Hitler, Adolf

Adolf Hitler (1889–1945) was the leader of Nazi Germany. In 1933, he declared himself dictator and set out to build a German empire. These acts led to World War II. He also began to persecute and kill all of the Jews in Germany. Hitler's armies tried unsuccessfully to conquer the Soviet Union. Allied forces finally defeated the Nazis in 1945.

hogan

Many Navajos live in houses called *hogans* that they built out of logs and earth. These are usually dome-shaped.

Holocaust

The Holocaust was the systematic destruction of European Jews between approximately 1941 and 1945 during World War II. German Nazis attempted to destroy the Jewish race. Six million people were killed in the Holocaust, and many more were imprisoned in concentration camps. Holocaust victims also included Gypsies, Poles, and homosexuals. *See Adolf Hitler.*

hologram

A hologram is a three-dimensional image, as opposed to a photograph that is two-dimensional. Hologram comes from the Greek words that mean "whole writing." This image begins with an intense light called a laser. It is split by a mirror into two parts—one part is reflected onto film and the other off of the object. Because the light waves are out-of-step, they create a pattern on film that can be read. That gives the hologram its extra dimension.

Holy Roman Empire

The Holy Roman Empire of central Europe was founded by Otto the Great of Germany. In 962 the Pope, the head of the Roman Catholic Church, crowned Otto ruler of the empire. By the late 1200s, the empire had crumbled, but the title Holy Roman Emperor continued until 1806.

Homer

According to tradition, Homer is the Greek poet who composed the epic poems, the *Iliad* and the *Odyssey*, which are set during and after the Trojan War. Although there is no factual evidence for the existence of Homer, tradition has it that he was blind.

homestead

A homestead is a farm on land provided by or purchased from the government. The United States Homestead Act of 1862 gave land to pioneers willing to farm it. Eager homesteaders came from the east and from Europe to settle on the Great Plains.

homing pigeons

Homing pigeons may use the sun to find their way, but they don't get lost when it's cloudy. They also may have a small amount of magnetic material in their brains. Scientists believe that this material may act something like a compass.

homographs

Homographs are words that have the same spelling but different definitions. Homographs often have different origins and sometimes have different pronunciations. The words *bass* (fish) and *bass* (male singing voice) are homographs. *See homophones.*

homophones

Homophones are words that have the same pronunciation but different spellings and meanings. *Wait* and *weight*, for example, are homophones, as are *their* and *there*. *See homographs.*

Hong Kong

Hong Kong is a British dependency on the southeastern coast of China. A small peninsula and several islands make up Hong Kong. In 1997, Hong Kong will revert back to Chinese control.

hormone

A hormone is a chemical substance that affects the growth and development of organisms.

horn

Horn is a the general name for any number of brass musical instruments which have what is called a "funnel mouthpiece."

Examples:
- cornet
- trumpet
- trombone
- French horn
- tuba

horsepower

Horsepower is a unit for measuring the power of engines. The idea of horsepower began with the Scottish engineer James Watt, who used it to compare the power of a steam engine to the power of a horse. Today, one horsepower is the power to lift 550 pounds one foot for one second. In the metric system of measurement, a horsepower equals 745.7 watts, a term used in honor of James Watt.

Houston

Houston is a city in southeastern Texas near the Gulf of Mexico. The largest metropolitan area in the southern United States and the fourth largest city in the country, Houston is a major commercial and industrial center. *See Gulf Coast.*

Hudson, Henry

Henry Hudson (?–1611), sailing for the Dutch in 1609, traveled up what later became known as the Hudson River and in 1611 explored Hudson Bay. He was searching unsuccessfully for the Northwest Passage—that is, a way north around North America to the Pacific Ocean.

Hudson's Bay Company

Hudson's Bay Company is a Canadian business firm. A group of English business people started the company in 1670 to buy and sell furs from North America. The company helped open western Canada to settlement.

Hughes, Langston

Langston Hughes (1902–1967), often called "the poet laureate of Black America," was born in Joplin, Missouri. He began writing poems when he was in high school. In addition to volumes of poetry, Hughes published an autobiography, short stories, novels, and children's stories.

humidity

Humidity is the amount of water vapor in the air. Most of the time humidity is expressed in percentages. For example, when it is raining, the humidity is 100 percent. That means that the air is full of water. Warm air can hold more humidity than cold air. The amount of humidity in the air is measured by an instrument called a *hygrometer.*

Hundred Years War

The Hundred Years War were a series of wars between England and France that lasted from 1337 to 1453. New weapons developed during the wars, such as the English longbows, reduced the effectiveness of knights' armor. As a result of the wars, England lost most of its land in mainland Europe to France.

hung jury

A hung jury is one that is unable to reach a unanimous verdict.

hurricane

A hurricane is tropical cyclone or windstorm originating in the West Indies. Hurricanes are usually accompanied by violent thunderstorms. More generally, a hurricane is any wind having a speed of more than seventy miles per hour.

Hutton, James

Until the nineteenth century, people believed the Earth was shaped by a series of catastrophic events such as earthquakes and volcanoes. James Hutton (1726–1797), a Scottish geologist, proposed the idea that rocks were formed in a layer-by-layer fashion, with the oldest layers at the bottom. He said that these processes were still happening today, just as they had in the past. Because of his book the *Theory of the Earth*, he is often referred to as "the father of geology." *See sedimentary rock.*

Huxley, Aldous

Aldous Huxley (1894–1963) was an English novelist. His most famous novel, *Brave New World*, presents a totalitarian utopia in which individual people have no rights.

hydroelectric plants

A hydroelectric plant is one that produces electricity using the power of water. Hydroelectric plants are located near dams. The water behind the dam is allowed to fall from a high level to a lower level. The falling water is directed over the blades of a turbine, a special kind of wheel. The turbine turns the magnetic coil of a generator, which produces electric energy. *See electricity.*

hymn

A hymn is a song of praise or adoration, usually with religious themes. The meter is regular and the verses, one or many, are most often rhymed. *See meter and rhyme.*

hyperbole

Hyperbole is a deliberate overstatement, an exaggeration to emphasize truth. Shakespeare's phrase "forever and a day" is an example of hyperbole. *See figurative language.*

hypertension

Hypertension is a condition in which blood pressure is consistently higher than normal. *See blood pressure.*

hyphen

A hyphen (-) is a punctuation mark most often used to divide a word at the end of a line of writing. The hyphen must always come after the syllable that ends the line. Hyphens are also used in a variety of other ways to prevent confusion, including joining words in compound numbers (twenty-three) and separating parts of some compound words (mother-in-law).

hypotenuse

In a right triangle, the side opposite the right angle is the hypotenuse.

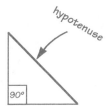

hypothermia

Hypothermia is a lowering of the body temperature usually caused by an excessive exposure to cold. *See frostbite.*

hypothesis

A reasonable guess about how or why an event happens is a hypothesis. Scientists test their hypotheses through experiments.

hypothesis contrary to fact

Hypothesis contrary to fact is a logical fallacy in which a person presents a hypothesis that is not true because any number of other variables could be possible.

Example:

If Adolf Hitler had not started World War II, someone else would have started it.

See logical fallacy.

Iberian Peninsula

The Iberian Peninsula is a peninsula in southwestern Europe bordered by the Mediterranean Sea and the Atlantic Ocean. The Iberian Peninsula contains the countries of Spain and Portugal. *See Europe.*

Icarus

In Greek mythology, Icarus was the son of Daedalus. When escaping from Crete on wings that Daedalus made, Icarus flew so high that the sun melted the wax on his wings, and he fell into the sea and drowned. *See Daedalus.*

Ice Age

During the Ice Ages, huge sheets of ice moved across a great part of the Earth's surface. The last great ice age began about 1.7 million years ago and ended about 10,000 years ago. The seas formed, as did the Great Lakes. Warm weather did not truly begin until about 5,000 B.C. Since then, the temperatures on the Earth have slowly risen. The only exception was the Little Ice Age, lasting approximately 400 years, between 1300–1700 A.D. *See glacier.*

icon

An icon is a painting of Christ, angels, or a saint that is considered sacred in the Eastern Orthodox Church. The word *icon* is also often used as a synonym for *symbol.*

idiom

An idiom is an expression or phrase whose meaning differs from the normal meanings of the individual words. For example, "hold one's tongue" is an idiom meaning "to remain quiet." Idiom is also used to describe word choice or sentence structure unique to a particular group of people or area of a country. For example, in one part of the country, a soft drink might be called *soda,* and in another part *pop. See dialect.*

igneous rocks

Igneous rocks are created when magma flows up from inside the Earth. The magma is a liquid rock containing water and gas. It passes through cracks in the crust of the Earth. As it moves into cracks, it cools and hardens. If the magma becomes solid in the cracks, it may form an igneous rock such as granite. If magma hardens above ground, it may form an igneous rock such as obsidian. *See lava and magma.*

imagery

In writing, images are word pictures, words, and phrases that help readers form ideas of what things look, sound, feel, smell, and taste like. Imagery often involves the use of figurative language. Below are lines from Walt Whitman's "Cavalry Crossing a Ford," describing horsemen crossing a river:

Example:

They take a serpentine course, their arms flash in the sun—hark to the musical clank.

Behold the silvery river, in it the splashing horses loitering stop to drink.

Behold the brown-faced men.

See figurative language.

Imhotep

Imhotep was an Egyptian physician who lived around 2650 B.C. He is the first known physician. He was also a statesman, engineer, and one of the first architects of pyramids. So great was his reputation as a healer, he was, upon his death, elevated to the status of a god.

immigrant

An immigrant comes into a new country or land to live. The United States is often described as a nation of immigrants. *See emigrant.*

immune system

The immune system is the body's natural defense against disease. If a person has an immunity against a particular disease—chicken pox, for example—it means that the person's body developed a resistance to it. Even though the person may be exposed to chicken pox, the person's body will be able to fight it off so that symptoms of the disease do not develop.

impeach

To impeach is to officially accuse a public official of wrongdoing in office. President Andrew Johnson was impeached by the U.S. House of Representatives, but the Senate did not find him guilty or remove him from office.

imperative sentence

An imperative sentence makes a command or a strong request. An imperative sentence will often have an understood subject such as *you.*

Example:
Sit down and be quiet.

See sentence.

imperialism

Imperialism is a policy in which one nation extends its authority over other countries, often by force. In the mid- to late 1800s, European nations established colonies in Africa to protect trading interests.

imply/infer

▷ *Imply* means to hint or to suggest something.
▷ *Infer* means to make a deduction or to draw a conclusion.

Example:

When the teacher implied that the exam would be difficult, the students inferred that they should study hard.

imports

The goods that come into and are purchased by a nation are its imports. The goods sent to other countries are exports.

impressionism

Impressionism is a style of painting in nineteenth-century France that focused on capturing the effects of light on natural scenes and people through the use of colorful and expressive brushstrokes.

improper fraction

In mathematics, a fraction whose numerator is greater than or equal to its denominator is an improper fraction. For example, 8/8 and 9/8 are improper fractions. *See denominator and numerator.*

Inca Empire

The Incas were an Indian civilization in eastern South America from about 1438 to 1532. Incas built many roads and bridges to connect their empire. They practiced terrace farming and irrigation methods, which were quite advanced for that time in history. Later, Spanish conquistadors took most of their gold and silver treasures. *See conquistador.*

incumbent

An incumbent is a person who holds public office. During an election, incumbents often have an advantage because their names are better known to voters than those of their challengers.

independence

Independence is freedom from another's control. The African nation of Kenya, for example, fought for its independence and in 1963 gained its freedom from Great Britain. Jomo Kenyatta, a national hero, became Kenya's first president.

independent clause

An independent clause presents a complete thought and, when removed from a sentence, can stand alone as a sentence. An independent clause is sometimes called a main clause.

Example:

 Dana went to the store because she wanted new shoes.

↖ independent clause

See clause, sentence, and subordinate clause.

index

An index is a list of topics in the back of a book that presents the page numbers on which information about those topics can be found. An index may also be a separate book that lists all of the topics, page numbers, and issues of particular magazines and newspapers. The *New York Times*, for example, has its own index.

India

India is a country in southern Asia. It is the second most populated nation in the world and the seventh largest in area. The people in India are diverse, speaking more than 1000 languages and dialects.

Indian Ocean

The Indian Ocean is the third largest ocean in the world. Lying between Africa on the west, Asia on the north, and Australia on the east, it provides an important trade route between Asia and Europe.

indirect object

In a sentence, the indirect object tells to whom or what or for whom or what the action of the verb is done. The indirect object usually comes before the direct object in a sentence.

Example:

I gave Meredith the tickets.

indirect object

See direct object and verb.

indirect quotation

An indirect quotation is a quotation that does not use the exact words borrowed from a source.

Example:

In his inaugural address, John F. Kennedy said we ought to uphold our duty as citizens.

See paraphrase and quotation.

induction

Induction is reasoning that begins with the examination of specific evidence (facts and examples) and moves to a conclusion or generalization based on that specific evidence. *See deduction.*

Industrial Revolution

The Industrial Revolution marks a time of change from manufacturing by hand to the use of machines. The Industrial Revolution began in England in the 1700s and spread to western Europe and the United States in the early 1800s. During the Industrial Revolution, many people moved from farms to work in factories in cities.

inertia

Inertia is the tendency of a moving object to stay in motion or of a resting object to stay still. In most cases, it takes more energy to overcome the inertia of a standing object than it does to keep that object in motion. That is, it takes more energy to push a car that is standing still than it would to push that same car if it were moving slightly.

inference

An inference is a reasonable conclusion based on information that has been stated or implied. In literature, inferences are often made by readers based on limited information presented about the characters and events.

infinitive

An infinitive is a verb, generally following the word *to*, used as a noun, adjective, or adverb.

Examples:

- to sing
- to dance
- to laugh

An infinitive is often used in an infinitive phrase, which consists of an infinitive and modifiers (to sing loudly and clearly). *See verb.*

inflation

Inflation is a general rise in prices resulting from an increase in the amount of money or credit. Essentially, during a period of inflation the value of money declines—a dollar is worth less because of an overly fast growth in the supply of money.

Inflection

Inflection is the change in the form of a word to show case (they-them), gender (widow-widower), person (I go-he goes), tense (throw-threw), or comparison (high-higher-highest). *See case, gender, personal pronoun, and tense.*

insects

Insects are the most common type of animals on Earth. All in all, there are over one million different kinds of insects. All insects have three main body parts. The head includes the mouth, eyes, and antennae. The thorax, or middle part of the insect, has wings and three pairs of legs. The abdomen, or rear part of the insect, comes last. Many insects, such as butterflies and moths, go through four stages of growth. Starting out as eggs, they soon develop into larvae. A larva eats a great deal and grows very rapidly. The third stage is the pupa. Many pupae are in cocoons, where they change into adults, the final stage.

pupa

eggs

larva

insomnia

Insomnia is difficulty getting to sleep and staying asleep.

instinct

An instinct is a behavior that animals are born with and do not have to learn from their parents. Homing pigeons, for example, do not have to be taught to return to the same place. They do it instinctively.

integers

Integers are whole numbers and their opposites. Some integers are + 3, -3, 0, +16, and -16.

integration

To *integrate* means "to make into a whole by bringing all the parts together." Integration refers to the idea of bringing together all races and people. Integration ensures that all people can use public places such as schools and housing. In 1954, the Supreme Court decided that schools should not be segregated—that is, blacks educated in black-only schools, whites in schools only for whites. Integrated schools are now the law of the land, so whites, Hispanics, Asians, and blacks are all educated together. *See segregation.*

interdependent

People are interdependent when they depend on each other for goods and services. The United States uses supplies from other countries to make certain products—coffee, for example, from South America. Other countries buy goods from America—for example, corn.

interference

In physics, when two waves overlap, they sometimes cancel each other out, or add or subtract from each other. This is interference.

interferon

Interferon is one defense the human body has when it is attacked by a virus. Interferon is a protein released by a cell when it is attacked. Interferon covers cells that have not been attacked from the virus and prevents them from becoming infected. Then antibodies, proteins produced to protect the body from infections, take over and attack the virus.

interjection

An interjection is an exclamation regarded as a part of speech. An interjection usually shows strong emotion or surprise.

Examples:
- Oh!
- Ah!
- Hurray!

interlibrary loan

Interlibrary loan is a system through which libraries can share materials. If a library does not own a book or other item a person needs, the library can often borrow the item from another library belonging to the same network.

interlude

The prefix *inter-* means "between." An interlude is a short piece of music played between acts of a dramatic work or sections of a musical composition.

internal rhyme

Internal rhyme is the rhyming of words within lines of poetry even though the lines might not rhyme at the end.

Example:

The dog in the fog sat on a log with a hog.

See rhyme.

International Date Line

The International Date Line, an imaginary line that runs north and south through the Pacific Ocean, is where each calendar day begins. It appears on a map near the 180th meridian or line of longitude.

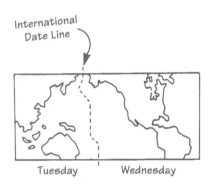

interrogative pronoun

An interrogative pronoun is a pronoun used in a question. For instance, *who, whose, what,* and *which* are interrogative pronouns.

Examples:

Who is coming to dinner?

Whose cousin are you?

See pronoun.

interrogative sentence

An interrogative sentence is a sentence that asks a question. An interrogative sentence begins with an interrogative pronoun or adverb and ends with a question mark.

Example:

What are you going to do this weekend?

See interrogative pronoun, question mark, and sentence.

intestine

Most people think that digestion takes place in the stomach, but in fact most digestion occurs in the small intestine. Saliva has chemicals that begin digestion. The stomach has even stronger liquids, called enzymes and acids, that break up food. The small intestine is where the strongest liquids for breaking up food are located. Bile comes from the liver, and other juices are sent to the small intestine from an organ called the pancreas. All of these break down the proteins, fats, and carbohydrates of the food.

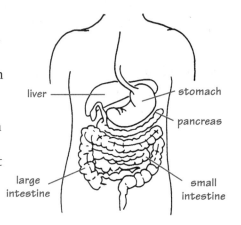

introduction

An introduction is the opening of a piece of writing. An introduction both gets the audience's attention and tells what the piece of writing will be about. In a composition, the introduction generally includes a thesis statement. *See thesis statement.*

inversion

In English, inversion is placing the verb before its subject.

Example:

Along the path stalked the spy.

Inverted sentences can be used for variety and emphasis.

invertebrate

snail

An invertebrate is an animal without a backbone. Snails, worms, and spiders are all similar in that none of them has a backbone. They are all invertebrates.

spider

worm

involuntary muscles

Involuntary muscles are muscles that move without conscious control. Smooth, cardiac, and some skeletal muscles are involuntary. *See voluntary muscles.*

ion

An ion is an atom or molecule that has lost or gained one or more electrons and thus has a positive or negative charge. Scientists refer to ions when talking about the atomic structure of molecules. *See atom, electron, and proton.*

Iran

Iran is a country in southwestern Asia south of the Caspian Sea. One of the oldest nations in the world, Iran has a culture that dates back nearly five thousand years.

Iraq

Iraq is a country in southwestern Asia west of Iran. The world's first civilization blossomed in what is now Iraq in the area between the Tigris River and the Euphrates River. Iraq's capital and largest city is Baghdad.

Ireland

Ireland is one of the British Isles. It is divided into the Republic of Ireland and Northern Ireland. The capital and largest city of the Republic of Ireland is Dublin. *See Northern Ireland.*

Atlantic Ocean

Irish Sea

IRELAND

Iron Curtain

First used by Sir Winston Churchill, the phrase "the Iron Curtain" described how the Soviet Union cut itself and its eastern European satellite countries off from non-Communist nations after World War II.

irony

In writing and speech, irony is an expression in which the intended meaning is the opposite of what is stated. If, for instance, someone does something incredibly silly and an observer comments, "How brilliant!" the words are meant to be ironic. In dramatic irony, the audience can see a character's problems even though the character cannot. More generally, irony describes any situation in which the opposite of what is expected actually occurs. A fire station burning down is an example of irony.

irradiation

Irradiation is the process of exposing matter to radiation to produce a specific change, either biological, chemical, or physical. Cancer cells, for example, are irradiated in an effort to destroy them.

irregardless

Irregardless is a nonstandard form of *regardless*, meaning "without regard to." Avoid the use of *irregardless* in writing.

irrigation

Irrigation is the artificial watering of land. Irrigation helped people of long ago farm and live in areas that did not receive enough rainfall. The Hohokam of the Southwestern United States, for instance, lived and farmed the dry lands of that region by perfecting methods of irrigation. Even today irrigation makes it possible to farm crops on more than 300 million acres of otherwise dry land.

Irving, Washington

Washington Irving (1783–1859) is sometimes called the "Father of American Literature." He wrote essays, novels, short stories, histories, and travelogues. His most famous stories are "Rip Van Winkle" and "The Legend of Sleepy Hollow."

Islam

Islam is a religion begun by Muhammad. Islam means submission, specifically to the power of Allah (God). Muslims follow the Koran, which contains the teachings of Muhammad. Today Islam is the main religion in the Middle East and parts of Asia and northern Africa. *See Koran and Muhammad.*

isobar

An isobar is a line on a weather map that connects places with the same average atmospheric pressure.

isolationism

The policy of avoiding political or economic relations with other countries is referred to as isolationism. Before World War I, the government of the United States tried to isolate itself from world events. Today, America tries to avoid a policy of isolation and instead pursues one of careful engagement—that is, sometimes becoming involved in the problems of other countries.

isometric exercise

Isometric exercise is exercise in which the muscles contract when working against a stationary object, but body parts do not move. *See calisthenics.*

isosceles triangle

A triangle with two congruent sides is an isosceles triangle. That is, two of the sides of the triangle are the same length, and two of the angles are the same.

two equal sides

isotopes

Isotopes are forms of an element with the same number of protons but different numbers of neutrons. Scientists speak of isotopes when discussing the atomic structure of compounds.

Israel

Israel is a country in southwest Asia bordering on the Mediterranean Sea. The area provided the ancient kingdom of the Jews, but Israel was not founded as a nation until 1948.

isthmus

An isthmus is a narrow strip of land with water on both sides that connects two larger bodies of land. Panama is an example of an isthmus.

italics

Italics is a slightly slanted form of printing (for example, *H.M.S. Belfast*) used to designate foreign words, the names of ships and aircraft, and the titles of books, magazines, movies, television shows, works of art, and so forth. Italics are also used to designate a word being defined, explained, or discussed. *See underlining.*

Italy

Italy is a country in southern Europe on the Mediterranean Sea. Rome, its capital and largest city, was the center of the ancient Roman Empire. *See Ancient Rome and Rome.*

its/it's

▷ *Its* is the possessive form of the pronoun *it*.
▷ *It's* is a contraction of *it is* or *it has*.

Example:
After that fumble, it's going to be difficult for the team to get up its morale.

Ivan III

The Grand Duke of Moscow, Ivan III (1440–1505) unified Russia and in 1480 declared himself ruler. He was nicknamed Ivan "the Great." His grandson, Ivan the Terrible, the first Russian czar, enlarged the empire and reformed the government.

ivory

Ivory is a hard, white substance used for carving. It is derived from the tusks of elephants and walruses and whale teeth. In an effort to preserve these natural creatures, most governments have banned the use of ivory.

Japan

Japan is a country made up of four large islands and many smaller islands in the western Pacific Ocean off the east coast of Asia. Japan is one of the leading industrial and commercial nations in the world. Most Japanese live in densely populated cities. *See Tokyo.*

jargon

Jargon is the technical terminology of a particular profession or activity. Medicine, basketball, and business all have their own jargon. *Slam, sky, board,* and *brick* are examples of basketball jargon. Jargon can also refer to any strange or confusing use of words. *See slang.*

jazz

Jazz is the general name for certain forms of popular music, begun around 1900 by black musicians in New Orleans. African rhythms, spirituals, and work songs inspired the various styles, including ragtime, blues, and Dixieland, among others. A strong, often irregular beat and rich melodic improvisation are typical of jazz.

Jefferson, Thomas

The third President of the United States, Thomas Jefferson (1743-1826) drafted the Declaration of Independence. As

President he greatly expanded the U.S. lands when he arranged for the Louisiana Purchase in 1803.

Jerusalem

Jerusalem, the capital of Israel, is located in the eastern part of the country. Jerusalem is a holy city for Jews, Christians, and Muslims. East Jerusalem contains the Old City with its many sacred churches, temples, and mosques. *See Israel.*

Jesus of Nazareth

Jesus of Nazareth (6 B.C.?–A.D. 30?) was one of the great spiritual leaders of the world. Four books of the Bible tell about the life of Jesus. Born in Bethlehem and raised in Nazareth, Jesus moved about Galilee teaching God's love and forgiveness.

Joan of Arc

A French national heroine and military leader, Joan of Arc (1412?–1431) led the French army to victory over the English in 1429. This became a turning point in the Hundred Years War. Two years later, the English burned her at the stake for witchcraft.

joint

A joint is a place in the body where bones come together. *See ligament.*

Jordan

Jordan is a country in southwestern Asia east of Israel. Located along the east bank of the Jordan River, Jordan contains most of the area of Palestine.

joule

A joule is a metric unit of measurement used to express the amount of energy or work. To move a small weight might require 2 joules; to move a large weight might require 20 joules.

journal

A journal is a written record of a person's daily experiences. Journals are generally written in chronological order. Writers often use them to record their experiences or ideas and feelings to use later in their other writing.

journalist

A journalist writes about current events for a newspaper or magazine. A broadcast journalist works in a radio or television station.

Joyce, James

James Joyce (1882-1941) was an Irish novelist who is often considered the most original and influential writer of the twentieth century. *Dubliners* is a collection of his short stories, and *A Portrait of the Artist as a Young Man* is his autobiographical novel. *Ulysses*, his stream-of-consciousness novel about a single day in the lives of a group of people, revolutionized modern fiction.

Judaism

The religion of the early Hebrews and of present-day Jews, Judaism teaches a belief in one God, the God of Abraham in the Old Testament. Judaism follows the spiritual and ethical beliefs outlined in the Bible and Talmud.

judicial branch

The judicial branch of government is its court system. The highest court in the United States is the Supreme Court in Washington, D.C. The Supreme Court settles arguments about what the laws mean. Judges on the Supreme Court are appointed for life by the President and approved by Congress. *See executive branch and legislative branch.*

Jupiter

The largest planet in the solar system is Jupiter. It would take 1,000 Earths to fill the volume of Jupiter. The *Voyager 1* & *2* spacecrafts traveled by Jupiter in 1979 on their way to view Saturn.

Justinian's Code

Justinian's Code is a set of laws organized by Justinian I, the Byzantine emperor, in the sixth century. Justinian directed the recording and revision of the Roman law system. This preserved for the future an important part of Roman culture. *See Ancient Rome.*

juvenile delinquency

People under the age of 18 are considered in most states to be juveniles. When they commit a crime, they become juvenile delinquents. The problem of youth crime is often referred to simply as juvenile delinquency.

juxtaposition

In writing, juxtaposition is the placing of two seemingly unrelated ideas or details next to each other in order to create a new meaning.

K

Kelvin, Lord

William Thompson, Lord Kelvin (1824–1907), was a British mathematician and physicist. He proposed the Kelvin, or "absolute zero," temperature scale. Kelvin attended lectures in mathematics when he was only eight years old, an early sign of his genius. *See absolute zero.*

Kepler, Johannes

Johannes Kepler (1571–1630) was a German astronomer who presented three important laws about the way that planets moved. He discovered, for instance, that the planets orbit around the sun in an elliptical pattern. He announced two of his laws in a book entitled *Astronomia Nova*, published in 1609. Kepler once wrote:

"So long as the mother, Ignorance, lives, it is not safe for Science, the offspring, to divulge the hidden causes of things."

kettle

In geology, a kettle is a depression left in the land by the melting of blocks of glacial ice. *See glacier.*

key

A key is an arrangement of notes that are tonally related, with the lowest note giving the key its name. There are most commonly two types (modes) of keys, one major and one minor, for each of the twelve tones of the chromatic scale, lettered from A to G. *See scale.*

keyboard

A keyboard is a bank of systematically arranged keys by which a machine or instrument is operated. Most personal computers have a keyboard that looks something like a typewriter keyboard. *See computer and piano.*

kiln

A kiln is a special high-intensity oven used to fire (bake) clay objects into hardened ceramic ware.

kilogram

A kilogram is a unit for measuring weight in the metric system. One kilogram equals 1,000 grams.

kilometer

A kilometer is a unit for measuring length in the metric system. One kilometer equals 1,000 meters. *See meter.*

kinetic energy

Kinetic energy is the energy of motion. The water of a river or stream has kinetic energy. The kinetic energy of an object is equal to half the product of its mass and the square of its velocity. The formula for figuring kinetic energy is:

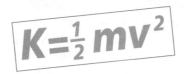

$$K = \tfrac{1}{2} mv^2$$

See energy and energy of motion.

King, Martin Luther, Jr.

Martin Luther King, Jr. (1929–1968), a minister and civil rights leader, fought discrimination against black people. He used nonviolent protest and civil disobedience to fight discrimination. He greatly helped the cause of blacks and other minorities. He was assassinated on April 4, 1968. His birthday, January 15, is observed as a holiday in the United States and is celebrated on the third Monday in January. *See civil rights.*

Knowles, John

John Knowles (b. 1926) is an American writer best known for his novel *A Separate Peace*. Knowles has also written magazine articles, essays, and short stories.

Koran

The Koran is the holy book of Islam. Muslims believe the Koran was revealed to Muhammad in small passages in the years between A.D. 610–632. The Koran explains the Muslim faith and guides its followers. Rules from the Koran have become law in many Arab countries. *See Islam and Muhammad.*

Korea

Korea is a peninsula in the southern part of East Asia between the Sea of Japan and the Yellow Sea. Korea is currently divided into two countries at the 38th parallel: noncommunist South Korea (Republic of Korea) and communist North Korea (Democratic People's Republic of Korea). Almost twice as many people live in South Korea as in North Korea. Seoul, the capital of South Korea, is the second largest city in the world. *See Seoul.*

RUSSIAN FED.

CHINA

Sea of Japan

NORTH KOREA

Yellow Sea

SOUTH KOREA

Korean War

The Korean War (1950–1953) was a conflict between North Korea and South Korea aided by United Nations forces. Communist North Koreans invaded South Korea. The United Nations, with help from the United States, sent troops to defend South Korea until a 1953 truce was reached. *See Korea.*

Kublai Khan

A Mongol emperor, Kublai Khan (1216–1294) was a grandson of the great warrior Genghis Khan. Kublai Khan governed a vast thirteenth-century Asian empire. Arts and science flourished at his court in China. Marco Polo spent about twenty years there. *See Marco Polo.*

Kyoto

Kyoto was the capital city of Japan from 794 to 1868. During this time, Japanese culture flourished. Today visitors to Kyoto can see many beautiful shrines and other examples of Japanese art and architecture. *See Japan.*

labor union

Workers who join together to deal as a group with their employers for better pay and working conditions form a labor union. Sometimes workers strike, or refuse to work, to pressure employers to meet their demands. *See strike.*

landscape

A landscape is the artistic depiction of an outdoor scene through drawing, painting, or photography.

laptop computer

A laptop computer is a computer small enough and light enough to be placed on the user's lap. *See computer.*

larva

The young, immature state of some insects that undergo further development is larva.

larynx

The larynx is located in the throat. Made of cartilage, the larynx is shaped like a box. Because it contains the vocal cords, the larynx is sometimes called the "voice box." *See cartilage.*

laser

A laser is a device that amplifies light. It causes atoms to give up light of only a certain wavelength. This results in a light of a single wavelength with all of the waves going in a single direction. A strong, intense beam of light is created.

latitude

The distance north or south of the equator, measured in degrees, is latitude. One degree of latitude equals about 69 miles (111 kilometers). *See longitude.*

lava

The molten rock flowing from a volcano when it erupts is lava. It comes from deep in the Earth and consists of a solution of silicate minerals raised to such a high temperature as to become a liquid. *See magma.*

Lavoisier, Antoine

Antoine Lavoisier (1743–1794) was a French scientist. Born to a wealthy Paris family, he was given an excellent education and devoted himself to chemistry. Lavoisier's most important contribution was his explanation of the chemical basis of combustion.

lay/lie

▷ *Lay* (laid, laid) means to put or to place and generally takes a direct object.
▷ *Lie* (lay, lain), which means to rest or to be at rest in a horizontal position, does not take a direct object.

Examples:

Lay that book on the table and then lie down on the couch.

After he laid the book on the table, he lay down on the couch.

See direct object.

LCD (least common denominator)

The LCD (least common denominator) is the least common multiple of the denominators of two or more fractions.

Example:

denominators

The least (or closest) common denominator is 6:

$1/2 \times 2/3 = 2/6$ ⟵ LCD

The LCD is used when fractions are added or subtracted. *See denominator.*

leach

To leach minerals is to wash them out of soil or some other material by running water through the material. Often as water moves through soil, it leaches harmful materials such as pesticides.

League of Five Nations

The Iroquois union formed around 1400 by the Senecas, Oneidas, Onondagas, Cayugas, and Mohawks was called the Iroquois League, or League of Five Nations. Eventually a sixth group, the Tuscaroras, joined the league in 1722.

leave/let

▷ *Leave* is a verb that means "to depart."
▷ *Let* is a verb that means "to allow" or "to permit."

Example:
The queen let the messenger leave the castle.

Lee, Harper

Harper Lee (b. 1926) is an American writer known for her only novel, *To Kill a Mockingbird*, which won the Pulitzer Prize for fiction in 1961. Set in a small Alabama town during the Great

Depression, *To Kill a Mockingbird* is about a young girl growing up and learning about social injustice.

Lee, Robert E.

Robert E. Lee (1807–1870) was a U.S. soldier and Confederate general during the Civil War. He was the commander of West Point in 1852. As Confederate Civil War commander, he was a skillful leader who worked against great odds. Lee eventually surrendered to General Ulysses S. Grant in 1865. *See civil war.*

left-wing

Individuals or groups that call for extreme measures to reform social or political problems are sometimes called *left-wing*. The term came into use during the French Revolution, when radicals sat on the left side of the French Revolutionary Assembly. *See right-wing.*

legend

A legend is a story handed down from the past. A legend may be based on actual people or events, but it is not thought of as historically accurate. Legends often deal with some important event in the history of a people. The stories about Arthur, king of ancient Britain, for example, are legends. *See fable, folklore, parable, tale, and tall tale.*

legislative branch

The legislative branch of government makes laws. The Senate and House of Representatives make up the legislative branch of the United States government. Together they make up the Congress. *See executive branch and judicial branch.*

Lenin, V. I.

V. I. Lenin (Vladimir Ilyich Ulyanov, 1870–1924) was one of the most famous Russian Communist leaders. He became the leader of the Bolshevik party and inspired the overthrow of the Russian government. He served as leader of the country from 1917 until his death in 1924.

less than (<)

In mathematics, the symbol < means "less than." A relation between two numbers with the lesser number given first is shown this way:

$$4 < 10$$

lever

A lever is a simple machine made of a rigid bar or plank that makes contact with a single pivot point called a *fulcrum*. A lever is often used to pry something loose or lift something heavy. *See fulcrum.*

lever

Lewis & Clark

Meriwether Lewis (1774–1809) and William Clark (1770–1838) were sent by President Jefferson to explore the lands west of the Mississippi River. Their 1804–1806 expedition opened the way for U.S. settlement in the West.

Lexington and Concord

The battles of Lexington and Concord (1775) marked the beginning of the American Revolution. Fighting broke out along the Lexington-Concord road between patriots and British troops marching to Concord, Massachusetts, to seize weapons and arrest colonial revolutionaries. A second battle took place the next day in Concord. *See American Revolution.*

libel

Libel is a written or published statement or picture that damages someone's reputation. When a person believes he or she has been libeled, that person sometimes goes to court and sues the publisher or writer.

Library of Congress System

The Library of Congress System is the system used in many college libraries and some public libraries to classify and arrange all of their holdings. Library of Congress classifications begin with capital letters followed by numbers. The first letter in a Library of Congress call number represents one of 21 general areas of knowledge.

Examples:

A: General Works

H: Social Sciences

K: Law

L: Education

Q: Science

The second letter represents a subclassification, and the numbers represent a specific topic.

Example:

See *call number* and *Dewey Decimal System.*

libretto

Libretto, an Italian word, refers to the "book" or words to which the music of an opera or an oratorio is set.

Libya

Libya is a North African country on the Mediterranean Sea, west of Egypt

MORE

and east of Algeria and Tunisia. Most of southern Libya is covered by the Sahara Desert. Tripoli is Libya's capital and largest city. *See Egypt and Sahara Desert.*

ligament

A ligament is a tough, white tissue that connects bones and holds body organs in place. *See joint.*

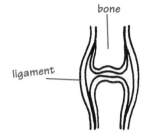

light bulb

Light bulbs contain a short piece of tungsten wire. This type of wire does not conduct electricity very well. As a result, when electricity flows through this wire, it begins to heat up. The wire becomes so hot that it gives off light. The wire does not burn up because it is in a vacuum (all air has been removed from the closed bulb). Thus, there is not enough air to feed the fire, and the result is simply light. *See Thomas Edison.*

light year

A light year is the distance that a pulse of light travels in one year. Since light travels 186,282 miles per second, a light year equals 5.88 trillion miles. Distances to and between stars are measured in light years. This is because the distances are so vast that usual measurements, such as meters and miles, would be too large to be practical.

lightning

Lightning is an electrical spark, but in the sky and on a giant scale. Scientists believe lightning occurs when a cumulonimbus cloud's light, rising water droplets collide with tiny pieces of ice, hail, and other heavy, falling particles. In this collision, the atoms of the heavy falling particles become negatively charged, while the atoms of the lighter, rising water droplets

become positively charged. Positive and negative charges attract, producing a rapid flow of charged atoms through the air. This flow produces electrical current that gives off sparks, or lightning. Lightning can take place between the negative and positive charged atoms within a cloud, between two clouds, or between a cloud and the ground.

lightning rods

One of Benjamin Franklin's most useful and practical inventions was also one of the simplest—the lightning rod. A lightning rod is fixed to the top of a house or building. It transfers lightning away from the house, through a metal cable, to a ground rod buried in the Earth. *See Benjamin Franklin.*

like/as

▷ *Like* is a preposition used to show comparison in a prepositional phrase.

Example:

Craig laughs like a hyena.

▷ *As* is a conjunction used to introduce clauses.

Example:

As the game ended, the crowd stormed onto the court and carried off the coach.

See conjunction and preposition.

limerick

A limerick is a humorous poem of five lines with a fixed rhythm and rhyme scheme.

Example:

There was a young woman named Sprite
Whose speed was much faster than light.
She set out one day
In a relative way
And returned on the previous night.

See poetry, rhyme, and rhythm.

Lincoln, Abraham

The sixteenth President of the United States, Abraham Lincoln (1809–1865) served during the Civil War. Lincoln insisted that the Union must be preserved to prove that democracy was a viable form of government. He is often considered the greatest U.S. President, in part because of his exceptional skills as a leader and a speech-maker. For example, he wrote and delivered the "Gettysburg Address," which reiterated the goals of the war and the importance of democratic government. An assassin, John Wilkes Booth, shot and killed Lincoln at a theater in Washington, D.C., in 1865. *See civil war and Gettysburg Address.*

Lindbergh, Charles

In 1927, Charles A. Lindbergh (1902–1974) flew all alone from New York City to Paris, France. His was the first solo nonstop flight across the Atlantic Ocean.

linking verb

A linking verb is a verb that shows state of being rather than action. A linking verb connects a subject with a noun, pronoun, or adjective that identifies or describes the subject. The word linked to the subject is the subject complement, predicate noun or pronoun, or predicate adjective. The most common linking verbs are forms of the verb *be*.

Examples:

- is
- are
- was
- were

Larry is a baseball fan, but Maria and Jackie are not fans.

liter

A liter is a unit for measuring capacity and volume in the metric system. One liter equals 1.0567 liquid quarts. *See quart.*

literary criticism

Literary criticism is the analysis, evaluation, and explanation of a piece of writing. Used in this sense, criticism may be positive as well as negative.

literature

Literature is the term used to describe writing, especially creative writing. The writings of a particular country are considered that nation's literature.

lithography

Lithography is a printing process employing a metal plate or flat stone.

loam

Loam is rich soil that contains a mixture of clay, sand, and silt. Loam is often deposited by river waters.

lobbyist

A person hired by a special-interest group to influence government decision-makers is a lobbyist. Congress can pass laws that greatly affect one industry or another—for example, farmers or steel-makers. To protect their interests and to be sure their concerns are heard, industries sometimes hire lobbyists to explain their positions to government officials.

lodestone

Lodestone is a mineral that attracts iron or materials with iron in them. The first magnets and compasses were made with lodestone. Compasses appear to have been used as early as about A.D. 1100. Englishman William Gilbert (1544–1603) first suggested that the

Earth itself acted as a magnet. Because of Gilbert's work, magnetic forces are now measured in units called *gilberts*.

logic

Logic is the principles of valid reasoning and correct inference. *See deduction, induction, and inference.*

logical fallacy

A logical fallacy is any reasoning, explanation, or argument that is contrary to the rules of logic.

Examples:

- ad misericordium
- argumentum ad hominem
- non sequitur
- post hoc

See logic.

London, Jack

Jack London (1876–1916) was an American writer whose novels and short stories were often about Alaska during the gold rush of the 1890s. His best-known novels are *Call of the Wild* and *White Fang.*

longhouse

Longhouses were the large, bark-covered homes in which Iroquois families lived. The Iroquois women controlled the longhouse and owned most of the property. *See League of Five Nations.*

longitude

Like latitude, longitude is a measure of distance. Longitude is the distance east and west on the Earth's surface. Usually geographers use Greenwich, England, as the point from which longitude is measured. *See latitude.*

Lorenz, Konrad

Austrian scientist Konrad Lorenz (1903–1989) studied the habits of birds and other animals in order to understand their behavior. He wanted, for instance, to learn how young birds recognize their parents. In one famous experiment, he spent so much time with baby geese that they considered him one of their parents.

Los Angeles

Los Angeles is a city on the Pacific Coast in southwest California. The second largest city in the United States, Los Angeles grew from 1.5 million people in 1945 to nearly 3.5 million people by 1990.

lose/loose

▷ *Lose* is a verb meaning to misplace.

▷ *Loose*, which can be used as an adjective or an adverb, means free or unattached.

Example:

It's easy to lose your loose change.

Louis XIV

Louis XIV (1638–1715) was a king of France. France gained power and prestige in the late seventeenth and early eighteenth centuries during his seventy-two-year reign. He spent vast sums of money fighting wars and building a huge palace located outside Paris in Versailles.

Louisiana Purchase

The Louisiana Purchase (1803) was territory bought from France by President Jefferson. The territory extended from the Mississippi River west to the Rockies. This land doubled the size of the United States and, in time, became part or all of fifteen new states. *See Thomas Jefferson.*

Low Countries

Belgium, the Netherlands, and Luxembourg in western Europe are known as the Low Countries. They are located between France and Germany along the coast of the North Atlantic. *See Europe.*

lunar eclipse

The moon revolves around the Earth. In rare instances, the Earth comes between the sun and the moon. The moon then passes through the Earth's shadow. This creates a lunar eclipse. During a lunar eclipse, the moon slowly gets dark and then gets light again. *See solar eclipse.*

lute

The lute is one of a family of fretted stringed instruments with half-pear-shaped bodies. The type best known today has an angled neck. Varieties of the lute have been known for several thousand years, but they were most popular in the seventeenth century. The strings are strummed by the fingers rather than by a pick. *See mandolin.*

lymphatic system

A system of lymph nodes and vessels runs throughout the human body. It is the system that allows nutrients to travel from the blood to individual cells. The lymphatic system also collects the fluid between cells and returns it to the bloodstream.

lyre

The lyre was popular in ancient times in Greece and the Middle East. It was similar to a harp but was played by stroking the strings with a plectrum (pick).

lyric poem

A lyric poem is a type of poem, usually short, that expresses the poet's ideas and emotions. For example, here is a lyric poem by Emily Dickinson:

> This is my letter to the World
> That never wrote to me—
> The simple News that Nature told—
> With tender Majesty
>
> Her Message is committed
> To Hands I cannot see—
> For love of Her—Sweet—countrymen—
> Judge tenderly—of Me

See ballad, epic, and poetry.

Macedonia

Macedonia is the name for an ancient country that lay north of Greece on the Aegean Sea. In the fourth century B.C., Philip, the Macedonian ruler, united the Greek states with Macedonia. His son, Alexander the Great, spread Greek culture throughout the Middle East. *See Ancient Greece and Athens.*

MacKenzie, Sir Alexander

Sir Alexander MacKenzie (1764–1820) was a Scottish-born Canadian fur trader and explorer. Between 1789 and 1793, MacKenzie led the first expedition known to cross North America north of Mexico. His journey encouraged Canadians to move west.

madrigal

The madrigal is a style of musical composition for three to six vocal parts, all carrying melodic lines that weave together harmoniously. Madrigals were most popular in sixteenth-century Italy and England and are again popular with choruses today.

Magellan, Ferdinand

Ferdinand Magellan (1480?–1521) led the first known expedition to sail around the world. He was killed in the Philippines, but some of his crew returned to Spain in 1522. This voyage greatly increased the understanding in Europe of the Earth's geography.

magenta

Magenta is the name of a color that is a deep, dark, purplish red.

magistrate

A magistrate is a type of judge who can hear cases for small offenses.

magma

Magma is melted rock that comes from deep inside the Earth. When magma cools slowly beneath the Earth's surface, it forms large crystals. Then it turns into rocks such as granite. Magma can also be pushed all the way up to the surface of the Earth, where it pours out of volcanoes as lava. When lava cools quickly, it forms such rocks as obsidian or pumice. *See lava.*

Magna Carta

The Magna Carta is a list of rights guaranteed to English nobles. In 1215, noblemen forced King John to sign the Magna Carta. It limited the king's power and was an important step toward the type of constitutional government we have today.

magnet

Magnets are used to pick up metal objects. One end of a magnet is the north pole, and the other end is the south pole. If two magnets are placed together, the south pole of one magnet attracts the north pole of the other magnet. However, the north pole of one magnet repels, or pushes away, the north pole of the other magnet. The same thing happens with the two south poles. In other words, opposite poles attract, and like poles repel.

maize

Maize is one of the most important grain crops in the world. Today's corn is descended from maize. Thousands of years ago, Indians of Latin America cultivated and developed a variety of food crops, including maize.

malapropism

A malapropism is a ridiculous misuse of words, caused by confusing two words that sound similar but have very different meanings.

Example:

In a right triangle, the side opposite the right angle is called the hippopotamus (hypotenuse).

malaria

Malaria is a disease that causes fevers, chilling sweats, and often death. Malaria is spread by mosquitos. Many colonists that landed at Jamestown in May 1607 died from malaria.

Malthusian theory

The idea that the world population is growing faster than the supply of food is the Malthusian theory. Thomas Malthus warned in the late eighteenth century that the lack of food would always be a problem unless war and disease kept the population in check.

mammals

Mammals are vertebrates—animals with backbones that feed their young on mother's milk. Mammals are warm-blooded, have lungs and hair, and give birth to live offspring. Only recently have scientists discovered two animals classified as mammals that lay eggs: the spiny anteater and the duckbill platypus.

mandolin

A mandolin is a fretted, stringed instrument smaller than a guitar. Like the lute, it has a small, rounded body and strings that are strummed with a pick. The mandolin originated in Italy and remains popular today, chiefly for folk music. *See lute.*

Manhattan Project

The Manhattan Project was the group organized in 1942 to produce the first atomic bomb. Physicist Robert Oppenheimer directed the design and building of the bomb. The first successful bomb test was in New Mexico in 1945.

Manifest Destiny

Manifest Destiny was the belief that the United States had a right to expand its borders and take over all of North America. Manifest destiny was the reason given for taking over Texas in 1845.

mantle

The layer lying between the crust and the core of the Earth is the mantle. Scientists have never been able to drill into the Earth's mantle because the crust is so thick. *See Earth.*

Mao Zedong

Mao Zedong (1893–1976) was the Chinese communist who led peasants and workers in a long struggle for power in China. In 1949, Mao and the Communists took control of the country by organizing the vast power of China's millions of peasants. They drove out the nationalist government of Chiang Kai-Shek, which fled to Taiwan.

Marathon

At Marathon, a plain twenty-five miles northeast of Athens, the ancient Greeks defeated the larger invading Persian forces in 490 B.C. Today's marathon races commemorate a messenger who died after he ran to Athens with the news of the Greek victory.

marble

Marble is a hard, crystalline metamorphic rock that can be polished to a smooth, shiny finish. It is often used in sculpture. Marble can be found in a variety of colors from Vermont white to Alabama cream and Tennessee pink.

Marconi, Guglielmo

Guglielmo Marconi (1874–1937) devised a wireless telegraph. He sent signals across the English Channel in 1898 and later across the Atlantic Ocean, improving the speed of worldwide communication.

Mariana Trench

The Mariana Trench is the deepest spot known in any ocean. The bottom of this trench is 36,198 feet—about 7,000 feet deeper than Mt. Everest is tall. The depth of the Mariana Trench became fully known on January 23, 1960, when Jacques Piccard and Don Walsh descended to its bottom.

marketplace

The place where people meet to buy and sell goods and services is the marketplace. Sometimes it is an open area in the center of a village. Marketplace today may also mean the business world in general, where ideas and inventions compete for notice.

Marquette, Father Jacques

Father Jacques Marquette (1637–1675), a missionary, along with Louis Jolliet (1645–1700), explored the Mississippi River from present-day Wisconsin to Arkansas. Following the Mississippi in order to discover where it led, they learned that it flowed south, probably into the Gulf of Mexico. *See Mississippi River.*

Mars

Mars is the fourth planet from the sun in our solar system. Temperatures range from -191° Fahrenheit in the winter to -24° Fahrenheit in the summer. An Italian astronomer named Giovanni Schiaparelli made detailed observations of Mars with a telescope. In 1877, he discovered lines on the planet, which he called "channels." This was mistranslated from his native Italian into English as "canals," which led to the idea that there was possibly life on Mars. The "canals" were thought to have been made by some form of intelligent life.

marsupial

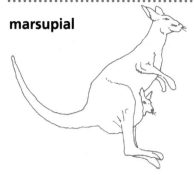

Marsupials are any mammals that give birth to live, but extremely immature, offspring and then complete the development of the offspring in pouches. A kangaroo, for example, is a marsupial.

Mason-Dixon Line

Before and during the Civil War, the Mason-Dixon Line stood for the division in the United States between free and slave states. Named for its two surveyors, it was a boundary line between Pennsylvania and Maryland, and between Maryland and part of Delaware.

mass

In physics, mass is the amount of matter in an object. The mass of an object can be measured by using a balance scale. An object is placed in a pan on one side of a balance, and another object is put into the pan on the opposite side of the balance. If the two sides of the balance are level with one another, the two objects have equal masses. Mass is, therefore, proportional to an object's weight.

mass media

The methods of modern communication that send information to millions of people are the mass media. Often when people mention mass media they are referring to radio, TV, newspapers, and magazines. Television and radio have, for example, dramatically changed the way people receive news and view the world.

Masters, Edgar Lee

Edgar Lee Masters (1868–1950) became famous overnight with the publication of *Spoon River Anthology* in 1915. The *Anthology* presents a series of "auto epitaphs" that present a realistic picture, good and bad, of small-town life.

matter

Matter can exist in one or more forms known as "states of matter." The three states of matter are:

- liquid
- solid
- gas

Water, for example, can exist in all three states of matter. As ice, it is a solid. As water, it is a liquid. And as steam, it is a gas. Albert Einstein discovered that energy and matter were different forms of each other. He also found that energy and matter could change back and forth into each other. This is known as the law of conservation of matter and energy. It means that the total amount of matter and energy in the universe is always constant. Neither can be destroyed or added to—only changed.

Maxwell, James Clerk

James Clerk Maxwell (1831–1879) was a scientist who showed that Saturn's rings were not solid. He also figured out the way molecules move in a gas and how they respond to heat. His crowning work, however, was developing a mathematical theory that described the relationship between electric and magnetic fields. *See electricity and magnet.*

Maya Empire

Mayan culture flourished in Central America between A.D. 250 and 900. Among Mayan accomplishments were an accurate calendar, a system of mathematics, astronomy, writing, and large stone pyramids. *See Central America.*

Mayflower Compact

The agreement by Pilgrim settlers on self-government was named the Mayflower Compact. When the *Mayflower* landed at Plymouth in 1620, the male adults signed the compact before going ashore.

McCormick, Cyrus

In 1831 Cyrus McCormick (1809–1884) developed the first successful machine for cutting ripe grain. The McCormick reaper greatly shortened the time it took farmers to harvest their grain.

mean

The mean is an average of a group of numbers. The mean is obtained by dividing the sum of the addends by the number of addends.

Example:

The mean of 2, 4, 5, 6, and 6 is (23/5), or 4.6.

See addend and median.

measure

A musical measure is a group of beats (typically from 2 to 5) in a composition, which is set off by bar lines on the staff and which has an accent on the first beat.

measuring sound

Sound can be measured in a number of ways. One way to measure sound is volume—the loudness or softness of a sound. A second way is pitch—how high or low a sound is. The more an object vibrates, the louder its sound and the higher its pitch. Objects that vibrate slowly have a low pitch and a low volume. It is also possible for an object to have a low pitch and a high volume (a bass guitar, for instance) or to have a high pitch and a low volume (a flute, for example).

Mecca

Mecca is the holiest city in the religion of Islam and the religious capital of Saudi Arabia. Mecca is the birthplace of the prophet Muhammad. A Muslim hopes to visit Mecca at least once, if possible. The word *mecca* has, therefore, come to mean any place that people have a strong desire to visit. *See Islam, Muhammad, and Saudi Arabia.*

mechanics

In writing, mechanics is the "machinery" of writing—capitalization, punctuation, spelling, and usage. *See capitalization and usage.*

median

The median is the middle number in a group of numbers when the numbers are listed in order.

Example:

2, 4, 5, 6, and 7

See mean.

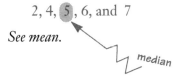

medley

A medley is a variety of tunes linked together in a series, forming a single piece of music.

megalopolis

A large metropolitan area containing two or more large cities is a megalopolis. In the northeastern United States, for instance, the cities of Boston, New York, and Philadelphia form a megalopolis.

melanin

Melanin is a brown or black pigment that determines the color of the skin and hair.

melody

Melody is created by a series of notes sounded one after the other and varying in pitch and in the length of the notes.

Melville, Herman

Herman Melville (1819–1891) was an American novelist. His most famous novel, *Moby-Dick*, is sometimes considered the greatest American novel ever written. *Typee* and *Omoo* are adventure novels based on his experiences in the South Seas.

Mendel, Gregor

Gregor Mendel (1822–1884) was an Austrian monk who formulated the basic laws of genetics. That is, he discovered the way parents pass along characteristics to their offspring—for example, why tall parents usually have tall children. Mendel grew peas in the garden of the monastery and carefully watched how various plants grew. He showed that certain characteristics did not blend together but remained distinct. His findings explained a great deal about Darwin's theory of natural selection. *See Charles Darwin and genetics.*

menopause

When women reach an age between 40 and 50 years old, most stop menstruating. This is menopause. Women's bodies go through several changes at this time, chief of which is that they are no longer able to conceive offspring.

menu

In computer jargon, a menu is list of options presented on a computer screen. A user can select an option from the menu.

mercantilism

Mercantilism was an economic system current in Europe between the 1500s and 1700s in which the state attempted to exert total control over imports and exports. Such countries as France and England attempted to maintain a favorable balance of trade—that is, more exports than imports—in the belief that large national reserves of gold and silver were beneficial. Since international debts were settled in gold and silver, a favorable balance of trade would cause precious metals to flow into, rather than out of, a country. England's mercantile policies may have been a factor leading to the American Revolutionary War because England discouraged colonial manufacturing to increase its own exports to the colonies. *See balance of trade.*

mercury

All of the metals that occur naturally in the world are solids when they are at room temperature—all, that is, except one. Mercury is the only metal that is a liquid at room temperature. Its liquid character makes it useful for thermometers, barometers, and other measuring devices. It can also be a dangerous poison.

barometer

meridian

A meridian is a north-south line on a globe or map from which longitude is measured. *See longitude.*

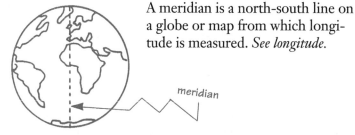

meridian

mestizo

A person of mixed descent, especially a person who is part Spanish and part Native American, is referred to as a *mestizo* in some Latin American countries.

metabolism

The sum of the chemical reactions that take place in the living cells of a person's body is the metabolism. The metabolism is the

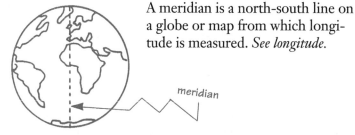

body's ability to take in food and release the energy stored in the food.

metamorphosis

A metamorphosis is a dramatic change in body size and shape of some lower animals as they develop from the time of birth until they reach maturity. For example, when a caterpillar changes into a butterfly, that dramatic change is a metamorphosis.

metaphor

A metaphor is a comparison, without using the words *like* or *as*, between things that don't seem to be alike. Shakespeare, for example, used the metaphor, "All the world's a stage." He also wrote: "Life's but a walking shadow, a poor player that struts and frets his hour upon the stage. . . ." *See figurative language.*

meteor

A meteor is a metallic or stony chunk falling through space that upon entering Earth's atmosphere begins to glow because of heat cuased by friction with the air. Every day meteors weighing a total of 1,000 tons strike the surface of the Earth. Most of them, however, are smaller than a grain of rice.

meter

In poetry, meter is the pattern of rhythm in the lines. Usually, the meter of a line of poetry is measured by the stressed and unstressed syllables. In the word *meter,* for example, the first syllable (me) is stressed. *See poetry and rhythm.*

meter

In the metric system, a meter is the base unit of measuring length. One meter equals 100 centimeters, or 39.3701 inches, which is slightly more than a yard. *See metric system.*

ANOTHER METER

meter

In music, meter, the basic structure of musical rhythm, is shown by pairs of numbers at the beginning of a composition.

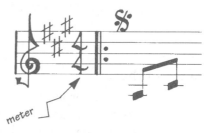

meter

metonymy

Metonymy is a figure of speech in which the name of something closely associated with a thing is substituted for the name of that thing.

> **Example:**
>
> Beth was drawn to the theater at an early age (theater as a substitute for a career as an actress).

See figurative language.

metric system

The metric system is a decimal system of weights and measures.

- The metric units of measurement for length are millimeters, centimeters, decimeters, meters, and kilometers.
- The metric units for capacity are milliliters and liters.
- The metric units for mass are grams and kilograms.
- The metric units for temperature are in degrees Celsius.

See customary units of measure.

metropolis

A large and important city is a metropolis. Any large city such as Mexico City, New York, London, or Hong Kong, for example, would be called a metropolis. *See megalopolis.*

metropolitan area

A metropolitan area is a city and the developed area around it that may include suburbs, villages, towns, and other smaller cities. Chicago and Los Angeles offer good examples. In both of them, the city and surrounding areas have grown to the point that they have joined completely. *See megalopolis and metropolis.*

Mexican Cession

The Mexican Cession was the land that the United States received from Mexico as a result of the Treaty of Guadalupe Hidalgo (1848). The land included present-day California, Nevada, Utah, and parts of New Mexico, Arizona, Colorado, and Wyoming.

Mexican War

The Mexican War (1846–1848) started as a boundary dispute in southern Texas. The war spread across the American Southwest, and Mexico ultimately gave up a large area of land in return for $15 million. *See Mexican Cession.*

Mexico

Mexico is a large country that lies south of the United States. The Maya, Toltec, and Aztec Indians created sophisticated civilizations before the Spanish conquered the country in the 1500s. The majority of people in Mexico are mestizos, offspring of the Indians and the Spanish settlers. *See mestizo and Mexico City.*

Mexico City

Mexico City, the capital of Mexico, is the largest city in the world. Approximately 21 million people live in the metropolitan area. Located in the central part of the country, it is Mexico's cultural, commercial, and industrial center. *See Mexico.*

mezzo-soprano

A mezzo-soprano is a female voice of the middle range.

microchip

A microchip is a miniature electronic device often used in computers. Microchips contain thousands of parts on a tiny piece of silicon. High-tech machines, such as com-

puters and communications satellites, depend upon microchips.
See computer.

microfiche

Microfiche is a sheet of film about the size of an index card on which information, especially from periodicals like magazines and newspapers, can be stored easily and economically in a library. *See microfilm and periodical.*

microfilm

Microfilm is a roll of film on which information, especially from magazines and newspapers, can be stored easily and economically in a library. *See microfiche and periodical.*

microprocessor

At first, computers were made with vacuum tubes and later with transistors. But eventually computers began using integrated circuits—a small set of many transistors all on a tiny chip. By the 1970s, all of the essential instructions for running a computer could be fit onto one chip, which was called the central processing unit, or microprocessor. Microprocessors allowed computers to be made smaller, to operate faster, and to cost less. *See chip and computer.*

microwave oven

When a microwave oven is turned on, microwaves penetrate the food and cause the water molecules in the food to vibrate. The molecules move so fast against each other that the friction releases energy in the form of heat. The heat then cooks the food. Since microwaves can pass through glass, paper, and some forms of china, containers of these materials do not heat up.

Middle English

Middle English is the form of English used after Old English but before the English used today. Middle English was used for approximately four hundred years between 1100 and 1500. *See Old English.*

Midway Island, Battle of

In the Battle of Midway Island (1942), U.S. forces defeated the Japanese, turning the tide of World War II in the Pacific. The Battle of Midway was fought completely by airplanes from land and aircraft carriers. *See World War II.*

migrate

To migrate is to move from one place to settle in another. Thousands of years ago, the first people arrived in North America. They probably migrated from Asia, following the animals they hunted.

mile

A mile is a unit for measuring distance in the customary system of measurement. A mile is equal to 5,280 feet or 1,760 yards. *See customary units of measure.*

militia

A military force made up mostly of civilians trained for emergency duty is a militia. Members of a militia are, essentially, citizen-soldiers.

Milky Way

Our solar system is part of the Milky Way galaxy. Stars, gases, and dust make up a hazy band of light, which we call the Milky Way. *See galaxy.*

Miller, Arthur

Arthur Miller (b. 1915) is an American playwright. *Death of a Salesman*, often considered his finest play, won both the New York Drama Critics' Circle Award and the Pulitzer Prize. Among Miller's other plays are *All My Sons* and *The Crucible*.

milliliter

A milliliter is a unit for measuring capacity or volume in the metric system. An eyedropper holds about 1 milliliter. *See metric system.*

millileter

million

In mathematics, million is the name for the number 1,000,000.

minerals

In the human body, minerals are nutrients that perform many functions in regulating the activities of cells. *See cell.*

minuend

A minuend is a number from which another number is subtracted.

Example:

95 - 68 = 27

minuend

minutemen

Before and at the beginning of the American Revolution, a citizen-soldier, said to be ready to fight at a moment's notice, was called a *minuteman.* In the 1770s, the American colonists formed themselves into militia and marched in the streets of Boston, readying themselves for war. *See American Revolution and militia.*

mirage

A mirage is an optical illusion. It is caused by refraction of light rays from a distant scene by air layers at different temperatures.

misdemeanor

A minor crime is a misdemeanor. A traffic offense such as speeding, for instance, is a misdemeanor. More serious crimes such as robbery are called felonies. *See felony.*

missionary

A missionary is a person who is sent by a religious organization to teach others about its beliefs. Missionaries often start churches and schools in the lands in which they settle.

Mississippi River

The Mississippi River is the longest river in the United States. Flowing from northern Minnesota to the Gulf of Mexico, it serves as the most important inland waterway in the United States. The Mississippi River and its tributaries also provided a route for explorers and settlers to follow in the seventeenth and eighteenth centuries. *See Gulf Coast and tributary.*

mitosis

Mitosis is the process of cell division. During this process, a cell divides and each new cell receives exactly the same number of chromosomes that the original cell had. *See cell and chromosome.*

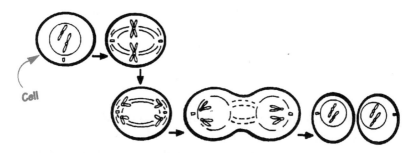

Cell

mixed number

A number that has a whole number part and a fraction part is called a mixed number.

Example:

3 1/2

mode

In mathematics, the mode is the number that occurs most often in a set of data.

Mode Example →

2, 4, 5, 6, and 6

mode

See median.

modifier

In English usage, a modifier is any word or group of words that limits the meaning of another word or group of words. Adjectives and adverbs, for instance, are modifiers.

Examples:
- blue jackets (not all of them, only the blue ones)
- worked slowly (describes one particular way of working)

See adjective and adverb.

modulation

Within a musical composition, modulation occurs when the music changes from one key to another by using a "pivot chord," a chord that is common to both keys. *See chord.*

Mohawk Trail

The Mohawk Trail ran from the Hudson River in New York to the eastern end of Lake Erie. First used by Native Americans, the Mohawk Trail helped open the upper Midwest frontier to Easterners in the early 1800s.

Mohs' scale

Friedrich Mohs (1773–1839), a German scientist, created the first scale to measure the hardness of minerals. Named the "Mohs' Scale of Hardness," the scale ranges from 1 to 10. The softest material is talc, which is like chalk, and the hardest is diamond. The Mohs' scale is one method scientists use to identify minerals. If a mineral will scratch a copper penny but not steel, for instance, the mineral falls between 3 and 7 on the Mohs' scale.

mold

In art, a mold is a hollow container or form in which a sculptural object can be created. By making a mold, an artist can create many copies of a sculpture in metal, bronze, and plaster, among other materials.

molecule

A molecule is two or more atoms joined together to form a particle that is the smallest unit into which a substance can be divided and still retain the chemical properties of the original substance. The atoms may be of the same element, or they may be of two or more separate elements.

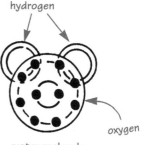

hydrogen

oxygen

water molecule

A molecule of water, for example, is composed of hydrogen and oxygen. Sugar is composed of molecules made of three elements—carbon, hydrogen, and oxygen. *See atom.*

mollusk

oyster

A mollusk is a soft-bodied invertebrate without bones that is usually covered by a hard shell. An oyster, for example, which has a soft body and hard shell, is a mollusk.

monarchy

A monarchy is a nation ruled by a king, queen, or emperor. The ruler, called a monarch, usually inherits the position. In a constitutional monarchy, laws restrict the leader's power. Historically, monarchs have had great power that they sometimes abused. *See despot and oligarchy.*

Mongols

The Mongols were a warlike people from northeastern Asia who held the largest land empire in history, reaching its peak in the late 1200s. The empire included much of Asia and parts of eastern Europe. *See Russia.*

monk

A monk is a man who gives up worldly things to devote his life to religion. Monks usually live in special places called monasteries. Medieval Christian monks preserved Greek and Roman literature. Being a monk is an honor for a Buddhist of Tibet.

monologue

A monologue is a single character's extended speech in a play or story. In Shakespeare's *Julius Caesar*, for instance, Marc Antony's famous monologue begins:

> Friends, Romans, countrymen, lend me your ears;
> I come to bury Caesar, not to praise him.

See dialogue and soliloquy.

monopoly

A business with no competition is a monopoly. It has complete control of a product or service. Generally the United States government tries to avoid letting any company become a monopoly. Instead, the government encourages free trade and competition so that there will be fair prices.

Monroe Doctrine

Begun by President James Monroe in 1823, the Monroe Doctrine was a statement about United States foreign policy. The Monroe Doctrine asserted that the United States would fight European aggression or colonization anywhere in the entire Western Hemisphere.

monsoon

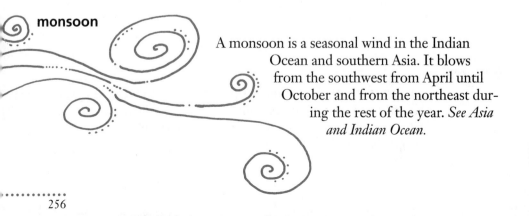

A monsoon is a seasonal wind in the Indian Ocean and southern Asia. It blows from the southwest from April until October and from the northeast during the rest of the year. *See Asia and Indian Ocean.*

moon

All of the planets in our solar system, except Mercury and Venus, have moons. The Earth and Pluto are the only planets with a single moon. One early theory of the moon's origin was that it was once part of the Earth and broke off, forming its own planet. Because the moon has no air, conditions there are not livable for humans. Temperatures on the moon also vary a lot. In the area directly below the sun, they can go as high as 266° Fahrenheit or as low as -280° Fahrenheit.

moon landing

On July 20, 1969, astronauts Neil Armstrong and Edwin "Buzz" Aldrin became the first humans to set foot on the moon. The Apollo space program had launched ten previous flights before these astronauts from *Apollo 11* made the first moon walk.

Mormon Trail

In 1845–47 more than 15,000 Mormons traveled west to Utah in search of a place where they could start a religious community. They eventually founded Salt Lake City. Mormons are members of the Church of Jesus Christ of Latter-day Saints.

Morrison, Toni

In 1993, Toni Morrison (b. 1931) became the first black American writer to win the Nobel Prize for literature. Her novel *Beloved* also won the Pulitzer Prize for fiction in 1988.

Morse, Samuel F. B.

Samuel F. B. Morse (1791–1872) made the first electric telegraph in 1837. He also created what is now known as the Morse code, a system of dots and dashes used for sending telegraph messages.

Examples:

A ● ▬
E ●
I ● ●
1 ● ▬ ▬ ●
2 ● ● ▬ ● ●

mosaic

A mosaic is a picture or decoration made of small, colored pieces of stone, tile, or glass affixed to a background. This art form dates back to Greek and Roman times, when mosaics were used on floors, ceilings, and walls. *See fresco and mural.*

Moscow

Moscow, the capital of Russia, is the largest city in Europe, with a population of about ten million. Located in the western part of the country, it is Russia's industrial, commercial, and cultural center. *See Russia.*

mosque

A mosque is a place of worship for Muslims, followers of Islam. Mosques are often domed and often have minarets—slender towers with balconies. At certain times each day, a holy man calls people to prayer from his minaret. *See Islam and Muhammad.*

Mother Teresa

Mother Teresa of Calcutta (Agnes Gonxha Bojaxhiu, b. 1910) is a Yugoslavian-born Roman Catholic missionary. She left teaching to care for India's ill and homeless people. In 1979 she was awarded the Nobel Peace Prize for her untiring work on behalf of the poor. *See India and missionary.*

motif

In any work of art, a repeated theme, pattern, or design is a motif.

mouse

In computer jargon, a mouse is a device used with a keyboard to enter data into a computer. A mouse may have one or more buttons that the user clicks. *See data and keyboard.*

movable type

The raised letters used in printing from about 1440 on are movable type. Type was first made of wood and later of metal. Before printing was invented in fifteenth-century Europe, all books had to be copied by hand. Movable type allowed for better and faster production of books—and thus the greater spread of information. *See Johannes Gutenburg.*

movement

In music, a movement is the principal division of a symphony, sonata, concerto, or other long work. *See symphony.*

Mozart, Wolfgang Amadeus

Wolfgang Amadeus Mozart (1756–1791) is often considered to be the finest purely classical composer who ever lived. His genius was recognized in childhood as he performed throughout Europe. His more than 600 compositions include the operas *Don Giovanni* and *The Marriage of Figaro* as well as many symphonies,

MORE NOTES →

concertos, other instrumental pieces, and sacred and secular vocal works.

muckraker

Journalists of the early 1900s who exposed social and political scandals, corruption, and social problems to public view were called *muckrakers*. Muckrakers earned this name because they dug up unpleasant material and exposed it to the public. Journalists such as Lincoln Steffens and Ida Tarbell were famous muckrakers.

Muhammad

The Arab founder of the Islam religion, Muhammad (570?–632) began at about the age of 35 to teach religion. He opposed worshipping idols and encouraged daily prayer and giving alms, money, or food for charity. In 630 Mecca became the holy city of Muhammad and his followers. *See Islam and Mecca.*

Muir, John

John Muir (1838–1914) was a naturalist. He did a great deal to establish national parks, particularly Yosemite National Park in California. He explored wilderness in the Sierra Nevadas and in Alaska, where he discovered Muir Glacier. Because of his travels and love of nature, he urged President Theodore Roosevelt to create a policy to preserve our national forests. Muir once said,

"In order for children to understand nature they must see how life and death work in nature. They must see the life of woods, meadows, plains, mountains, and streams. In so doing they will learn that death is as beautiful as life."

multiplicand

A number that is multiplied by another number is the multiplicand.

Example:

$$27 \times 3 = 81$$

multiplicand

See multiplier and product.

multiplier

A number that multiplies another number is a multiplier.

Example:

multiplier

$$27 \times 3 = 81$$

See multiplicand.

mural

A large painting done either directly on or fastened to a wall or ceiling is a mural. Murals painted on wet plaster are called frescoes; murals on dry plaster are seccos. Murals are also painted on canvas, which is later attached to a wall or ceiling. *See fresco.*

muscles

Muscles are organs composed of tough tissues that affect the movement of the human body. The body has more than 600 muscles. Some, such as those in a person's arms and legs, are voluntary muscles because they can be controlled. Others, such as those in a person's stomach, are involuntary muscles because they cannot be controlled. Inside of muscles, lactic acid and a substance called glycogen interact to provide strength for the body.

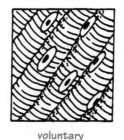 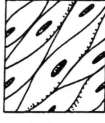

voluntary   involuntary

mutation

A mutation is a change within a gene or chromosome of a living organism. When a mutation occurs in a cell, the DNA of that cell is permanently changed. *See cell and DNA.*

myth

A myth is a story once believed to be true that usually explains a phenomenon of nature or illustrates a religious belief. There are, for instance, Greek myths about the beginning of the world, the origin of humankind, and the roles of good and evil. The term *myth* can also refer to any fictitious story or imaginary person or event.

NAACP

The National Association for the Advancement of Colored People (NAACP), founded in 1909, works for the civil rights of black people and other minority groups. *See civil rights.*

Napoleon I

A French general and emperor, Napoleon Bonaparte (1769–1821) was a soldier during the French Revolution. Seizing power in 1799, he became emperor of France in 1804. Napoleon wanted to establish an empire for France, so he fought wars all across Europe. Ultimately, Napoleon was defeated at the Battle of Waterloo and sent into exile in 1815. *See France and Napoleonic Code.*

Napoleonic Code

The Napoleonic Code, created by Napoleon Bonaparte, modernized French laws in the early 1800s. This code set up a system of government that improved the lives of French people. *See Napoleon I.*

narcotic

Drugs such as opium, morphine, codeine, and heroin are narcotics. As a group, they are depressants that interact with the central nervous system. Possession of narcotic drugs is illegal

MORE

without a prescription, but certain narcotics are sometimes used for medical purposes—to kill pain, for example.

narrative

A narrative is a story. Short stories, novels, and biographies are all narratives. Any writing that tells a story or recounts an event is narration.

narrator

The narrator is the person telling a story. A narrator tells a story from a particular point of view. *See point of view.*

NASA

The National Aeronautics and Space Administration (NASA) manages the United States space exploration program. NASA is responsible for choosing crews and directing launches of space-crafts.

national anthem

The official, patriotic song of a country is its national anthem. The "Star-Spangled Banner" is the national anthem of the United States. Francis Scott Key wrote the words during the War of 1812 when, after one battle, he saw the American flag still flying.

national debt

A national debt is the total amount of money that a nation has borrowed. A government borrows money just like anyone else. It sometimes spends more money on services, such as building roads, than it collects in taxes. When it does, it creates a debt.

National Road

The National Road was the pioneer road from Cumberland, Maryland, to Vandalia, Illinois. It was started in 1811. The completed trail carried many settlers through the Appalachians to the Midwest. After railroads were developed, the importance of the National Road diminished.

NATO

The North Atlantic Treaty Organization (NATO) was created in 1950 as a cooperative military defense agreement. The purpose was to protect Western Europe and the United States from possible attacks by the Soviet Union.

natural resource

Natural resources are anything in or on the Earth that people use to meet their needs. Renewable resources, such as wind and sunlight, can be used over and over. Nonrenewable resources, such as oil and natural gas, need to be conserved because they cannot be replaced.

nauseated/nauseous

▷ *Nauseated* means ill or sick.
▷ *Nauseous* means sickening or disgusting.

Example:
The nauseous odor in the chemistry lab made the students nauseated.

nebula

A nebula is a cloud of gas and dust in outer space. *See Milky Way.*

negative number

In mathematics, a negative number is one that is less than 0.

Examples:
- -5
- -7
- -24

less than 0

-3 -2 -1 0 1 2 3

nerve endings

The human skin has many different nerve endings. Each nerve ending performs a special function. Some nerve endings only gather information about heat. Others are only sensitive to pain, cold, pressure, or touch. Most of the time

WAIT, THERE'S MORE!

several kinds of nerve endings work together. For example, two different types of nerve endings signal that something is hot and should not be picked up. *See nerve signals and nervous system.*

nerve signals

When a person feels pain, an electrical signal moves along the nerves in the direction of the brain. The brain then sends other signals back along the nerves to cause the body to react. The nerve signals that travel to and from the brain move at speeds of 3 to 300 feet per second. *See nerve endings and nervous system.*

nervous system

The nervous system is the system within the body that provides paths for the brain to communicate with the rest of the body. The nervous system consists of the brain, the spinal cord, and the nerves. The nervous system has billions of cells connected in a pathway of nerves throughout the body. *See nerve endings and nerve signals.*

network, computer

A computer network is a system of computers, terminals, and databases connected by communications lines. *See database and terminal.*

neutrality

Neutrality is a country's policy of taking neither side in a dispute, argument, or war. Switzerland, for example, has followed a policy of neutrality for so long that it is known as the "peace capital of the world."

neutron

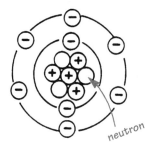
neutron

A neutron is a particle that has no electric charge. It may be found either by itself or in a nucleus of an atom. Along with electrons and protons, neutrons are one of the main parts of the atomic structure of matter. *See electron and proton.*

New Deal

President Franklin D. Roosevelt's program for relief, recovery, and reform during the Great Depression of the 1930s was called "the New Deal." It gave direct relief to the unemployed and began public works projects such as the Tennessee Valley Authority. In 1935, Roosevelt began a Second New Deal, which began the Social Security program and developed additional public works programs that created jobs for workers.

New York City

New York City is a seaport in southeastern New York State. With a population of about 7.3 million people, it is the largest city in the United States. The United Nations has its headquarters in New York City.

newton

A newton (N) is a metric unit of measurement that tells the strength of a force.

Newton, Isaac

Isaac Newton (1642–1727) was an English scientist who made two of the world's most fundamentally important scientific discoveries. One was his discovery of the spectral composition of light. That is, he discovered that light is in fact composed of many different colors, even though we cannot see them all.

MORE

Second, he discovered the law of gravity, which states that all things have a gravitational pull in proportion to their mass. Newton once wrote:

> "I do not know what I may appear to the world; but to myself I seem to have been only like a boy playing on the seashore, and diverting myself in now and then finding a smoother pebble or a prettier shell than ordinary, whilst the great ocean of truth lay all undiscovered before me."

See Newton's laws.

Newton's laws

In his book *Mathematical Principles of Natural Philosophy*, Isaac Newton presented three laws about how the world works.

1. The first law of motion stated that a body at rest tends to remain at rest, and that a body in motion tends to remain in motion at a constant velocity if no outside factors interfere.
2. The second law described force as an equation of M (mass) and acceleration.
3. The third law stated that for every action there is an opposite and equal reaction.

See Isaac Newton.

Nile River

The Nile River is a river in North Africa that flows into the Mediterranean Sea. Running more than 4,000 miles, the Nile is the longest river in the world. Since the beginning of civilization, it has provided people with transportation and irrigation. The Nile Valley includes the fertile banks of the Nile River. The Nile Delta is the fertile region at the mouth of the Nile. *See Egypt.*

Ninety-five Theses

The Ninety-five Theses are a list of criticisms of the Roman Catholic Church. In 1517, a German priest, Martin Luther, made the list public and started a great controversy. He broke with the Roman Catholic Church and began the Reformation, which led to Protestantism.

Nobel Prize

Established by Alfred Nobel, a Swedish chemist and inventor, the Nobel Prize is given to individuals or groups for outstanding work in the sciences, literature, economics, and peace.

nomad

A nomad moves from place to place in search of food. Prehistoric people were nomadic hunter-gatherers who lived by following food sources. Today nomads still move about to find pastures for their herds.

nomination

When candidates are selected to run for a political office, they are nominated. The nomination of a candidate, then, means the selection of a candidate by his or her party.

non sequitur

A non sequitur is a logical fallacy in which a person presents a conclusion that does not follow from the premises.

Example:

Luis is a great athlete. He can play any sport well. Therefore, when he says to vote for Senator Valdez, I'm going to vote for her.

See logical fallacy.

nonfiction

Nonfiction is any writing that is not about imagined characters and events. For example, Martin Luther King's speech "I Have a Dream" is nonfiction.

nonpartisan

A nonpartisan is a person who is not affiliated with a political party. The two major parties in the United States are the Democratic and the Republican. A person belonging to one of them is a partisan of that party. A person belonging to neither party is a nonpartisan. A proposed law that favors neither party is also nonpartisan.

nonrenewable resource

Something that is nonrenewable cannot be made again. Often when people refer to a resource such as oil as nonrenewable, they mean that once the oil is used, it cannot be replaced. Wind is an example of a renewable resource. *See natural resource.*

Nonstandard English

Nonstandard English is any version of English used by people who do not speak or write standard English. Nonstandard English, characterized by excessive slang, idioms, dialect, and odd sentence structure, is inappropriate in formal writing. *See dialect, idiom, and slang.*

Normandy Beach

The World War II invasion of northern France by Allied forces occurred at Normandy Beach. This invasion on June 6, 1944, called "D-Day" by the invasion's planners, began the Allied drive to retake France from the Nazis. It is considered the turning point in the war. *See World War II.*

North America

North America, the third largest continent in the world, lies between the Atlantic Ocean in the east and the Pacific Ocean in the west. North America includes the United States, Canada, Greenland, Mexico, the countries of Central America, and the islands of the Caribbean Sea.

Northern Ireland

Northern Ireland is a self-governing country in northeastern Ireland that is part of Great Britain. It covers about one-sixth of the area of Ireland. The majority of the people in Northern Ireland are the descendants of English and Scottish settlers. *See England and Ireland.*

Northwest Passage

The mythical ship route that joins the Atlantic and the Pacific oceans is the Northwest Passage. Much of America was explored and discovered in the sixteenth century as Europeans searched unsuccessfully for a northwest sea passage to Asia.

Norway

Norway is a mountainous country in northern Europe on the Scandinavian Peninsula. It borders on both the Atlantic Ocean and the Arctic Ocean. *See Scandinavia.*

notes and rests

Notes and rests are the symbols used to write music. A note shows how long a sound is held. The notes are called:

- whole
- half
- quarter
- eighth
- sixteenth

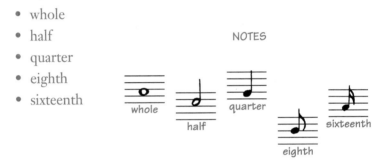

Rests have the same names and show how long a silence is held:

- whole
- half
- quarter
- eighth
- sixteenth

noun

A noun is a word used to name a person, place, thing, or idea.

Examples:

- William Shakespeare
- New York
- book
- freedom

Nouns may be common or proper, abstract or concrete, or collective. Nouns are most often used in sentences as subjects, indirect objects, direct objects, objects of prepositions, and predicate nouns.

noun clause

A noun clause is a subordinate (dependent) clause that is used as a noun in a sentence.

Example:

That Kristi is an excellent student is widely known.

└── noun clause used as the subject of the sentence

See noun and subordinate clause.

novel

A novel is a story with characters and a plot long enough to fill one or more book volumes. Famous American novels include *The Adventures of Huckleberry Finn, The Great Gatsby,* and *The Catcher in the Rye. See fiction.*

nuclear energy

Nuclear energy is produced when the nuclei of atoms are split or joined together. A great deal of energy is then released in a short amount of time. Large amounts of heat are also created. The exploding of an atom bomb and shining stars are both the result of atoms releasing nuclear energy. Uranium is the natural material that is the main source of nuclear energy. It was discovered by Martin Klaproth in 1789 in a heavy black ore called pitchblende. This new material was named uranium after what was then a newly discovered planet, Uranus. *See nuclear fission, nuclear fusion, and nuclear reactor.*

nuclear fission

The process of splitting heavy nuclei into lighter ones is nuclear fission. It is done because it releases an enormous amount of energy. *See nuclear energy and nuclear fusion.*

nuclear fusion

The process of joining light nuclei to make a heavier nucleus is nuclear fusion. *See nuclear energy and nuclear fusion.*

nuclear reaction

When one type of nucleus is changed into another, the process is a nuclear reaction. Either nuclear fusion (joining nuclei) or nuclear fission (splitting a nucleus) produces a nuclear reaction. The first self-sustaining nuclear chain reaction was demonstrated on December 2, 1942, in a laboratory at The University of Chicago. This research is known now as the Manhattan Project. This historic event started the atomic age and eventually led to the development of the atomic bomb and nuclear reactors. *See Manhattan Project, nuclear energy, and nuclear reactor.*

nuclear reactor

A nuclear reactor usually uses the element uranium for fuel. The atoms inside the uranium are split, which results in the release of large amounts of heat. That heat then heats water inside of the reactor. The water changes to steam and flows through pipes to a special kind of engine called a turbine. The steam turns the blades of the turbine, which are connected to a generator. A generator is a motor that produces electricity, and this electricity is sent out over power lines. *See nuclear energy and nuclear reaction.*

nucleus

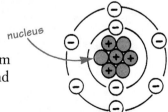

The positively charged core of an atom is the nucleus. It contains neutrons and protons. *See neutron and proton.*

number

In language, number indicates whether a word is singular (one) or plural (more than one). A singular subject must take a singular verb.

Example:

Katie graduates from college this week.

A plural subject must take a plural verb.

Example:

The boys jump in the lake.

See subject and verb.

numerator

In mathematics, the number above the line in a fraction is the numerator.

Example:

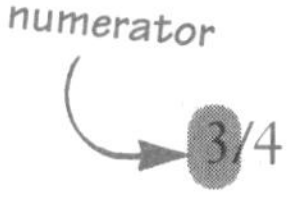

numerator

3/4

See denominator.

nutrients

Nutrients are food substances necessary for the growth and maintenance of cells. *See cell and nutrition.*

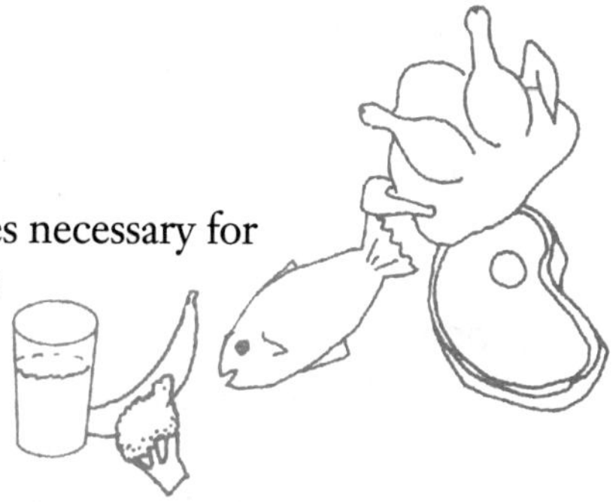

nutrition

Nutrition is the science of nutrients and how the human body uses them. Scientists who study nutrition look at people's diets and what nutrients are contained in different foods. *See nutrients.*

o

obesity

Obesity is the condition of having a high percentage of body fat.

objet d'art

Objet d'art is a French phrase for a relatively small artistic object such as a vase or figurine.

oboe

The modern oboe, a member of the orchestra's woodwind section, is a long, tube-like instrument with a double reed in the mouthpiece, openings along the front, and keys that the oboist presses to change the pitches. The oboe family includes the English horn and the bassoon.

obtuse angle

In geometry, an obtuse angle is one with a measure greater than 90° and less than 180°. *See acute angle.*

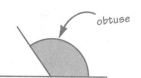

obtuse

ocean currents

The water in the ocean is always moving. Although some ocean currents are deep underwater, most currents are near the surface

MORE

of the ocean. These currents are created by a combination of the wind and the movement of the Earth as it rotates. The direction of the wind and shape of the land under the sea also affect ocean currents.

oceanographer

An oceanographer is a scientist who studies oceans and the plant and animal life of oceans and seas. Jacques Cousteau is a famous oceanographer. *See Jacques Cousteau.*

octagon

An octagon is an eight-sided polygon. *See polygon.*

octagon

octave

In music, the first and the eighth tone of the major-minor diatonic scale creates an octave. Any two notes that create this interval have twice or half the frequency of each other. When sounded together, the two notes sound like duplicates—the higher note brighter than the lower note. *See notes and rests.*

ohm

An ohm is a unit used to express the amount of electrical resistance. That is, an ohm measures how easily or with how much difficulty electrical current is transmitted. *See electricity.*

oil spills

Millions of tons of oil are spilled into oceans around the world each year. In 1967, for example, the *Torrey Canyon* spilled 100,000 tons of crude oil into the Atlantic. In 1990, the *Exxon Valdez* spilled an enormous amount of oil into the ocean off the coast of Alaska. Much pollution is also caused by supertankers flushing their tanks clean with seawater.

Exxon Valdez

Old English

Old English is the first form of English that was recorded in writing. Old English was used from approximately 500 to 1100. *See Middle English.*

oligarchy

In an oligarchy, a small group of people rule a country. The rest of the people have little or no representation in government. An oligarchy may have a premier, or leader, supported by a political party.

Olympus

In Greek mythology, Olympus was the home of the gods. It is a mountain in Thessaly, a section of Greece.

ombudsman

An ombudsman is a nonpartisan public official with the power to investigate a complaint against government. *See nonpartisan.*

onomatopoeia

The use of words that sound like their meaning is onomatopoeia.

Examples:
- buzz
- woof
- quack
- hiss

See figurative language.

OPEC

OPEC (Organization of Petroleum Exporting Countries) has thirteen member nations. These nations, which produce and export a great deal of oil, formed this group to work together to increase profits from the sale of oil.

opera

Operas, like plays, tell a story with actors, scenery, and costumes; but the actors sing their lines, with the orchestra accompanying them and adding to the dramatic effect. Drama has been set to music since the days of ancient Greece, but the opera of today has grown out of operatic styles of the late sixteenth and seventeenth centuries. Among the best known operas are *Madame Butterfly, Carmen, Rigoletto,* and *The Barber of Seville. See drama.*

optical fiber

An optical fiber is a narrow, transparent tube through which light travels, even around curves. Telephone calls, for example, are often transmitted via optical fiber lines.

oral history

Information and ideas told from one generation to the next are oral history. Before written records, people kept track of names and events by repeating them over and over during ceremonies and other special occasions. That was the only way people could remember and keep track of what had happened in the past.

oratorio

An oratorio is a musical composition for chorus, soloists, and orchestra that develops a religious or meditative story (libretto). Unlike opera, it is performed without action, scenery, or costumes. *See libretto and opera.*

orbit

An orbit is the path an object takes around another object. The moon, for example, orbits around the Earth. The orbit of the Earth around the sun is elliptical—more like an oval than a circle. A planet's distance away from the sun determines the planet's year—the time it takes to complete one orbit. Since the Earth takes 365.2433 days to go completely around the sun, its year is 365 days. Once every four years, one day is added—February 29 of a leap year. Mercury, on the other hand, makes a complete revolution around the sun in 88 "earth" days. Pluto has a year equal to 247 "earth" years.

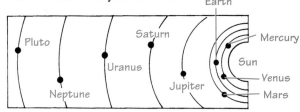

orchestra

An orchestra is a large group of musicians who play together under the direction of a conductor. A symphony orchestra includes strings (violin, viola, cello, double-bass, harp), woodwinds (flute, clarinet, oboe, English horn, bassoon), brass (trumpet, French horn, trombone, tuba), and percussion (drums, cymbals, and instruments for special effects). Modern orchestras have between eighty and one hundred musicians.

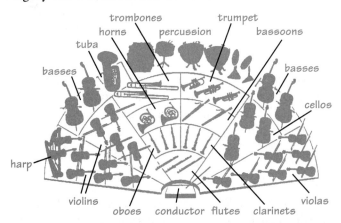

ordered pair

In mathematics, an ordered pair is any two numbers written in a meaningful order so that one can be considered the first and the other considered the second of the pair.

ordinal number

An ordinal number is a number, such as third or seventh, used to tell order or position in a series.

Oregon Trail

The Oregon Trail was the route used by people bound for the Oregon Territory beginning in the 1840s. It began in Independence, Missouri, and continued 2,000 miles across the Great Plains and the Rocky Mountains to Fort Vancouver in Oregon.

organ

The pipe organ has one to five keyboards (manuals) played by the hands and a pedal board played by the feet. As the organist plays, air is forced through a bellows into pipes of many lengths and shapes to create a great variety of musical tones. Electric organs have a similar keyboard design, but there are no pipes. The tones are created electronically.

Orient Express

The *Orient Express* was a luxury train that ran from Paris to Constantinople (Istanbul). It ran with some interruptions from 1883 to 1977. Writers, impressed by its glamor, helped to make the *Orient Express* famous.

Orwell, George

George Orwell (1903–1950) was the pen name for Eric Blair, a British journalist, novelist, and essayist. His two most famous novels are *Animal Farm* and *1984.*

osmosis

Osmosis is the process by which tiny molecules pass through the membranes (or linings) of cells. Trees, for example, get water through the process of osmosis. The water molecules seep into the membrane of larger molecules and cells. In this way, water passes from the soil in the ground into the cells in trees and plants. *See cell and molecule.*

Otis, Elisha

Elisha Otis (1811–1861) invented the first safe elevator to move people from one floor of a building to another. A store in New York installed the first elevator in 1857. Passenger elevators made modern skyscrapers practical.

Ottawa

Ottawa is the capital of Canada. It is located in the southeastern part of the province of Ontario just above New York State. *See Canada.*

Ottoman Empire

The Ottoman Empire flourished in Turkey between the fourteenth and twentieth centuries. Ottoman Turks conquered the Byzantine capital of Constantinople in 1453. Their rule of the Mideast ended with their defeat in World War I in 1918.

ounce

An ounce is a unit for measuring weight in the customary system. A slice of bread, for example, weighs about 1 ounce.

outline

An outline is an organized, sequential plan for a piece of writing. Outline forms use numbers and letters to show relationships among ideas and pieces of evidence. *See prewriting.*

overture

An overture is an instrumental composition. Best known are the operatic overature, which introduces an opera, and the concert overture, an independent work such as Brahms's *Academic Festival Overture.*

ovulation

Ovulation is the release of a mature egg from the ovary. When the egg is released, a female is able to conceive a child.

oxidation

Oxidation is a process by which certain minerals combine with oxygen in the air or water. When copper, for example, changes color from a reddish brown to green, oxidation is the process that causes that change. Rust is another form of oxidation.

ozone

Ozone is a molecule that is made up of three atoms of oxygen. Ozone provides a protective layer high up in the Earth's atmosphere. Without ozone, the Earth might not be a livable planet.

Pacific Ocean

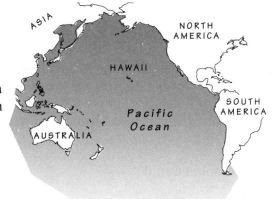

The Pacific Ocean is the largest of the four oceans in the world. Bordered on the east by North America and South America and on the west by Asia and Australia, the Pacific Ocean is larger than all of the Earth's continents combined.

pacifist

A pacifist is a person who opposes war. Pacifists advocate settling all conflicts by negotiation—talking things over. In time of war, some pacifists choose to perform public service rather than join the armed forces.

paddy

A paddy is a flooded field with raised sides for growing rice. Hundreds of years ago, Asian farmers developed this method of irrigation. Building paddies made it possible to grow rice, even on hillsides.

palette

A palette is the board or the table where an artist arranges

MORE ➔

his or her paints. A palette is also the group of colors an artist selects for a painting.

palindrome

A set of letters that read the same forward as they do backward is a palindrome.

Examples:

- level
- eye
- dad

Pan

In Greek mythology, Pan was the god of forests and pastures and the protector of shepherds and their flocks. He was depicted as half human and half goat.

Panama Canal

The Panama Canal offers a waterway across the Isthmus of Panama connecting the Atlantic and Pacific oceans. It allows ships to travel from California to New York without going all the way around South America. Trade with Asia increased greatly after the canal's completion in 1914.

panorama

A panorama is a picture or picture series that presents an unlimited, continuous view of a landscape or event.

papier-mâché

The term *papier-mâché* in French means "chewed paper." It is a strong, lightweight art material used in sculpture and made by combining torn paper with paste. *See sculpture.*

papyrus

In ancient times Egyptians made paper by placing the thin, wet strips of the water plant papyrus together, putting them in the sun, and pressing them flat. *See parchment.*

parable

A parable is a story that uses a specific situation to teach a moral lesson. The Bible, for example, includes many parables such as the story of the Good Samaritan.

paradox

A paradox is an apparent contradiction that is somehow true on a deeper level. Mark Twain, for example, stated the paradox, "It takes a heap of sense to write good nonsense." Another paradox is the saying, "The more we learn, the less we know." *See figurative language.*

parallel

In geography, a parallel is any of the imaginary circles around the Earth that run parallel to the equator. The parallels form degrees of latitude, showing how far north or south something is from the equator. *See latitude.*

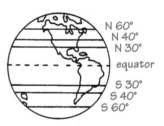

parallel lines

In geometry, lines in a plane that never meet are parallel lines.

parallelism

In English usage, parallelism is the use of similar forms for words and phrases that have similar structure. For instance, infinitives (*to show up* for the game and *to play hard*) are used together, as are gerunds (*Eating* quickly and *drinking* fast can cause indigestion.). *See gerund and infinitive.*

parallelogram

A parallelogram is a quadrilateral with opposite sides parallel and congruent. *See parallel lines and quadrilateral.*

parallelograms

paraphrase

A paraphrase is a restatement of the meaning of a passage in other words than the original. *See indirect quotation and plagiarism.*

parasite

A parasite is an organism that lives in or on another organism, called the host, and usually harms that organism. The parasite feeds itself on the host. A tapeworm, for example, is a kind of parasite. It lives in the intestine of an animal, taking its nourishment and harming the host by doing so.

parchment

Parchment is a smooth, durable writing material made from the skin of a sheep or goat.

parentheses

Parentheses ( ) are punctuation marks used to enclose explanatory information added to a sentence.

Example:

Senator Paul Simon (Illinois) is meeting with the President today.

Paris

Paris is the capital and largest city of France. It is located in the northern part of that country. For many centuries, Paris has been an international center of art and education. *See France.*

parliamentary system

In a parliamentary system of government, a group of representa-

tives called a *parliament* make and carry out the laws. The system
began in the thirteenth century in England when elected representatives from towns, boroughs, and shires (counties) were included
in the King's council of nobles.

participle

A participle is a verb used as an adjective. Participles generally end
in *-ing* or *-ed*. Participles are sometimes used in phrases called participial phrases.

Examples:

The *diving* heron caught the fish.

Diving into the lake, the heron caught the fish.

See adjective and verb.

Pascal's law

Pascal's law states that, if the pressure of a liquid in one part of a
container changes, the pressure changes throughout the container.
This law is named after Blaise Pascal (1623–1662), a French
philosopher, scientist, and mathematician who discovered it.

passed/past

▷ *Passed* is a verb that forms the past tense of *pass*.

▷ *Past*, which may be used as a noun, adjective, adverb,
or preposition, means "in time gone by" or "beyond."

Example:

In the past, Samantha has always passed the exams with
honors.

passenger pigeon

The last passenger pigeon in the world died on September 1, 1914,
in a zoo in Cincinnati. In 1800, there were an estimated three to
five billion passenger pigeons in North America. In a little more
than one hundred years, they were complete wiped out. Many died
because they were hunted for their meat.

pastel

A pastel is a chalk-like crayon made by mixing finely ground color with gum. This word is also used to name a picture created with such crayons. A soft, pale shade of a color is called *pastel* as well.

Pasteur, Louis

Louis Pasteur (1822–1895) invented pasteurization, a process that kills disease-bearing germs in milk. Pasteur proved that diseases are spread by bacteria, and he developed antiseptics, making surgical operations much safer for people. He also developed vaccines to prevent anthrax in farm animals and the spread of rabies from animals to humans.

patent

A patent is a government document giving a person the rights to an invention. A patent keeps other people from taking and manufacturing the invention.

pathogen

A pathogen is a disease-causing organism or virus.

patron

A patron is a wealthy person who supports people who are working in the arts. During the Renaissance, for example, rich patrons paid writers, painters, architects, and sculptors to create works of art.

Pearl Harbor

Pearl Harbor is a naval base in Hawaii. The Japanese air force attacked Pearl Harbor on December 7, 1941, bringing the United States into World War II. President Roosevelt called it, "a date which will live in infamy." *See World War II.*

Peary, Robert Edwin and Henson, Matthew

Robert Edwin Peary (1856–1920) and Matthew Henson (1867–1955) explored the Arctic. Peary mapped the northern limits of Greenland. In 1909, Peary and Henson, along with four Inuit men, reached the North Pole.

Peloponnesian War

The Peloponnesian War (431–404 B.C.) was a war between the city-states of Athens and Sparta. After a long destructive struggle, Sparta defeated Athens. One of the first historians, Thucydides, fought in the war and later wrote an accurate account of it. *See Athens.*

penicillin

Penicillin is an antibiotic medicine. Alexander Fleming developed penicillin from a kind of mold. He observed that the mold was killing bacteria in a laboratory dish. This accidental discovery of the penicillin mold led to the creation of one of the most widely used medicines of all time. Penicillin was perfected during World War II to help wounded soldiers. Fleming received the 1945 Nobel Prize for his work on penicillin.

peninsula

A peninsula is land that is surrounded by water on all sides but one. Florida, for example, is a peninsula, as is Scandinavia.

pentagon

A pentagon is a five-sided polygon. *See polygon.*

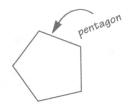

pentagon

percent (%)

Percent is a word meaning "hundredths" or "out of a hundred." Forty-five percent (45%), for instance, means 45/100 or .45. *See decimal.*

percussion

 Percussion is any type of musical instrument that produces sound when struck or shaken. Some produce definite pitches (marimba, xylophone, celesta, chimes, kettledrum); some do not (snare drum, bass drum, tambourine, cymbals, triangle).

perfect square

In mathematics, a perfect square is an integer whose square root is an integer. For example, 9 is a perfect square because its square root is 3. *See integers.*

perimeter

In mathematics, a perimeter is the sum of the lengths of the sides of a polygon.

Example

The perimeter is 26.

See polygon.

period

 A period (.) is a punctuation mark most often used to end a sentence that makes a statement or a command that is not an exclamation. Periods are also used after initials, abbreviations, and as decimal points. *See abbreviation and declarative sentence.*

periodic sentence

A periodic sentence is a sentence in which the most important thought is not completed until the end.

Example:

Following my teacher's heated command that I be quiet, I shut my mouth.

See sentence.

periodic table

The periodic table lists all of the elements known to us. At present, 109 elements are included in the table. The periodic table was first created by a Russian chemist named Dmitri Mendeleev (1834–1907). Mendeleev pointed out that certain elements had similar properties. He noticed that these properties occurred in patterns and predicted that other elements would be discovered. Three new elements were discovered within fifteen years of Mendeleev's publication of his periodic table.

periodical

A magazine or journal that is published at regular intervals, but not daily, is a periodical. *TIME*, *Sport*, and *Teen* are all examples of periodicals. Most libraries have a periodical room or section that contains current issues and back copies of periodicals.

periodical guide

A periodical guide is an index that lists the names of articles, authors, issues, and publications related to particular topics. *See index and periodical.*

peripheral

In computer jargon, a peripheral is a device connected to a computer. A printer and an external disk drive are examples of peripherals. *See computer.*

permafrost

Soil that stays permanently frozen is permafrost. Parts of Siberia in Russia, for instance, have permafrost. *See Russia.*

perpendicular lines

Lines that intersect to form right angles are perpendicular lines.

90°

Perry, Matthew

An American naval officer, Matthew Perry (1794-1858) is credited with persuading the Japanese to open up their ports to trade in 1854. This began a period of modernization in Japan. Perry sailed with his fleet of ships into Tokyo Bay and persuaded the *shoganate* in power to sign a treaty with the United States. *See Japan.*

Persephone

In Greek mythology, Persephone was the daughter of Demeter. Hades fell in love with her and carried her off to rule the underworld with him. Her Roman name was Proserpina. *See Demeter and Hades.*

personal pronoun

A personal pronoun is a pronoun that changes form when used in the first person (the person speaking), second person (the person spoken to), and third person (the person or thing spoken about).

Example

First person pronouns are *I, me, we,* and *us.*

The second person pronoun *is you.*

The third person pronouns are *he, him, she, her, they, them,* and *it.*

See pronoun.

personification

Personification is a form of figurative language in which an idea, object, or animal is given human feelings, thoughts, or attitudes. For example, "Sunday Rain," by John Updike, depends on personification. In the poem, a window screen is trying to do its crossword puzzle but appears to know only vertical words. *See figurative language.*

perspective

Perspective is an artistic technique, developed during the Renaissance, for creating the illusion of three-dimensional depth or volume on a two-dimensional surface. *See Renaissance.*

perspiration

Perspiration is a fluid made up of water, organic compounds, and salts excreted through the pores in the skin. Another word for perspiration is sweat.

Peter the Great

Peter the Great (1672–1725) became the sole ruler of Russia in 1696. His battles gave Russia ports on two seas. He established a powerful navy, strengthened the central government of the country, started schools, and built a new capital city. *See Russia.*

petition

A petition is a request by citizens. During many elections, voters will be asked to vote on issues that have been put on the ballot by petitions. If citizens collect enough support, then the issue can be put on the ballot and voted upon. A citizen can also petition the government or a judge to correct a wrong or to enforce a right. A request of any kind is sometimes referred to as a petition as well.

pewter

Pewter is a metal alloy—a combination of tin and two or more other metals—with a silvery, grayish luster often used for candlesticks and silverware.

pH scale

The pH scale is a range of numbers from 0–14 that indicate how acidic or basic a solution is. A pH of less than 7 indicates an acid. A pH of exactly 7 indicates a

WAIT, THERE'S MORE!

neutral solution, and a pH of greater than 7 indicates a base, a substance that produces hydroxide ions in water.

Phaethon

In Greek mythology, Phaethon, the son of Helios, tried unsuccessfully to drive the sun chariot. *See Helios.*

pharaoh

Pharaoh is the name for a king in ancient Egypt. This title came into general use after 1554 B.C.

philosopher

A philosopher looks for and studies the underlying truths about the world. For example, Socrates, the ancient Greek philosopher, taught his students to question everything.

phonics

Phonics is the study of the sounds associated with letters and groups of letters of the alphabet. For example, the long *a* sound can be spelled *a* (fate), *ea* (great), and *eigh* (eight).

photon

A photon is an elementary particle that is the basic unit of electromagnetic energy. Photons travel at the speed of light. *See atom and energy.*

photosynthesis

Photosynthesis is the process in which plants use light energy to change carbon dioxide and water into carbohydrates. Green plants make food from water and carbon dioxide by using energy they absorb from sunlight. The light is first absorbed by the chlorophyll in the plant. The plant splits the water into hydrogen and oxygen

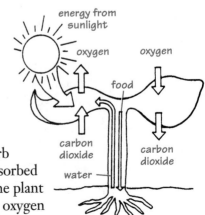

but uses only the hydrogen. The oxygen and extra water produced during photosynthesis escape through holes in the plant leaves.

phrase

A phrase is a group of two or more related words that lacks a verb and its subject. A phrase functions as a single part of speech. Common types of phrases are gerund phrases, infinitive phrases, participial phrases, and prepositional phrases. *See gerund, infinitive, participle, and prepositional phrase.*

physical and chemical changes

An object undergoes a physical change when what it looks like changes but what it is made of does not change (an ice cube changing to crushed ice, for instance). Melting a stick of butter is another example of a physical change. An object undergoes a chemical change when it forms a new substance with new properties. Examples of chemical changes include the burning of wood and the digestion of food.

physical fitness

Physical fitness is the ability of body systems to work together efficiently. *See cardiovascular fitness and total fitness.*

physics

Physics is the study of energy and matter. The energy might be heat, electrical, mechanical, or nuclear. Some physicists study the movement of bodies—why an apple falls to the ground or why the Earth revolves around the sun. Albert Einstein studied the movement of light through space and the energy that can be released by splitting an atom. *See Albert Einstein, energy, and matter.*

physiology

Physiology is the study of how organisms carry out life processes. A physiologist might study how organisms digest food, how they breathe, and how blood enables them to live. Physiologists may study the life processes of humans, of single-cell organisms like amoeba, or plants.

Pi (Π)

Pi is the number obtained by dividing the circumference of any circle by its diameter. A common approximation for Π is 3.14.

piano

The piano has been the most popular keyboard instrument since the early nineteenth century. Each key of the eighty-eight on the keyboard is attached to a small padded hammer. When a key is pressed, its hammer strikes the strings for that key, creating the sound, which can vary from soft to loud. The Italian word *pianoforte* (meaning "soft-loud") is the piano's original name.

pigment

Pigment is a coloring matter, generally in powder form, which is mixed with oil or water to make paint.

pilgrimage

A journey to a sacred place is a pilgrimage. Followers of Islam, for example, hope to make at least one pilgrimage to Mecca, their holy city, during their lifetime.

pint

A pint is a unit for measuring capacity in the customary system. A pint equals 2 cups.

pioneer

A pioneer is an early settler in a region of a country. Someone who does something first, preparing the way for others, is also often called a pioneer. Astronauts, for example, are pioneers in space.

pistil

The female reproductive organ of a flower is a pistil. It consists of the ovary, style, and the stigma.

pitch

In music, pitch is the height or depth of a musical tone. The pitch of a tone depends on the frequency of the vibrations of the sound.

pituitary gland

Human growth is controlled by a small gland at the bottom of the brain called the pituitary gland. This gland releases a substance that controls the growth of the body. When a person is young, tiny amounts of this chemical are released into the body. By the time a person is between the ages of 9 and 12 years old, larger amounts of the chemical are released, and a growth spurt occurs.

Pizarro, Francisco

Francisco Pizarro (1478?–1541) invaded Peru and executed the Inca emperor, Atahualpa. He conquered the Incas and seized their gold and silver treasures. *See conquistador.*

place value

The number each digit represents is determined by the position the digit occupies—that is, its place value.

Example:

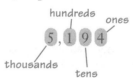

placenta

The placenta is a special organ that most mammals develop during pregnancy. It enables food and oxygen from the mother's blood to pass to a developing fetus and fetal wastes to pass back to the mother's blood. *See fetus.*

plagiarism

Plagiarism is the stealing of and passing off as one's own another person's ideas or words. Sources must be cited any time another person's ideas or words are used in a piece of writing.

plaintiff

The person who begins a lawsuit against someone else is the plaintiff. The person who is accused of doing wrong is the defendant.

plane

In geometry, a flat surface that extends without end in all directions is a plane.

plank

During elections, political parties take positions on the issues. For example, they take a particular stance or position on health care for the elderly or on raising taxes. Those positions are called *planks*.

plankton

Plankton are tiny, free-floating protists, plants and animals that live near the surface of the water. Plankton drift with the ocean currents. They are extremely small but important in the food chain in the ocean. *See food chain.*

plant cell

The cells of plants are composed of several parts. The cell wall covers and protects each cell. Inside each cell is a cell membrane that lets water, food, and gases in and out of the cell. The nucleus controls the work of the other cell parts. The space inside the cells is filled with vacuoles, or tiny sacs of water. The vacuoles float in a jellylike material known as cytoplasm, which usually contains cellulose produced in the cytoplasm. The part of a plant cell that gives it its green color is the chloroplast. *See cell.*

chloroplast
nucleus
large vacuole
cell wall

plant classification

Plants have been studied since Greek and Roman times. Most studies group plants into species, and most species of plants fall into one of two major groups. One group is plants that use seeds to reproduce. This group includes trees and many kinds of flowering plants. The other group is plants that do not have seeds. This kind of plant includes mosses, ferns, fungi, and algae.

plantation

A plantation is a large farm or estate, especially one that grows such crops as cotton, rice, and tobacco. In the pre-Civil War South, plantations depended on slave labor. The plantation system was an important part of the Southern economy.

plasma

In physics, plasma is a gas that is broken up into positively and negatively charged particles. In biology, plasma is the name of the liquid part of blood. *See blood.*

plaster of Paris

Plaster of Paris is a heavy, white, calcium-based powder which, when mixed with water, can be used for casts, molds, and sculptures.

plastic

Plastic, developed in the United States in 1869, is an artificial substance made from raw materials such as coal and water. Celluloid, an early plastic, was invented to make billiard balls. In 1909, Leo Baekeland created the first completely synthetic plastic, called *Bakelite.*

plate tectonics

Plate tectonics is the theory that the Earth's crust is composed of plates whose movements have created mountains, ocean trenches, and major faults. *See Earth and fault.*

plateau

A large, flat area of elevated land is a plateau. The flattened top of a mountain, for example, is a plateau.

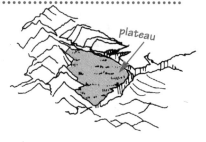

platelet

A platelet is a disc-like structure that develops from cells produced in bone marrow. Platelets help to stop the bleeding from a cut or other injury to the blood vessels. *See blood.*

Plato

Plato (427?–347? B.C.) was a Greek philosopher and teacher whose dialogues strongly influenced Western culture. He founded the Academy, a school famous in ancient times. In *The Republic*, he discussed the ideal state or society and what it means to be an individual in society. *See Aristotle and Socrates.*

plea bargaining

In a court case, the person accused of a crime sometimes will agree to plead guilty to one offense but not to another, more serious offense. This is plea bargaining. The accused person and his or her lawyer make a bargain with the court. They are able to do this because sometimes it is very difficult to prove without a doubt someone's guilt.

Pliny

Pliny the Elder (A.D. 23–79) was a Roman scholar. He wrote a book called Natural History, marking him as one of the earliest scholars interested in scientific matters.

plot

The plot is the organization of the events in a story or play. Most plots include a sequence of introduction, rising action, climax, falling action, and resolution. *See climax.*

climax

introduction

rising action

resolution

Plymouth Colony

The Plymouth Colony was a settlement established by English Pilgrims in 1620. They migrated from Europe to present-day Massachusetts for religious freedom. Miles Standish and William Bradford were early leaders of the colony. *See Mayflower Compact.*

pocket veto

When the President of the United States receives a bill within the last ten days of a session of Congress, he can kill the bill by using a pocket veto. That is, he can stop the bill by delaying it (carrying it around in his pocket) until the end of the session. This is only one way that a President can veto a bill. *See veto.*

Poe, Edgar Allan

Edgar Allan Poe (1809–1849) was an American poet, literary critic, and short-story writer best known for his tales of horror. His most famous stories include "The Tell-Tale Heart," "The Pit and the Pendulum," "The Cask of Amontillado," and "The Fall of the House of Usher." His most famous poem is "The Raven."

poetry

Poetry is imaginative writing using vivid, colorful words carefully and concisely arranged to have a particular sound and rhythm. Poems are most often organized in lines and stanzas. *See rhyme, rhythm, and stanza.*

point

In mathematics, a point is an exact location in space. *See ordered pair.*

point of view

Point of view is the perspective from which a story is told. Stories can be told from a variety of points of view, but the two most common are first person and third-person omniscient (all-knowing).

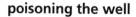

poisoning the well

Poisoning the well is a logical fallacy in which a person tries to discredit the speaker or writer before the argument is even presented.

Example:

Here comes Erin! If she tells you about what she says I said about Tyler, don't believe her. She has a crush on Tyler, and she'd say anything. Don't believe a word of what she says.

See *argumentum ad hominem* and *logical fallacy.*

police state

A state in which the government exercises great power is often called a *police state*. In such a country, the freedoms of citizens are often ignored. The police arrest or stop whomever they want whenever they want for whatever reasons they want.

polio

Polio, or poliomyelitis, is an inflammation of the brain and spinal cord. It is caused by a virus that infects the gray matter of the brain and spinal column. Often it cripples its victims. Dr. Jonas Salk was determined to find a medicine to prevent polio. In 1955, he developed a vaccine that was given to millions of children throughout the United States. His work, along with that of Albert Sabin, is responsible for almost completely eliminating the disease.

political party

A political party is a group of people who share similar ideas about how to run and improve their government. The United States Constitution does not mention political parties. However, people in the United States began to organize them in the late eighteenth century.

political scientist

A person who studies government and politics is a political scientist. Political scientists often study past governments in order to predict possible future events. Aristotle, the ancient Greek philosopher, is considered one of the earliest political scientists.

poll tax

A poll tax refers to a charge for voting in public elections. It was first used in the South around 1890 to keep blacks from voting.

pollution

Pollution is the contamination of the environment, especially with waste materials. Living things can be hurt or killed by pollution. Pollution comes in various forms.

1. Thermal Pollution. When factories empty heated water into lakes and streams, it raises the temperature of the water and can kill some plant and animal life.
2. Water Pollution. This type occurs when sewage and other pollutants are put into water sources. The pollutant might be waste, such as oil, or it might be weed killer that washes into a nearby stream.
3. Air Pollution. Carbon monoxide from cars and sulphur dioxide from factories are the most common air pollutants.

Polo, Marco

Marco Polo (1254–1324?) was an Italian merchant and traveler. With his father and his uncle, Polo crossed Asia to China between 1271 and 1274. There they stayed with the ruler, Kublai Khan, for almost twenty years. Polo's book about his travels stirred European curiosity about the outside world and especially the peoples in the East.

polygon

A polygon is a closed plane figure made by line segments called *sides*. Each side of a polygon meets two other sides, one at each of its endpoints. Triangles, quadrilaterals, and pentagons are all polygons.

three polygons

polyhedron

A polyhedron is a solid figure made up of four or more flat surfaces called *faces*. Each face of a polyhedron is a polygon. *See polygon.*

polymer

A polymer is a large, chainlike molecule that is formed by joining many smaller molecules chemically. Wool is a natural polymer; nylon is a synthetic polymer.

Polynesians

Polynesians are Asian people who, traveling in rafts or dugout canoes and using only the stars to guide them, began to colonize the Pacific islands about A.D. 500. Over the years, they discovered and settled countless islands.

Ponce de Leon, Juan

In 1513, Juan Ponce de Leon (1471–1521) set out to search for a legendary "Fountain of Youth." He explored present-day Florida and claimed the land for Spain. *See conquistador.*

pop art

Pop art was an art movement in the United States during the 1960s which used popular everyday objects from the world of mass media (advertising, packaging, and comic strips) as the basis of their art. Andy Warhol and Roy Lichtenstein are two well-known pop artists.

population density

Population density is the average number of people living in a certain area. Population density is the measure of how crowded with people a place is. If 1,000 people live inside an area of one square mile, then the population density is 1,000 per square mile. In a rural area, the population density might be 5–10 per square mile.

porcelain

Porcelain, developed in ancient China, is a fine, hard, white, translucent, earthenware used in ceramics.

portrait

A portrait is a painting, sculpture, or photograph of a person, especially of his or her face. A portrait may be of the head only, the head and shoulders, or of the whole body. A self-portrait is a portrait painted by an artist of himself or herself.

Poseidon

In Greek mythology, Poseidon was the god of the sea. His Roman name was Neptune.

possessive pronoun

A possessive pronoun is a personal pronoun used to show ownership. Possessive pronouns modify nouns the way adjectives do. In fact, possessive pronouns are sometimes called possessive adjectives.

Examples:

The possessive pronouns are *my, mine, his, her, hers, our, ours, their, theirs, your, yours,* and *its.*

See *adjective, personal pronoun,* and *pronoun.*

post hoc

Post hoc is a logical fallacy in which a person assumes that because event B follows event A, event A must have caused event B.

Example:

Jen started dating Sam in February. Her grades third quarter were poor. If she wants to make honor roll, she had better stop dating Sam.

The term post hoc comes from the Latin phrase *post hoc, ergo propter hoc,* meaning, "after this, therefore because of this."
See *logical fallacy.*

precede/proceed

▷ *Precede* means "to go before" or "to come before."
▷ *Proceed* means "to advance" or "move along."

Example:
Proceed to the theater and buy the inexpensive tickets that precede the first show.

precedent

Legal decisions are made every day. When someone refers to a decision made in an earlier legal case, he or she is referring to a precedent. Lawyers use precedents to help persuade a judge and jury how to decide a case similar to the ones given as precedents.

precinct

A precinct is a neighborhood district arranged for government or administrative purposes. A city council is often made up of representatives from each of a city's precincts.

precipitation

Any moisture that is released by clouds and falls to the ground is precipitation. Rain, snow, ice, hail, and sleet are all types of precipitation.

precis

A precis is a brief, accurate summary of the main ideas of a piece of writing or a speech.

predator

Predators are animals that capture and eat other animals. The animals that predators capture and eat are known as prey. For example, frogs are predators, and flies and other insects are their prey. Lions are predators, and antelope, among other animals, are their prey.

predicate

The predicate of a sentence is the part that says something about the subject. The simple predicate is the principal word or words in the predicate. The simple predicate is often called the *verb*.

Example:

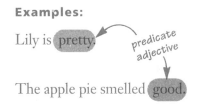

See sentence, subject, and verb.

predicate adjective

A predicate adjective is an adjective separated from the word it modifies by a linking verb.

Examples:

See adjective and linking verb.

predicate noun

A predicate noun (or pronoun) is a word that follows a linking verb and renames the subject.

Example:

Mr. Smith is the (principal.) predicate noun

A predicate noun (or pronoun) is sometimes called a *predicate nominative*. See *linking verb and noun*.

prefix

A prefix is a letter or group of letters added to the beginning of a word to change the word's meaning. The prefix *im-*, for example, changes the word *possible* to *impossible*. See *root and suffix*.

prejudice

An opinion formed without caring about or considering the facts is a prejudice. Prejudice can cause discrimination. People are sometimes prejudiced because of a person's religion, race, sex, or age. Any opinions formed about a person ought to be based upon facts, not upon some beliefs about someone's sex, race, religion, or age.

premise

A premise is an idea or statement assumed to be true that serves as a basis for a discussion or argument.

preposition

A preposition is a word placed before a noun or pronoun to show the relationship of that noun or pronoun to another word in the sentence. A preposition always appears in a phrase that ends with a noun or pronoun called the *object* of the preposition.

Example:

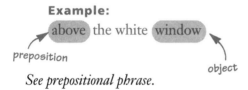

above the white window

preposition

object

See prepositional phrase.

prepositional phrase

A prepositional phrase is a group of words beginning with a preposition and ending with an object. A prepositional phrase may be used as a noun, adjective, or adverb.

Examples:
- across the lake
- around the bend
- through the window

See preposition.

prewriting

Prewriting is all of the activities a writer does before he or she begins to write. Prewriting includes, among other activities, brainstorming, clustering, gathering information, taking notes, planning, organizing evidence, and outlining. *See brainstorming, outline, and writing process.*

Priestley, Joseph

 Joseph Priestley (1733–1804), an English chemist who lived around the time of Benjamin Franklin, is remembered for his work with gases. At the time he began work, only three gases were known: carbon dioxide, hydrogen, and air. He is credited with discovering oxygen and with isolating and identifying nitrous oxide and sulfur dioxide.

primary colors

The three primary colors from which all other colors are derived are red, yellow, and blue. They are primary colors because, unlike other colors, they cannot be produced by mixing any other colors. *See color.*

primate

A primate is a mammal that has well-developed fingers and toes with nails, as well as well-developed brains and forward-facing eyes. Monkeys, for example, are primates.

prime factor

A factor that is a prime number is called a *prime factor.* The prime factors of 10, for example, are 2 and 5. The prime factors of 30 are 5, 3, and 2. *See prime number.*

prime meridian

The imaginary line that acts as a starting point for measuring longitude on the globe is the prime meridian. It is also known as the Greenwich meridian because it runs through Greenwich, England. *See longitude and meridian.*

prime number

A prime number is a whole number, greater than 1, that has exactly two factors: itself and 1.

Examples:

- 3
- 5
- 7
- 11
- 13
- 17

principal/principle

▷ *Principal* is used as a noun meaning chief or leader and as an adjective meaning leading or important.

▷ *Principle* is used as a noun meaning belief or doctrine or rule.

Example:

The principal explained the new program's principles to the students.

prism

In mathematics, a prism is a polyhedron with two parallel, congruent faces called *bases*. All other faces are parallelograms. In science, a prism-shaped transparent object that separates light into its different wavelengths (colors) is also called a prism. *See parallelogram and polyhedron.*

product

In mathematics, a product is the number found by multiplying numbers.

Example:

$$27 \times 3 = 81$$

product

See multiplicand and multiplier.

program, computer

Programs are codes used to tell a computer what to do. In computer jargon, then, a program is a sequence of coded instructions placed in a computer. Programs are written in various languages, such as Fortran, Basic, Cobol, and Pascal. These languages are in some ways as different as French, Spanish, and English. However, each of them allows people who work with computers to create complicated instructions in a simple way. *See computer.*

Prohibition

Prohibition was a period in the United States when laws prohibited making or selling alcoholic drinks. A national prohibition amendment to the Constitution (the 18th Amendment) was ratified in 1919 and went into effect in 1920. Thirteen years later, the 21st Amendment repealed the 18th Amendment, ending Prohibition.

proletariat

The term *proletariat* refers to working-class people. This word is used often when discussing communist or socialist beliefs or governments.

pronoun

A pronoun is a word that takes the place of a noun and acts like a noun. A pronoun refers back to a noun, its antecedent. Pronouns may be personal, possessive, demonstrative, interrogative, or relative. *See antecedent, noun, and demonstrative, interrogative, personal, possessive, or relative pronoun.*

proofreading

Proofreading is the careful reading of a piece of writing to find and correct any flaws. Proofreading is generally the final step before the completion of a piece of writing. *See revision.*

proper noun

A proper noun is a noun that names a particular person, place, or thing.

Examples:
- Michael Jordan
- Seattle
- Veterans Stadium

See common noun and noun.

property of zero

The property of zero states that the sum of zero and a number is that number ($0 + 5 = 5$). The product of zero and a number is zero ($0 \times 5 = 0$).

prose

Prose is any writing that is not poetry. A letter, for example, is prose, not poetry. A newspaper story, essay, and report are also examples of prose writing. *See poetry.*

prosecutor

A lawyer in charge of the government's side of a case against an accused person is the prosecutor.

protagonist

The protagonist is the main character in a story or play. The protagonist is often also called the hero or heroine. *See antagonist.*

proton

A proton is a positively charged particle found in the nucleus of an atom. *See atom, electron, neutron, and nucleus.*

protractor

A protractor is a device used to draw or measure angles.

proverb

A proverb is a traditional saying that presents some general truth.

Examples:

A stitch in time saves nine.

The early bird gets the worm.

An apple a day keeps the doctor away.

See epigram.

psalm

There are 150 psalms in the Old Testament of the Bible. These Hebrew songs of praise or prayer have been the most frequently used texts for Judeo-Christian music throughout the centuries.

Ptolemy

Ptolemy (100?–165?), was an ancient Greek astronomer. He developed an entire system of astronomy based upon the idea that our solar system revolved around a stationary Earth. He was one of the first astronomers to estimate the distance between the moon and the Earth. He also gathered information about the planets, predicting the position of planets and identifying constellations. The Ptolemaic system of astronomy was greatly admired and accepted as authoritative until 1543, when Copernicus published his theory on the movement of Earth and the planets around the sun. As a mapmaker, Ptolemy realized that the Earth was a sphere and then created a map showing the Earth as round. *See Nicolaus Copernicus.*

puberty

Puberty is a time in one's life when the body begins to produce sex hormones.

pueblo

Early Indian villages of the Southwest were called *pueblos*. Groups of homes, made of a sun-dried brick called *adobe*, were often clustered together in a pueblo.

MORE

Indians who lived there came to be called "Pueblo Indians." *See adobe.*

Pulitzer Prize

Joseph Pulitzer, a Hungarian-born journalist and publisher, established the Pulitzer Prize awards in his last will and testament. Since 1917, these prizes have been awarded to Americans for outstanding work in journalism, drama, literature, and music.

Pullman, George

George Pullman (1831–1897) developed a railroad sleeping car that made it more comfortable for people to travel long distances by train. His factory also produced other railway cars, such as diners.

pulsar

A pulsar is an object in space that sends out radio waves of short duration in regular pulses. Scientists believe pulsars are neutron stars—that is, stars that retain their original mass but have collapsed in on themselves.

pun

A pun is a play on the multiple meanings of a word or on two words with the same sound but different meanings.

Example:
Touching an electrical socket is a shocking experience.

purpose

In writing, the purpose is a writer's goal for composing a particular piece of writing.

pyramid

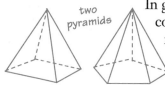

two pyramids

In geometry, a pyramid is a polyhedron formed by connecting points of a polygon to a single point not on the face of the polygon. The polygon and its interior form the base of the pyramid. *See polygon and polyhedron.*

Pyramids

Pyramids are massive stone monuments. The great Pyramids of Giza, begun about 2600 B.C. as tombs for Egyptian kings, were one of the Seven Wonders of the Ancient World. Indians of Central America were also building pyramids for ceremonies between A.D. 250 and 800.

pyrite

Iron pyrite is often referred to as "fool's gold" because it looks like real gold. During the days of the great Gold Rush, miners sometimes mistook pyrite for gold. One test to determine the difference between gold and pyrite is to heat it. Gold will not be changed by heat, but pyrite will smoke and produce a foul odor.

Pyrrhic victory

A Pyrrhic victory is one won at a greater cost than it is worth, leaving the winners suffering as much as the losers. General Pyrrhus, when he defeated the ancient Romans, reportedly said, "One more such victory, and Pyrrhus is undone."

Pythagoras

Pythagoras (580–? B.C.)was a Greek philosopher and mathematician who as an adult lived in Crotona, Italy. He was the first person known to have taught that the Earth was round. He pointed out that the Earth, sun, and moon all had their own orbits. He also developed the Pythagorean theorem.

Pythagorean theorem

The Pythagorean theorem states: In a right triangle the sum of the squares of two sides equals the square of the hypotenuse. The theorem is named for Pythagoras, the ancient Greek who discovered it. *See Pythagoras.*

Pytheas

Pytheas was a Greek astronomer, writer, and explorer. In the late 300s B.C., Pytheas sailed the western coasts of Spain, Gaul, and the British Isles. He was the first man to formulate a relationship between ocean waves and the moon.

quadrilateral

In mathematics, any four-sided polygon is a quadrilateral. *See polygon.*

quark

The basic unit that makes up neutrons and protons is a quark.

quart

A quart is a unit for measuring capacity and volume in the customary system of measures. Two pints equal one 1 quart. *See pint.*

quasar

A quasar is an extremely bright object in the sky that looks much like a star but whose spectrum reveals that it is traveling away very fast. Some astronomers think quasars are exceptionally bright cores of distant galaxies.

question mark

A question mark (?) is a punctuation mark most often used to end a direct question (interrogative sentence). A question mark is placed inside quotation marks in a direct quotation.

Example:

Lauren asked, "Where are we going tonight?"

See interrogative sentence and quotation marks.

quiet/quite

▷ *Quiet* means "silent" or "not noisy."
▷ *Quite* means "completely" or "actually."

Example:

The teacher was quite certain the class needed to be more quiet.

quorum

A quorum is the number of members an assembly must have present if the business done is to be legal or binding. Congress, for example, needs a minimum number of members present to pass laws. That minimum number is called a quorum. *See judicial branch.*

quotation

A quotation is a group of words taken from another person and subsequently used in a speech or a piece of writing. In writing, a quotation must be placed within quotation marks.

Example:

Shakespeare wrote in *Julius Caesar*, "Cowards die many times before their deaths; the valiant never taste of death but once."

See quotation marks.

quotation marks

Quotation marks (") are punctuation marks most often used before and after a direct quotation, a speaker's exact words. Single quotation marks (') are used to punctuate a direct quotation within another direct quotation. Periods and commas are always placed inside quotation marks, and colons and semicolons are always placed outside. A question mark or exclamation point is placed inside quotation marks when it punctuates the quotation and outside the quotation marks when it punctuates the sentence the quotation is in. *See quotation.*

quotient

The answer after dividing one number by another is the quotient.

Example:

$$75 \div 5 = 15$$

quotient

See divisor.

R

radar

Radar sends out radio electromagnetic waves that bounce off an object and return, telling the location, direction, and speed of a fixed or moving object. Radar is used, for example, by pilots of airplanes to scan and track objects that they cannot see. Radar and sonar, which is used similarly but under water, are critical in air, sea, and space travel.

radiation

The sun radiates solar energy—that is, it shines light outward. Light is energy that can travel through empty space. When solar radiation strikes an object, it causes the particles in the object to move faster. By doing so, it warms the object. The energy given off by nuclear fission and by radioactive materials such as uranium is also radiation. A nuclear reactor, for example, would give off radiation from nuclear fission. *See nuclear fission and nuclear reactor.*

radio galaxy

Galaxies send out light, which is why we can see them. But some galaxies also send out powerful radio waves and thus are known as *radio galaxies.* The cause of these radio signals from distant galaxies is not yet understood. *See galaxy.*

radio telescope

A radio telescope is a device made up of a radio receiver and a large, bowl-shaped antenna that detects and receives radio waves from space. *See galaxy, radio galaxy, and reflecting telescope.*

radiocarbon dating

Radiocarbon dating is a method of determining how old an ancient object is by measuring its radiocarbon content. Because all radiocarbon atoms decay or break down at an exact rate, it is possible to determine the approximate age of very old objects, such as rocks and fossils, by measuring individual atoms or electrons emitted by those atoms. The older the object is, the smaller the emission.

radius

In a circle, a line segment that connects the center of the circle with a point on the circle is the radius. *See circumference and diameter.*

ragtime

Ragtime is a type of music with roots related to early jazz. It is especially associated with a style of piano composition with a highly complicated melody and a regular rhythmic bass. The most famous composer of ragtime was Scott Joplin (1868–1917), a black pianist.

railway locomotive

A railway locomotive is the engine that pulls a train. Inventor Richard Trevithick (1771–1833) designed and built the first steam locomotive in 1801. A locomotive builder, George Stevenson, constructed the first public railway in 1825.

rain shadow

More rain falls on the exposed side of mountains, the side facing the direction from which storms usually come. The clouds collect on the exposed side of the mountains and produce rain. The sheltered side is said to be in a *rain shadow*, since most of the rain has already fallen before it reaches there.

raindrops

Raindrops fall from clouds at different speeds, depending upon their size. Small raindrops can fall at a speed of as little as 7 feet per second, and large raindrops fall at speeds of as much as 30 feet per second. This occurs because wind resistance slows the speed at which the drops fall. The weather term used for rain is *precipitation. See precipitation.*

ratify

To ratify something is to approve or confirm it in a formal way, often by a vote. International treaties, for example, are ratified, as are union contracts.

ratio

A pair of numbers that names the rate of a comparison is a ratio. Often a ratio is expressed this way: 3:5, and is described as "three is to five."

raw material

A substance in its natural state that will eventually be processed in some fashion is a raw material. Coal, iron ore, cut timber, and animal hides are examples of raw materials.

ray

In geometry, a ray is a set of points (a straight line) that has one endpoint and that extends without end in a particular direction.

ray

ray

Reader's Guide to Periodical Literature

The Reader's Guide to Periodical Literature is an index that lists the names of topics, articles, and authors for more than two hundred magazines. *The Reader's Guide* is updated approximately monthly so that people can find information on current topics. Hardcover copies of *The Reader's Guide* contain references to articles dating back more than ninety years. *See periodical guide.*

realism

Realism is a type of literature or art that attempts to portray the world and life accurately and honestly as observed through the senses. Realism tends to portray ordinary characters in everyday settings and situations. To paint the inside of a subway car, showing tired people and litter, is to paint realistically. *See romanticism.*

Wyeth, Andrew. *Christina's World*, 1948.

recession

A period of slow business activity is a recession. In contrast, a period of very slow business activity—for some companies, business stops all together—is a depression. A recession is a little less serious than a depression. *See Great Depression.*

recital

A recital is a performance given usually by one musician and an accompanist, or one in which a number of musicians perform as soloists.

Reconstruction

Reconstruction was the name given to the period of time after the American Civil War, when the Southern states were reorganized and restored to the Union. This period lasted from 1865 to about 1877. *See civil war.*

recorder

Recorders (soprano, alto, tenor, and bass) belong to a family of flute instruments, each with a whistle mouthpiece at one end. Recorders were popular in the sixteenth and seventeenth centuries and have been back in use since the early 1920s. They have a soft, slightly reedy sound.

rectangle

A parallelogram with four right angles is a rectangle. *See parallelogram.*

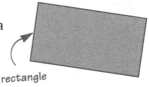

rectangle

Red Cross

Started in 1864 to help people around the world who were hurt or homeless because of war, the Red Cross today also works closely with victims of natural disasters such as earthquakes, floods, and hurricanes.

reef

A reef is a chain of rocks and sand at or near the surface of the water. Coral, which sometimes forms a reef, is created from the skeletons of sea animals called *polyps.* Reefs generally form in warm, shallow water. *See Great Barrier Reef.*

reference

Any book that contains useful facts or information is a reference. References include almanacs, atlases, dictionaries, encyclopedias, and indexes. Most libraries have a reference room or section that contains numerous references on a wide variety of subjects. These references may be used in the libraries but not taken out. *See almanac, atlas, and index.*

referendum

A referendum is a bill that is submitted to people for approval or rejection by direct vote. For example, the people of a particular area may vote on a referendum that determines if a new school will be built. *See bill.*

reflecting telescope

Reflecting telescopes use a series of mirrors to gather light coming to Earth from distant stars. A refracting telescope, on the other hand, gathers light with a lens or series of lenses, the way Hans Lippershey's first telescope did. *See radio telescope.*

Reformation

The Reformation, begun in Europe by Martin Luther (1483–1546), was an attempt to reform the Catholic Church. Some Protestant churches were founded in the sixteenth century as part of the Reformation. *See Ninety-five Theses.*

refugee

A person who seeks safety in another country is a refugee. Often during a time of war or disaster, refugees from one country flee to other countries. For example, refugees fled to the United States from Cuba after Fidel Castro came to power there in 1959.

reggae

Reggae is a kind of dance music that originated in Jamaica. It has a distinct rhythm and vocal style, combining elements of Latin music and American jazz. Probably the most famous reggae artist was Bob Marley (1945–1981).

Reign of Terror

The Reign of Terror (1793–1794) was a particularly violent period in the French Revolution. During this time, the French leader, Robespierre, ordered the executions of many people who opposed the rule of the leaders of the National Convention, a legislative body running the government. *See French Revolution.*

relative pronoun

A relative pronoun is a pronoun that begins a subordinate clause. A relative pronoun is always related to its antecedent, a noun or pronoun stated or understood elsewhere in the sentence. Commonly used relative pronouns are *who, whom, whose, which,* and *that.*

WAIT, THERE'S MORE! ➜

Example:

antecedent   relative pronoun

The airplane, which travels at eight hundred miles an hour, will reach London soon.

See adjective clause, antecedent, and pronoun.

remainder

The number that is left over after dividing one number by another number is the remainder. When 20 is divided by 6, for example, the remainder is 2. *See divisor and quotient.*

Renaissance

The Renaissance was the period of a great European revival of learning from the early 1300s to about 1600. During this time, classical Greek and Roman culture inspired artists, writers, and scientists, such as Leonardo da Vinci, Martin Luther, Shakespeare, and Cervantes. The term *renaissance* is now also used to describe any time period in which there is a renewed interest in learning.

renewable resource

If something is capable of being made again, it is renewable. The term is often used when talking about resources. Solar energy, for example, is a renewable resource because it comes from the sun and cannot be used up. *See natural resource and nonrenewable resource.*

reparations

After a war, the country that is defeated is sometimes made to pay for the damages caused by the war. The payments for these damages are called *reparations*.

repeating decimal

A repeating decimal is one in which the same figure or series of figures is repeated indefinitely.

> **Examples:**
> .2323
> .33333
> *See decimal.*

repetition

In writing, repetition, the intentional repeating of a word or idea, is often used for emphasis. Repetition of key words, for example, can suggest strong feeling or emotion.

reptile

Reptiles are cold-blooded animals that have backbones and breathe with lungs. Many reptiles lay eggs, but some give birth to live young. Snakes, lizards, turtles, and crocodiles are reptiles. *See amphibians.*

reservoir

A reservoir is a place where energy is collected and stored for future use. A water reservoir, for example, can be created by a dam.

resolution

The outcome or solution of the plot in a story or play is the resolution. The resolution comes after the climax. *See climax, denouement, and plot.*

respiration

The process of breathing is respiration. During respiration, cells change oxygen and sugar into carbon dioxide and water—thereby releasing energy. *See respiratory system.*

respiratory system

The respiratory system is the body system that brings oxygen to the bloodstream and eliminates carbon dioxide from the bloodstream. The lungs are the central part of the respiratory system. *See respiration.*

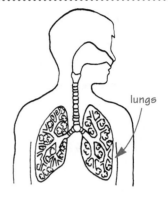

lungs

retina

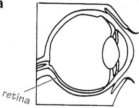

retina

The retina is the eye's back inside lining that is sensitive to light and receives optical images.

revision

Revision is the general term used for all of the activities a writer does while changing and improving a piece of writing. Revision includes, among other activities, adding material, deleting material, reorganizing information, clarifying ideas, changing vocabulary, and correcting errors. Proofreading is also sometimes considered part of revision. *See proofreading and writing process.*

revolution

A revolution is an attempt to overthrow an established government. In the French Revolution, for example, the common people in the Estates-General seized power from the king and his nobles. *See American Revolution and French Revolution.*

revolution

In physics, revolution is the movement of one object around another object. The planet Mercury, for example, takes 88 Earth-days to make a complete revolution around the sun. The Earth, on the other hand, takes 365 days to make one complete revolution around the sun. *See orbit.*

rhetorical question

A rhetorical question is a question that expects no answer because the answer should be obvious. Rhetorical questions are sometimes used in writing to introduce ideas or to make points dramatically.

rhombus

A rhombus is a parallelogram with four equal sides, usually having two obtuse angles and two acute angles. *See parallelogram.*

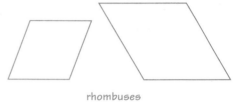

rhombuses

rhyme

Rhyme is the repetition of two or more words which sound alike. *Bite*, *fight*, and *height*, for example, all rhyme. Rhyme can occur at the end of or within a line of poetry.

> **Example:**
> "The Fool and the Poet" by Alexander Pope
> Sir, I admit your general rule,
> That every poet is a fool,
> But you yourself may serve to show it,
> That every fool is not a poet.

See rhyme scheme.

rhyme scheme

Rhyme scheme is any pattern of rhyme at the end of lines within a stanza of poetry. The analysis of rhyme scheme involves labeling with an *a* the first rhyme and any words that rhyme with it. The second rhyme is labeled with a *b*, the third with a *c*, and so forth. For example, the rhyme scheme of Pope's four lines in the *rhyme* entry is *aabb*. *See rhyme and stanza.*

rhythm

In writing, rhythm is the flow of sound the words make. Rhythm is especially important in poetry. Poets most often plan the rhythm of their poems carefully. A rhythm that repeats in a regular pattern is called *meter. See meter and poetry.*

rhythm and blues

The phrase *rhythm and blues* refers to a style of popular American music that was first developed in the 1940s. Often played on electric guitars, it combines loud, rhythmic tunes with lyrics on blues themes.

right-wing

Conservative or traditional people or ideas are sometimes called *right-wing.* Conservatives prefer to keep policies as they are or to change things slowly. The term came about because conservatives sat on the right side of the French Revolutionary Assembly. *See left-wing.*

RNA

RNA (ribonucleic acid) is a single-stranded molecule that is important in protein synthesis and genetic transmission. *See DNA.*

rock 'n' roll

Rock 'n' roll became popular in the 1950s, growing out of rhythm and blues. Elvis Presley and Chuck Berry were two of the earlier and best-known performers of rock. Since its beginnings, rock has branched out into a number of variations: soft rock, hard rock, acid rock, punk rock, and so on. *See rhythm and blues.*

CHUCK BERRY
NEW JUKE BOX HITS

rocket

Space travel could be accomplished only after the invention of rockets. A Soviet scientist, Konstantin Tsiolokovsky, was a theoretical pioneer in this field. The first successful rocket was launched in 1926 by American scientist Robert H. Goddard. *See space age.*

Rocky Mountains

The Rocky Mountains, which extend from Alaska to New Mexico, is the longest mountain system in North America. The Rockies form the Continental Divide of the United States.

romanticism

Romanticism is a type of literature or art that emphasizes imagination and emotions. Romanticism tends to portray extraordinary characters in unusual settings and situations. *See realism.*

Rome

Rome is the capital of Italy. It was the city from which the ancient Roman Empire expanded to encompass all of the land bordering the Mediterranean Sea and much of Western Europe, including Britain. Vatican City, within Rome, is the center of the Roman Catholic Church and the home of the Pope. *See Ancient Rome and Italy.*

Roosevelt, Eleanor

American stateswoman and wife of
President Franklin Roosevelt, Eleanor
Roosevelt (1884–1962) continued her
active role in politics after her husband
died in 1945. She was the United
States delegate to the United Nations
General Assembly from 1945 to
1951. *See Franklin Delano Roosevelt.*

Roosevelt, Franklin Delano

Franklin Delano Roosevelt (1882–1945), the 32nd American
President, was elected in November 1932 at the height of the
Great Depression. Roosevelt's New Deal program attempted to
help the U.S. recover from the Depression. Elected for four terms
in office (1932, 1936, 1940, and 1944), he led the nation during the
difficult years of the worst depression and war in American history.
See Eleanor Roosevelt, Great Depression, and New Deal.

Roosevelt, Theodore

The 26th American President, Theodore Roosevelt (1858–1919) is
remembered for leading a group of soldiers called the "Rough
Riders" during the Spanish-American War, as well as being an
early conservationist and proponent of honest government. After
Roosevelt became President in 1901, he persuaded Congress to
build the Panama Canal. *See Panama Canal and Spanish-American
War.*

root

In English, the term *root* refers to the original core of a word.
Many new words are formed in English when prefixes and suffixes
are added to roots.

Example:

Add the prefix *ex-* and suffix *-ate* to the root *culp* (blame). The
resulting word, *exculpate*, means "to make free from blame."

See prefix and suffix.

rotation

A rotation is a change in location of a figure by turning it about a point. More specifically, rotation is the action of an object that makes one full spin around an axis (the imaginary line that goes through the center of an object). The Earth completes a rotation once every twenty-four hours. In other words, one rotation for the Earth equals one day.

rounded number

A rounded number is one expressed to the nearest 10, 100, 1000, and so on. For example, 368 rounded to the nearest 10 is 370. Rounded to the nearest 100, 368 is 400.

368 is rounded to 370

350   360   370

run-on sentence

A run-on sentence is an incorrect combination of two or more sentences. A run-on sentence usually lacks proper punctuation or a correct conjunction.

Example:
We ran around the building and we slipped in the back door and we screamed as loud as we could to scare my sister and she chased us.

See sentence.

rural

Rural means "in the country." A rural region may have farms or ranches and possibly small towns or villages. Since its beginning, the United States has changed from a rural to an urban, or city-centered, nation. *See urban.*

Russia

Russia is the world's largest nation. It covers a large portion of both Europe and Asia. Between 1922 and 1991, the Republic of Russia dominated the communist Union of

MAP
AND
MORE
→

Soviet Socialist Republics (USSR). *See Asia, Europe, and Moscow.*

Russian Revolution

The overthrow of Czar Nicholas II in Russia began the Russian Revolution (1917–1918). Several groups struggled for power until the Bolsheviks took over the government. They renamed themselves the Communists and set up a dictatorship with V. I. Lenin in charge. *See V. I. Lenin.*

Rutherford, Daniel

In 1772 Daniel Rutherford (1749–1819), a Scottish physician, discovered something he called "phlogisticated air," which we now call nitrogen. He spent a good part of his life studying the gases that make up air—especially what remained after the oxygen was removed from it.

Sacagawea

Sacagawea (1787?–1812), a Shoshone Indian guide and interpreter, guided the Lewis and Clark expedition from present-day North Dakota through the Rocky Mountains. The expedition reached the Pacific in 1805. *See Lewis and Clark.*

Sahara Desert

The Sahara is the world's largest desert. Located in northern Africa, the Sahara is approximately the size of the United States. *See Africa.*

Saladin

A Muslim leader of the twelfth century, Saladin ruled the eastern Mediterranean area and Egypt. He fought the English leader Richard the Lion-Hearted during the Third Crusade.

Salem Witch Trials

The Salem Witch Trials, held in Salem, Massachusetts, in 1692, occurred when several young girls accused other people in Salem of being witches. The accused were tried and convicted of witch-craft on little or no evidence. Today a public accusation with little proof is sometimes called a "witch hunt." *See witch hunt.*

Salinger, J. D.

Jerome David Salinger (b. 1919) is an American writer best known for his novel *The Catcher in the Rye*, about a high school dropout wandering around New York City. Salinger's other books include *Nine Stories* and *Franny and Zooey*.

saliva

The liquid in a person's mouth is saliva. It is produced by the salivary glands in the mouth. With the help of the tongue, saliva softens food and begins the digestion process on starches.

Salk, Jonas Edward

Jonas Edward Salk (b. 1914) discovered a way to protect people from polio. He created a vaccine—that is, a way to give people a small dose of a virus to protect them from ever catching the virus again. By receiving a small amount of the virus, the body is able to create antibodies that help it fight the virus. *See vaccine.*

salutation

A salutation is the greeting in a letter. A comma is used in the salutation of a friendly letter, and a colon is used in the salutation of a business letter.

Examples:
- Dear Jennifer,
- Dear Sir:
- Dear Ms. Juarez:

sample

In research, a sample is a group upon which an experiment or survey is conducted. A sample is a representative group of a much larger population. Television ratings, for example, are based on a sample of the population, because it would be far too difficult to survey all television viewers.

samurai

The samurai were a Japanese military class. Samurai served as warriors, feudal lords, and as the shogun, the top military leader. Their feudal way of life lasted from the thirteenth to the nineteenth century. The samurai code of honor was similar to, although more strict than, that of the European knights of the Middle Ages.

San Andreas Fault

The San Andreas Fault is a fracture between two plates—the Pacific and the North American—in the Earth's outer shell. The fault runs along much of the coast of California. It was responsible for the great earthquake that occurred in San Francisco in 1906, which destroyed thousands of buildings and hundred of lives. In 1990, another rumbling along the fault caused a great deal of damage to buildings and roads. Scientists believe that within the next hundred years there will be another major earthquake along this fault. *See earthquake and fault.*

Sandburg, Carl

Carl Sandburg (1878–1967) was an American poet and historian. His four-volume history, *Abraham Lincoln: The War Years*, won a Pulitzer Prize for history in 1939. His *Complete Poems* won the Pulitzer Prize for poetry in 1951.

Sanskrit

Sanskrit is the language of the ancient Aryans who conquered India. By about 500 B.C., Indian scholars were using Sanskrit as the language for religion, politics, and the arts. *See India.*

Santa Fe Trail

Early in the nineteenth century, the Santa Fe Trail was a trade route between Santa Fe, then in Mexico, and Independence, Missouri. Wagon trains carried goods to and from Santa Fe. California-bound pioneers also used this route west.

Saratoga

The Battle of Saratoga (1777) was a turning point of the Revolutionary War. The colonial army proved it could defeat the British at Saratoga, New York. After that, other nations began to support the colonies and helped them win the war against British rule. *See American Revolution.*

satellite

A satellite is any object that orbits around another object. Earth and other planets circle the sun. Communications satellites, launched into space, orbit the Earth.

satellite

In politics, a satellite is a weak country that is controlled by a stronger country. For example, for a long time after World War II, Poland was a satellite of the former Soviet Union. *See orbit.*

satire

Satire is writing that makes fun of human errors or weaknesses. Satire is often used to question current social trends or political decisions. Swift's *Gulliver's Travels* is an example of satire.

saturated fat

Saturated fat is a solid or semi-solid animal fat, such as butter, that contains mainly saturated fatty acids. *See unsaturated fat.*

Saturn

Saturn is the sixth planet from the sun and the second largest planet in our solar system. The rings of Saturn, though they look solid, are in fact made up of billions of ice particles. One of the first scientists to discover multiple rings around Saturn was Jean Domenique Cassini. The gap between the rings is still called "Cassini's division."

Saudi Arabia

Saudi Arabia is a country on the Arabian Peninsula in southwest Asia. It is the largest petroleum exporter in the world. Mecca, the holiest city of Islam, is located in Saudi Arabia. *See Mecca.*

savanna

A level, tropical grassland with scattered trees is a savanna. Africa is well known for the variety of animals that live on the savannas. *See Africa.*

saxophone

The saxophone, invented in 1840 by Adolph Sax, comes in several sizes. It is very popular as a band instrument, blending well with both brass and woodwinds because its design shares their qualities. It is made of brass like a horn, has a single reed like a clarinet, and is shaped like a mix of the two. *See horn.*

scalawag

During Reconstruction, some white Southerners participated in the new state governments that were established. Other Southerners, opposed to the new governments, considered the first group traitors to the South and called them *scalawags. See Reconstruction.*

scale

A scale is the relationship between the size of a plan, map, drawing, or model and the actual size of the object or area being represented. Usually in one corner of a map or drawing, there is a key that shows how the scale works.

scale

In music, the term scale (a musical "ladder") refers to various patterns of rising pitches. Specific scales are the major and minor (seven-toned), the whole-tone (six-toned), and the pentatonic (five-toned).

scalene triangle

A triangle with no congruent sides is called a scalene triangle. *See triangle.*

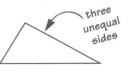

three unequal sides

Scandinavia

The peninsula in northern Europe made up of Norway and Sweden is Scandinavia. *See Europe.*

scansion

Scansion is the analysis of verse to determine its meter. Scansion involves marking off the lines of verse into feet. *See foot, meter, and verse.*

scavenger

Scavengers are animals that eat dead organisms. Two of the best-known scavengers are the vulture and the hyena. They feed on the remains left by other animals. The hyena, however, is also a skillful hunter in its own right.

scherzo

Scherzo is an Italian word meaning "joke." Music labeled *scherzo,* usually the third section or movement of a symphony, is fast and often playful or abrupt in style.

science fiction

Science fiction is highly imaginative fiction often set in the future and dealing with space and other universes. The plot frequently contains events that are plausible according to accepted or possible scientific theories. The TV show "Star Trek" is an example of science fiction. *See fantasy and fiction.*

score

The written notes to be performed by singers and instrumentalists make up the score. A score for orchestra or chorus has a separate line, known as the staff, for the notes of each vocal or instrumental part. *See notes and rests.*

Scotland

Scotland is a division of Great Britain located north of England. The Highlands are the mountainous areas that cover approximately the northern two-thirds of Scotland. *See England.*

scroll

A scroll is a roll of parchment or paper. Many early cultures used scrolls for writing and illustrations. Ancient Egyptians glued strips of papyrus together to make scrolls. *See papyrus and parchment.*

sculpture

In art, a sculpture is a three-dimensional form created by modeling, carving, or assembling. The sculptor can model a sculpture from clay, carve an image out of wood or stone, or assemble a sculpture from metal. The one constant about sculpture is that the final work has height, depth, and width and is not two-dimensional like a painting.

sea level

The level of the surface of the ocean is called *sea level.* Glaciers and icebergs contain vast amounts of water. If all of the ice in Antarctica and Greenland melted, the sea level all over the world would rise about two hundred feet. That would mean that the Statue of Liberty would probably have only her arm and the torch above the water.

search warrant

A court order that allows the police to search a place is a search warrant. The warrant is issued only if there is a good reason to believe that evidence of a crime will be found.

secede

To secede is to withdraw formally from an organization. Eleven southern states seceded from the Union prior to the start of the American Civil War. They formed the Confederate States of America. The move to secede by these states was the chief cause of the Civil War. *See civil war.*

sediment

Sediment is made up of rocks, sand, and soil carried by wind, ice, or water. The Mississippi River, nicknamed "Big Muddy," is brown because it carries so much sediment in its water. *See Mississippi River.*

sedimentary rock

The rock that forms much of the Earth's surface is sedimentary rock. Sedimentary rocks are formed from layers of mud, sand, silt, or plant and animal life that settle out of water, ice, or air. The top layers press down on the bottom layers, and eventually the sediment begins to harden. This process occurs over many millions of years. Sandstone is an example of sedimentary rock. The chalk used in classrooms is a type of limestone, another sedimentary rock. *See sediment.*

sedition

A speech or action that causes discontent or rebellion against a government is sedition. *See traitor and treason.*

seed dispersal

Dispersal is the scattering of seeds. Seeds need to get away from the parent plant in order to grow properly. Dispersal can take place in several ways. Some seeds are scattered by the wind, which may blow few feet or several miles from their parent plant. Other seeds are carried by water, and still others are scattered by animals. Some seeds stick to the fur of animals, while others pass through their bodies.

segregation

The separation of one race, people, or group from another or from the rest of society is segregation. The Civil Rights movement ended most of the segregation of blacks practiced in the United States. *See civil rights.*

seismologist

A scientist who studies earthquakes and other movements of the Earth's crust is a seismologist. *See Earth, earthquake, and fault.*

self-determination

Self-determination is the term for allowing the people of a nation to decide what form of government they will have, without interference from another country. Some central European countries have recently set up new governments through self-determination.

Selma

Selma is a city in central Alabama. In 1965, Martin Luther King, Jr., led a civil rights march of 4,000 people from Selma to Montgomery. He carried a petition to protest discrimination against blacks.
See Martin Luther King, Jr., and segregation.

semicolon

A semicolon (;) is a punctuation mark used most often to separate independent clauses not joined by a comma and coordinating conjunction *(and, but, for, nor, or, yet)*. Semicolons are also used to separate other closely related independent clauses and to separate phrases in a series that already contains commas.

Example:

Example:

Kortney is a superb diver; she finished third in the state meet.

See coordinating conjunction and independent clause.

sentence

A sentence is a group of words that expresses a complete thought. A sentence begins with a capital letter and ends with a period, question mark, or exclamation point. A sentence has at least two parts, a subject and a predicate. Sentences can have four kinds of structures: simple, compound, complex, and compound-complex. The four types of sentences, based on their purposes, are

- declarative
- interrogative
- imperative
- exclamatory

sentence fragment

A sentence fragment is a group of words incorrectly used as a sentence. A fragment is an incomplete thought usually lacking a subject or predicate.

Examples:

Brought the sodas.

Carl who works for the post office.

See run-on sentence and sentence.

Seoul

Seoul, the capital of South Korea (Republic of Korea), is the second largest city in the world. Its population is more than 9.5 million people. Seoul is the cultural and economic center of South Korea. *See Korea.*

separation of church and state

People who believe in the separation of church and state think that government must not endorse or favor any religion. The United States Constitution forbids an official national religion. It also guarantees that people are free to practice any religion they wish or none at all.

Serra, Junípero

Junípero Serra (1713–1784), a Roman Catholic missionary from Spain, began in 1769 to convert the Indians in California to Christianity. He and his followers built a string of missions along the California coast. *See missionary.*

setting

The setting is the time and place in which a story, play, or poem occurs. For example, the setting of the story of *Johnny Tremain* is the Revolutionary War.

Seward's Folly

Alaska, at the time of its purchase by the United States in 1867, was called "Seward's Folly" or "Seward's Icebox." Secretary of State William Seward arranged for the United States to buy Alaska from Russia for $7,200,000. At the time, some people called it a waste of money.

Shakespeare, William

William Shakespeare (1564–1616) was an English poet and playwright who is often considered the greatest writer who ever lived. His plays have been produced more than those of any other playwright. His works have been read more around the world than those of any other writer. Shakespeare's tragedies include *Romeo and Juliet*, *Macbeth*, *Othello*, and *Hamlet*. His comedies include *A Midsummer Night's Dream* and *Twelfth Night*.

shale

Shale is a fine-grained rock that is formed from hardened clay, mud, or silt in thin layers. *See sedimentary rock.*

shall/will

▷ *Shall* is seldom used except for special emphasis.

Example:

You shall not disobey your mother!

▷ *Will* is generally used to show both future tense and determination.

Examples:

Rita will go to the party.

I will pass the science test.

sharecropper

A sharecropper farms land for a landowner in return for part of the crops. Sharecropping was very common in the South in the era between the Civil War and World War II.

sharp

In music, the symbol for a sharp (#) indicates a pitch raised by a half-step. It is placed in front of the note being raised or is written at the beginning of each staff of the score to indicate the key signature. Singing or playing "sharp" indicates performing at pitches slightly higher than the correct ones. *See score.*

sheik

A sheik is an Arab chief or the head of a family, village, or tribe.

Shiite

A Shiite is a member of a sect of Islam that believes Moslem leadership passed from Muhammad to his son-in-law. Most Shiites live in Iran and Iraq. *See Islam and Muhammad.*

Shinto

Shinto, the native religion of ancient Japan, is still practiced today. Followers of Shinto worship nature deities and ancestral heroes.

short story

A short story is a brief work of fiction. It has characters, a theme, and a plot with a clear beginning, middle, and ending. *See fiction.*

shrine

A shrine may be a church, an altar, a tomb of a holy person—any sacred place. People visit shrines, such as Lourdes in France, to show respect and to worship.

siege

During a siege, an army surrounds a fortified place and tries to capture it. General Ulysses Grant's siege of Richmond led to the surrender of the Confederate forces in the Civil War.

signature

Two kinds of signatures are used in music. The key signature indicates the key of a composition by the number of sharps, flats, or lack of either noted at the beginning of each staff of the score.

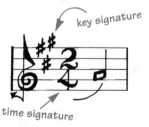

key signature

time signature

The time signature, written next to the key signature on the first staff, tells how many beats are in each measure and also what kind of note gets the beat. Both key and time signatures may change as the piece continues.

Sikorsky, Igor

Russian aircraft designer Igor Sikorsky (1889–1972) built the first four-engine airplane in 1913. After moving to the United States, Sikorsky designed the first successful helicopter in 1939.

silkscreening

Silkscreening is a printing process, often used for posters and cards, in which a stenciled design is placed on a screen of silk or fine fabric. Areas that are not to be printed are blocked out with impermeable film. Then ink is squeezed onto the cloth and forced through the open portions of the design.

simile

A simile is a comparison between two unlike things using *like* or *as*. Shakespeare's line "Glory is like a circle in the water" is a simile. *See figurative language and metaphor.*

simple sentence

A simple sentence is a sentence with one independent clause and no subordinate (dependent) clauses.

Example:

The catcher threw the ball to second base.

See complex sentence, compound sentence, and sentence.

simple subject

The simple subject is the principal word or words in the subject of a sentence.

Example:

The large (truck) stopped at the intersection.

simple
subject

See subject.

simple *vs.* compound machines

▷ Simple machines make it easier to do work and are made of very few parts.

Examples:

- lever
- wheel and axle
- inclined plane or ramp
- pulley
- screw

▷ Compound machines are machines made of two or more simple machines.

Examples:

- bicycles
- can openers
- wheelbarrows

sit/set

▷ *Sit* is a verb that usually means "to rest or to occupy."

Example:

A person sits down.

▷ *Set* is a verb that usually means "to place or to put."

Example:

A person sets something down.

Sitting Bull

A Hunkpapa Sioux medicine man, Sitting Bull (1834?–1890) planned the strategy that led to the defeat of General George Custer at the Little Big Horn in 1876. Sitting Bull fled to Canada to escape retaliation, but he finally surrendered in 1881.

sketch

A sketch is a first drawing or design done by an artist. A sketch is often done quickly and without much detail in preparation for a larger, more finished work.

skin

The largest organ of the human body is the skin. The weight of the skin of an average adult is about six pounds. The skin completely replaces itself about every fifteen to thirty days.

hair
skin
epidermis

slang

Slang is the informal, nonstandard vocabulary unique to a particular group. In this sense, a gang, team, or any other group may have its own slang.

Examples:

- dude
- scuz
- bro

See jargon.

slash and burn

The term *slash and burn* refers to a type of agriculture. To clear a field for planting, farmers in tropical forests often cut down (slash) and burn them. The ashes fertilize the soil for a few years. When the soil is worn out, the farmers move on and start over.

slave

A slave was a person considered the property of another person. The first slaves in America were brought into various colonies in the early 1600s. In 1865, the Thirteenth Amendment to the U. S. Constitution ended slavery in the United States. *See Emancipation Proclamation.*

slum

An old, dirty, run-down part of a city is a slum.

smallpox

Smallpox was an infectious disease caused by a virus. Dr. Edward Jenner, an English physician, discovered a way to prevent smallpox. He injected a boy with cowpox, which was a disease of cattle that was like smallpox. The boy then became infected with cowpox. Several months later Jenner injected the same boy with smallpox—and the infection did not affect him. It was a risky thing to do, because if the experiment had not worked, the boy might have died. As it turned out, Jenner's discovery of the vaccine saved thousands of lives and led to the eradication of the disease. *See vaccine.*

snail

A snail is a slow-moving mollusk with a spiral shell. Snails live on land, in fresh water, and in salt water. They leave behind a mucus, or slimy liquid, when they move. This liquid enables them, for instance, to crawl along the edge of a razor blade without cutting themselves.

snake bites

Many snakes have hinged mouths. This means they can open their mouths very wide. In the top of a poisonous snake's mouth are one or more small glands that contain poison. When the snake bites something, small tubes in the snake's fangs send poison from the gland into the victim. The venom of some poisonous snakes either kills the victim or stuns it so that it can't move. *See venom.*

snare drum

A snare drum has a circular shell and is twelve to eighteen inches in diameter. It produces a brilliant, rattling sound.

socialism

Socialism, like capitalism, is a system of government. In socialism, the government or groups of workers control or own everything. No one person owns a business; the government owns and controls all businesses. The former Soviet Union developed a form of socialism, called Communism, after 1917. *See communism.*

society

A society is all of the people who live together as a group. Each society has a culture that is unique to itself. *See culture.*

sociologist

A sociologist investigates human societies, especially present-day societies. Population, human behavior, and social change are some of the topics that a sociologist studies.

Socrates

Socrates (469?–399 B.C.) was the first of the great ancient Greek philosophers and teachers. His mode of teaching, later called the "Socratic Method," was that of questioning his students to draw out the knowledge he believed was inside them. His teachings focused on the nature of humans and what it means to be good. He was convicted of corrupting the youth of Athens and was sentenced to death. Although Socrates never wrote down his teachings, they were collected by his student Plato. *See Aristotle and Plato.*

software and hardware

Software consists of programs loaded into a computer that tell the computer what to do. Software is run on a computer. For example, a word-processing program is software. Hardware, on the other hand, is the term for the physical parts of a computer system—the keyboard, monitor, disk drive, and printer.

soil

Soil is a combination of many things, including rock, mineral particles, air, water, and decayed materials. The decayed material, or humus, comes from plants and animals. It provides the soil with the nutrients needed to sustain plant life. The richest types of soils are usually those with dark colors, indicating a large quantity of humus.

solar collector

A solar collector is used to generate solar energy—that is, energy collected from the light of the sun. Sunlight hits small solar cells in each solar collector. Special silicon material in the cells creates a tiny electric current. These small amounts of current are collected until they are strong enough to be used. In other cases, solar collectors are black metal plates covered by glass. As sunlight heats the metal, it also heats a liquid in the solar collector. The liquid then flows through pipes to a large water heating container. The water is heated by this warm liquid from the solar collector. *See solar energy.*

solar eclipse

Usually the moon's path does not place it between the sun and the Earth. When it does, the moon blocks sunlight from reaching the Earth—and a solar eclipse occurs. During a solar eclipse, the sun appears to be covered by the moon, and sections of the Earth become dark.

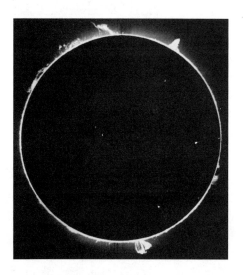

solar energy

Radiant energy that comes from the sun is solar energy. The sun generates a tremendous amount of energy every minute. At its center, the sun reaches temperatures of 27 million degrees Fahrenheit. Only about 1 two-billionth of the sun's energy reaches our atmosphere. About 34 percent of the energy from the sun is reflected back into space by clouds and the atmosphere. About 19 percent is absorbed by the clouds and gases in the Earth's atmosphere. The remaining 47 percent reaches the ground and oceans. Efforts to collect heat from the sun and use it to heat our homes are improving each year. Right now, we only know ways to collect a tiny portion of the solar energy that reaches the Earth each day. *See solar collector.*

solar system

The sun, the nine planets and their moons, and all the other objects that orbit the sun are known as "the solar system." A large model of the solar system would include all the planets and their moons, as well as several asteroids.

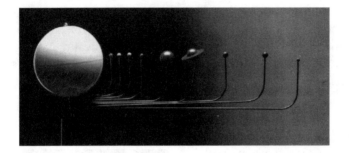

solid figure

A solid figure has three dimensions: length, height, and width. *See cone, cube, polyhedron, and sphere.*

soliloquy

A soliloquy is a monologue in a play during which a character presents his or her innermost thoughts aloud. The character speaks only to himself or herself and the audience, not to other characters. In Shakespeare's *Hamlet*, for example, Hamlet's famous soliloquy begins:

> To be, or not to be, that is the question:
> Whether 'tis nobler in the mind to suffer
> The slings and arrows of outrageous fortune,
> Or to take arms against a sea of troubles,
> And by opposing end them?

See dialogue and monologue.

solo

A solo is a musical part for one voice or one instrument. A person who performs a solo part is called a soloist, whether the part stands alone or has an accompaniment.

solstice

Two times during the year, the sun reaches a point in its orbit when it is as far as it can be from the celestial equator. These times are called the *summer solstice* and *winter solstice*. *See equinox.*

solubility

The ability of one substance to be dissolved in another is its solubility. Salt, for example, is soluble in water, but oil is not.

sonata

A sonata can be a composition for a piano or an instrument with piano accompaniment. A sonata is also the most common musical form used by nineteenth-century composers for symphonies, concertos, and instrumental quartets. The most common pattern for the sonata is described by the tempos of its four movements: allegro (quick), lento (slow), presto (very quick), and allegro. *See symphony.*

sonnet

A sonnet is a form of poetry that has fourteen lines and a particular type of meter, iambic pentameter. *See meter and poetry.*

Sophocles

Sophocles (496–406 B.C.) was a Greek playwright whose tragedies focused on the struggle of a hero against his or her fate. His plays *Antigone* and *Oedipus Rex* are considered classics and are still performed today. *See Aeschylus and Euripides.*

soprano

A soprano voice is the highest woman's voice or the highest unchanged voice of a boy. It is the highest part of a choral composition.

sound

Sound is caused by tiny vibrations. A person hears sound because the vibrations enter the ear canal and cause the eardrum to vibrate. Those vibrations cause three bones in the middle ear to vibrate. The vibrations then pass into the inner ear, which has a tube filled with a special liquid. That liquid vibrates, moving tiny hairlike nerve endings inside the tube. The nerve endings send sound signals to the brain.

Sound travels at different speeds through different types of materials. For example, sound travels at about 1,085 feet per second through the air, but it can travel at 17,100 feet per second through steel. The reason for this is that sound is energy. Sound occurs when vibrations are set off. How fast the sound waves move through a medium, such as steel or air, determines the speed of sound. *See ear and energy.*

soundbite

In media jargon, a soundbite is a short bit of film that catches the highlight of a longer speech. Political campaigns, for instance, use soundbites on television. This makes maximum use of the television time but can only give a glimpse of a larger event. Politicians try to be careful in creating soundbites for television because the impressions of viewers are often shaped by them.

South Africa

South Africa is the country at the southern tip of Africa. It is the wealthiest country in Africa and the world's leading producer of gold. Known for apartheid, its system of discrimination against blacks and other nonwhite people, South Africa repealed its last apartheid laws in 1991. *See apartheid.*

South America

South America is a continent that lies between the Pacific Ocean on the west and the Atlantic Ocean on the east. It is connected to North America by the Isthmus of Panama. Approximately 308 million people live in South America. *See Central America.*

sovereignty

Sovereignty is supreme power or authority of a single ruler or a single state or nation. In 1789, for example, the French people rejected the sovereignty of the French king and started the French Revolution.

space age

The space age began with Sputnik 1 on October 4, 1957. Sputnik was a satellite launched by the Soviet Union. It was about as big as a football and carried a radio transmitter. *See rocket.*

Spanish Armada

The Spanish Armada was a huge fleet of Spanish warships that sailed from Spain in 1588. In a sea battle off the coast of Britain, faster English ships and bad weather defeated the Armada. England was then able to challenge a weakened Spain for power in America. *See Elizabeth I.*

Spanish-American War

The Spanish-American War (1898) was a brief war in which the United States defeated Spain. As a result of the war, Cuba was freed from Spanish control, and the U.S. gained islands in the Pacific and the Caribbean. These islands were considered important for trade and the defense of the United States.

spawning

Spawning is a process in which fish lay eggs. *See fish.*

species

A species is a group of organisms that are alike. Members of the same species interbreed naturally and produce offspring capable of reproducing.

spectrum

A spectrum is a pattern, sometimes visible, formed by the separation and sorting of radiant energy or charged particles according to wavelength, energy, mass, and so on. Such a pattern can be measured and reported by scientific instruments. *See atom and energy.*

sphere

A sphere is a solid figure with all points the same distance from a given point, the center. A basketball, for example, is a sphere. *See solid figure.*

spider webs

Spider webs are made of silk that comes from small glands in the spider's abdomen. Certain glands make silk for each part of a spider's web. One gland makes a sticky silk to capture insects. Another gland makes silk for the structure of the web. Each thread of the web has several strands to give it strength. In addition to webs, spiders make their homes from silk.

split infinitive

A split infinitive is an infinitive phrase with an adverb placed between *to* and the verb.

Example:

to quickly speak

Because split infinitives sometimes sound awkward, they should be avoided in formal writing. *See adverb and infinitive.*

split ticket

When a person votes for some candidates from one party and some candidates from another, he or she is voting a split ticket. If a person votes for all candidates of one party (say, all Democrats or all Republicans), he or she is voting a straight ticket.

spore

A spore is a reproductive cell capable of developing into a new organism.

sprain

A sprain is an injury to ligaments and muscles. *See strain.*

square

In geometry a square is a rectangle with four congruent sides. *See polygon and rectangle.*

squares

square root

A number *x* is the square root of a number *y* if *x* times $x = y$.

Examples:

$3 \times 3 = 9$, so 3 is the square root of 9
$5 \times 5 = 25$, so 5 is the square root of 25

squeegee

A squeegee is a tool with a thick rubber blade that is pulled across a silkscreen frame, forcing ink down through the screen and onto the paper to create a print. *See silkscreening.*

Stalin, Josef

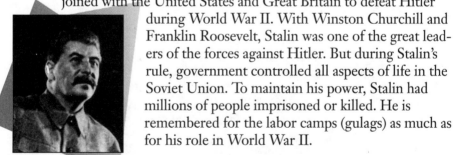

Josef Stalin (1879-1953), the Soviet dictator from 1929-1953, joined with the United States and Great Britain to defeat Hitler during World War II. With Winston Churchill and Franklin Roosevelt, Stalin was one of the great leaders of the forces against Hitler. But during Stalin's rule, government controlled all aspects of life in the Soviet Union. To maintain his power, Stalin had millions of people imprisoned or killed. He is remembered for the labor camps (gulags) as much as for his role in World War II.

Stalingrad, Battle of

The Battle of Stalingrad (1942–1943) was an important and bitter battle between Russians and the invading Nazi army during World War II. When the Nazi army attacking Stalingrad surrendered, the course of World War II turned in favor of the Allies. *See Adolf Hitler and World War II.*

stamen

The male reproductive part of a flower is the stamen. It is composed of the filament and anther.

standard of living

A standard of living is the measure of the quality of everyday life. This measure includes the availability of such items as food, housing, and medical care. The income of a nation's people affects its standard of living. Rich countries, such as Japan and the United States, have a high standard of living. Poor countries have a low standard of living. *See Third World.*

Stanley and Livingstone

Henry Stanley (1841–1904) and David Livingstone (1813–1873) were famous English explorers. Stanley, a reporter, and Livingstone, a medical missionary, both explored parts of Africa in the 1860s and 1870s. Livingstone was the first European to see Victoria Falls, one of the most famous waterfalls in the world. In 1869, Stanley was sent by a New York newspaper to find Livingstone, who was believed lost. Upon reaching Livingstone on the shore of Lake Tanganyika in 1871, Stanley uttered the now-famous line, "Dr. Livingstone, I presume?" *See Africa.*

stanza

A stanza is a group of consecutive lines in a poem that forms a single unit. Here, for example, are the first two stanzas of Paul Lawrence Dunbar's "We Wear the Mask."

> We wear the mask that grins and lies,
> It hides our cheeks and shades our eyes—
> This debt we pay to human guile;
> With torn and bleeding hearts we smile,
> And mouth with myriad subtleties.
>
> Why should the world be overwise,
> In counting all our tears and sighs?
> Nay, let them only see us, while
> We wear the mask.

See poetry.

star

A star is a gaseous, shining heavenly body that is usually spherical. About 3,000 stars are visible on a clear night. The closest star to the Earth, not counting the Sun, is Proxima Centauri, which is 25 trillion miles away.

stationary/stationery

▷ *Stationary* means "standing still" or "not movable."
▷ *Stationery* is writing material such as paper and envelopes.

Example:

The stack of the President's official stationery lay on the desk between the stationary guards.

statistics

Statistics are numerical facts that are collected, organized, and analyzed. Governments may, for example, gather statistics on population trends or financial issues.

statute

Statutes are laws. Statutes are created by a legislature for a city, state, or country. *See legislative branch.*

STD

STD is an abbreviation for "sexually transmitted disease." It refers to a communicable disease spread by sexual contact.

stegosaurus

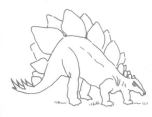

The stegosaurus was one of the larger dinosaurs. It was about eight feet tall at the hips, twenty feet long, and weighed nearly two tons. The word *dinosaur* means "terrible lizard." It was coined by Richard Owen in 1841. He was one of the first scientists who devoted himself to learning about dinosaurs. *See dinosaurs.*

Steinbeck, John

John Steinbeck (1902–1968) was an American writer who won the Nobel Prize for literature in 1962. His stories often dealt with the problems of poor people, especially ranch hands and migrant fruit pickers in California during the Depression. *The Grapes of Wrath*, considered his finest novel, won the Pulitzer Prize in 1940. His other novels include *Of Mice and Men*, *East of Eden*, and *The Winter of Our Discontent*. *See Great Depression.*

Steinmetz, Charles

Charles Steinmetz (1865–1923), a German-born mathematician and engineer, developed the theory of alternating current, an important component in the creation of today's efficient electrical energy system. *See electricity.*

stenciling

Stenciling is the process of cutting a design in paper, cardboard, plastic, or metal and brushing or squeezing paint or ink through it in order to transfer the image.

steppe

A steppe is a vast, treeless plain in southeastern Europe or Asia. *See taiga.*

stereo

Stereo is short for stereophonic, which describes the use of two or more microphones or speakers in recording and amplifying sound. This process creates a richer, more complete reproduction of the original sound than is possible with only one microphone or speaker.

stereotype

A stereotype is anything conforming to a set, predictable pattern. In literature, a stereotype is a conventional character, plot, or setting that presents no individuality.

stigma

The stigma is the sticky top part of the pistil of a flower. The stigma traps pollen grains that fertilize the flower. *See pistil.*

still life

A still life is an arrangement that is the subject matter for a work of art.

stomata

Tiny openings in a leaf are stomata. Oxygen enters the leaf and carbon dioxide leaves the leaf through the stomata. In other words, they enable a plant to breathe.

stomata

Stone Age

The term *Stone Age* refers to a period in all human cultures during which people made and used stone, rather than iron, tools. Although some groups continued to use stone tools into the twentieth century, the Stone Age is generally considered to have begun about two million years ago and ended about 3000 B.C.

straight ticket

When a person votes for all candidates from one party, he or she votes a straight ticket. If a person votes for some candidates from one party and some from another party, he or she votes a split ticket. *See split ticket.*

strain

A strain is an injury to tendons and muscles caused by too much effort or stretching. *See sprain.*

stratosphere

The stratosphere is the second layer of the atmosphere above the Earth. It begins from between six to ten miles above the Earth and extends thirty miles upward. The stratosphere is characterized by horizontal air movements.

strength

Strength is the amount of force a person's muscles can produce.

stress

Stress is the body's reaction to a demanding situation.

strike

A strike occurs when workers stop work. Workers generally strike to force their employer to improve their pay or working conditions. Usually they also stand outside the place of work and picket, or hold signs, keeping any other workers from entering the business.

stroke

A stroke is the loss of the ability to feel or think or move due to a broken or blocked blood vessel in the brain.

stucco

Stucco is a type of fine plaster or cement used to coat inside or outside walls and create relief ornaments. The texture of stucco can be rough, wavy, or smooth.

style

In literature, style is the particular way in which an author writes. Style involves the writer's personal selection and arrangement of words rather than the message of the writing.

Styx

In Greek mythology, Styx was the river that the souls of the dead had to cross to reach Hades. *See Hades.*

subject

The subject of a sentence is the part about which something is said.

Example:

The (ten-speed bicycle) broke down along the highway.

See simple subject.   subject

subject complement

A subject complement is a noun, pronoun, or adjective connected to a subject by a linking verb. A subject complement identifies or describes the subject.

Example:

(Dina) is a silly (person).

subject   subject complement

submersible

A submersible is a submarine-like machine that is used to explore the ocean. In 1930, two pioneers, William Bebe and Otis Barton, descended into the ocean in a "bathysphere" to study the depths of the ocean. Since 1960, research scientists have created more and more advanced submersibles to explore the ocean depths, even the Mariana Trench. *See Mariana Trench.*

subordinate clause

A subordinate (dependent) clause does not express a complete thought and can never stand alone as a sentence. A subordinate clause is always combined with an independent clause. A subordinate clause acts like a noun, adjective, or adverb in a sentence.

Examples:

Examples:

subordinate clause

When the train pulled into the station, it sounded its whistle.

The engineer sounded the horn because he wanted the tracks clear.

subordinate clause

See clause, independent clause, and sentence.

subordinating conjunction

A subordinating conjunction is a conjunction that joins a subordinate clause with the main clause of the sentence.

Examples:

- although
- as
- because
- if
- since
- unless
- when
- where
- while

See adverb clause and conjunction.

subsistence farming

The word subsistence means "barely enough." Subsistence farming produces only enough for food and clothing for the farm family. Early pioneers in America were often subsistence farmers at first. Little of the food they produced was left over for sale to others.

subtract

To subtract is to find out what is left when a quantity is taken away.

Example:

6 - 2 = 4

2 is taken away from 6, leaving 4

Suez Canal

The Suez is a canal in northeastern Egypt connecting the Mediterranean Sea and the Red Sea. Started in 1859 by a French company, the canal took ten years to build. The canal shortened trade routes by saving shippers a long voyage around southern Africa, much like the Panama Canal saves shippers a long voyage around South America. *See Panama Canal.*

suffix

A suffix is a letter or group of letters added to the end of a word to change the word's meaning. The suffix *-ness*, for example, changes the word *natural* to *naturalness. See prefix and root.*

suffrage

Suffrage is the right to vote. After a long struggle for suffrage, American women were enfranchised (that is, allowed to vote) in 1920 by the Nineteenth Amendment to the U. S. Constitution.

suite

The suite is a form of instrumental music most popular during the Baroque period. It is made up of several sections (movements), all in the same key. Each movement is based on a different dance rhythm.

sum

A sum is the number found by adding two or more numbers.

Example:

$$8 + 4 = 12$$

sum

See addend.

Sun Yat-sen

Sun Yat-sen (1866–1925), a Chinese revolutionary leader, inspired the overthrow of the Manchu dynasty in 1911 and the establishment of a republic. His dream of unifying China was accomplished in the 1930s and 1940s by General Chiang (Jiang) Kai-shek.

supernova

A supernova is the explosion of a massive, dying supergiant star.

Sutter's Mill

Sutter's Mill was the site of the discovery of gold in California in 1849. With news of the discovery, thousands of people moved to California—and the gold rush began.

swastika

A swastika is an ancient symbol resembling a cross with the arms bent. Swastikas were thought in early times to bring good luck. A swastika turned in the opposite direction symbolized the German Nazi party.

Swift, Jonathan

Jonathan Swift (1667–1745) was an Anglo-Irish writer best known for his satire. *Gulliver's Travels*, his most famous work, is considered a comic masterpiece. Swift's essay "A Modest Proposal" protested the British treatment of the Irish.

syllogism

A syllogism is a form of deductive reasoning that has three parts: a major premise (a general statement), a minor premise (a particular case), and a conclusion (the deduction that follows logically from the two premises).

Examples:

All graduates of Lincoln High School are well educated.
Liz is a graduate of Lincoln High School.
Therefore, Liz is well educated.

All trees have roots.
Oaks are trees.
Therefore, oaks have roots.

See deduction.

symbiosis

Symbiosis occurs when two species live together in a close relationship. One example of this relationship is wolves and caribou: the life cycles of both species are very closely intertwined.

symbol

A symbol is any object, concrete or real, used to represent an idea. The flag, for instance, is a symbol of our country. In literature, a symbol can represent more than one idea. A black cloak, for example, might represent death, sadness, or evil.

symmetry

A symmetric figure is a plane figure that can be folded in half so that the two halves match.

symphony

A symphony is a sonata for orchestra. Because of the large variety of musical sounds available, a symphonic work is usually longer and more complex than a sonata for a soloist or a small group. Among the most famous composers of symphonies are Haydn, Mozart, Beethoven, Brahms, Schubert, and Mahler. *See sonata.*

synonym

A synonym is a word that has a meaning similar to the meaning of another word.

Examples:
- country and nation
- sea and ocean

See antonym.

syntax

The relationship of words and word groups in sentences is syntax. *See sentence.*

synthesizer

A synthesizer is a computer that creates electronic music by mixing, modifying, and changing tones.

taiga

The swampy, needle-leaf forest land of the subarctic Siberia between the tundra and the steppes is the taiga. The word *taiga* also describes the climate of a wide stretch of land that runs across northern Europe and North America. The climate produces long, hard winters and brief summers. *See tundra.*

take the fifth

The Fifth Amendment to the Constitution states that a person cannot be made to incriminate himself or herself. A person "takes the fifth" if he or she refuses to testify at a trial. Often people will not testify if they believe that it will get them in trouble.

tale

A tale is a true or fictitious story, a narrative. Tall tales and folk tales are types of tales. *See folklore, narrative, and tall tale.*

tall tale

A tall tale is a humorous narrative that presents strange or impossible events. Tall tales are often about folk heroes. The story of Paul Bunyan, for example, is a tall tale. *See folklore and tale.*

tambourine

A tambourine is a shallow, hand-held drum with metal bangles set into its

MORE

sides. It is struck on the palm of the hand and shaken to produce an emphatic, jangling sound.

tariff

A tariff is a tax that the government charges on imports and exports. *See exports and imports.*

tautology

A tautology is the needless repetition of an idea or statement.

Example:
The airplane flew in the air in the sky.

technology

The word *technology* refers to the tools people use to meet their needs. Technology influences where and how people live. Steam engines, for example, were once a great advance in technology. Now the introduction of calculators and computers is another great advance that affects the lives of millions of people.

telephone

The first telephone was invented by Alexander Graham Bell in 1876. The telephones we use today are very different from the one Bell first designed. His first phone only ran between two rooms, and the first phone conversation was between Bell and his assistant. A lifelong interest in deafness prompted Bell to study speech and the way sounds are created. *See Alexander Graham Bell.*

telescope

An instrument that magnifies objects seen from a great distance is a telescope. The first telescope was invented in 1608 by Dutch optician Johann Lippershey, a lens grinder who sold glasses. By adjusting the space between two lenses, he discovered that distant objects looked closer. He put the lenses in tubes and sold them, making

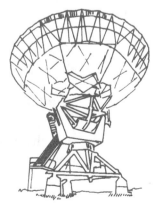

him the first telescope manufacturer. *See radio telescope and reflecting telescope.*

television

When a television camera takes a picture, it changes the light into electricity and then into radio waves. These radio waves are sent out over the air. When those signals reach a household, an antenna picks them up and transmits them to the television. When the signals reach a television set, they are changed back to electricity and then into light that is seen on the TV. Today more than 88 million households in the United States have television sets.

temperance movement

The temperance movement was a crusade in America against the use of alcohol. In 1920, because of the efforts of the temperance movement, the production and sale of alcohol was prohibited in the United States. Prohibition was repealed in 1933.

temperature and heat

Temperature is a measure of how fast an object's particles are moving. Heat is the flow of energy from a warmer object to a cooler one. Thus, two objects with the same temperature can give off different amounts of heat. A lake gives off more heat than does a nearby puddle, even though both may have the same temperature.

tendon

The tough, cordlike tissues that attach the muscles to bones are tendons.

tenor

In music, the highest male voice is a tenor.

tense

In language, tense refers to time. A verb may be used in the present tense (she smiles), past tense (she smiled), present perfect tense (she has smiled), past

WAIT, THERE'S MORE!

perfect tense (she had smiled), or the future perfect tense (she will have smiled). *See verb.*

tepee

A tepee is a the tent used by the Native Americans of the Great Plains. A tepee was made of hides sewn together and stretched over poles. It could be packed and moved easily as Indians traveled to hunt for food.

Tereshkova, Valentina

Valentina Tereshkova (b. 1937), a Russian cosmonaut, was the first woman to fly a spacecraft. Her 1963 flight in *Vostok VI*, which she operated with manual controls, orbited the Earth for about three days.

terminal

A terminal is a keyboard and display screen or printer connected directly to a central computer or a computer network. *See network.*

terminating decimal

A terminating decimal is a decimal that, after a number of decimal places, is stated in full.

Examples:

.3

.35

.357

See decimal and repeating decimal.

terrorism

The use of threats or violence to create fear within a group, organization, or government is terrorism. Terrorists kill people, hijack planes, and set off bombs. To gain publicity for their causes, they attack people or organizations that oppose them.

testes

The male sex organs that produce sperm are the testes.

texture

In a work of art, especially a painting, the texture is the special surface quality of the work. Such a surface may be rough, smooth, sandy, and so on.

than/then

▷ *Than* is a conjunction introducing the second part of a comparison.

▷ *Then* is an adverb meaning "after" or "at that time" or "therefore."

Example:

If the temperature is higher than 92°, then turn on the air conditioner.

their/there/they're

▷ *Their* is the possessive form of the pronoun *they*.

▷ *There* is an adverb meaning "place."

▷ *They're* is a contraction of *they are*.

Example:

They're going to put away their equipment in the cabinets over there.

theirself/theirselves

Both *theirself* and *theirselves* are nonstandard forms of *themselves*. Avoid *theirself* and *theirselves* in writing.

theme

In literature, a theme is the idea about life the writer wishes to convey about his or her subject. A theme may be stated or implied.

theocracy

A government headed by religious authorities is a theocracy. In a theocracy, religious law is inseparable from civil law. The Puritan government in colonial Massachusetts and the present government in Iran are examples of theocracies.

thermal pollution

When hot water is added to a body of cooler water, such as a stream or lake, thermal pollution occurs. If the temperature of a lake rises, the heat might well kill off species that live in the lake. *See pollution.*

thermostat

A thermostat keeps a constant temperature by turning a heat source on and off. A thermostat controls the temperature in a house, for example, by controlling when the furnace or air conditioning goes on or off.

thesaurus

A thesaurus is a reference book that contains words and their synonyms. A thesaurus may also include technical terms or other information about a particular field of study. *See reference and synonym.*

thesis statement

The thesis statement is the sentence, generally near the beginning of a piece of writing, that states the central idea of that piece of writing and the writer's attitude toward the idea. *See central idea.*

Third Reich

The Nazi government in Germany during the 1930s and 1940s was called the *Third Reich*, which means "third empire." Adolf Hitler, the Nazi leader, believed his was the third empire, after the Holy Roman Empire and the nineteenth-century German Empire. *See Adolf Hitler.*

Third World

The term *Third World* refers to underdeveloped or developing countries. Developing nations of Asia, Latin America, and Africa are often referred to all together as the Third World. The African country of Somalia, for example, is poor and might be described as a Third World country.

Thoreau, Henry David

Henry David Thoreau (1817–1862) was an American writer and naturalist. *Walden*, his most famous book, presents his reflections about the two years he spent living alone in a cabin he built by Walden Pond. His best-known essay, "Civil Disobedience," stressed his belief that a person must follow his or her conscience, even if it means breaking the law. Thoreau's writing influenced political leaders such as Mahatma Gandhi and Martin Luther King, Jr. *See Mohandas K. Gandhi and Martin Luther King, Jr.*

threw/through

▷ *Threw* is the past tense of the verb *throw*.
▷ *Through*, which can be used as a preposition or an adverb, means "in one side and out the other."

Example:
Greg threw the ball through the picture window.

thunder

Thunder always occurs where there is lightning. This is because thunder is produced by the rapid heating and expanding of the air through which lightning passes. The rumbling noise of thunder is caused by the air wave produced by the bolt of lightning farthest away from the observer. *See thunderstorm.*

thunderstorm

Thunderstorms usually occur in the summer when there is a large amount of warm, moist air. If this air is pushed up

MORE

rapidly by winds and is replaced by rapid downdrafts of cool air, then thunderstorms form. A thunderstorm can also form when a cold front begins to push warmer air ahead of it. At any given time, day or night, about 18,000 thunderstorms are taking place throughout the world. Lightning is created by an electrical charge between clouds. The passage of an electrical charge from the lightning generates heat. That sudden heat path created inside a cloud creates the sound waves that we call *thunder.*

tides

Tides are caused by the gravitational pull of the moon on the Earth's surface. As the moon travels around the Earth, it pulls on the part of the Earth closest to it. As ocean water moves in the direction of that gravitational pull, there is a high tide or rise in the water level. In areas of the Earth where the moon is not pulling, the water level is low. This is a low tide. The Bay of Fundy in Canada has the greatest extremes in tides of any place on Earth. The difference between high tide and low tide at Fundy can be as much as 53 1/2 feet. In most places, however, tides will vary from a few feet to perhaps 12 to 20 feet.

Tigris River

The Tigris River is a river in southwestern Asia that flows from eastern Turkey through Iraq into the Persian Gulf. The area between the Tigris River and Euphrates River is often called "the cradle of civilization," because it was there that Western culture first developed. *See Euphrates River.*

time line

A chart that has information about past history is a time line. A time line presents the sequence, or order, in which events occurred.

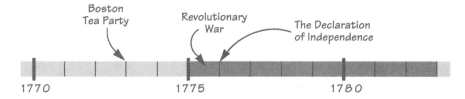

time zone

A time zone is an area in which the same time is used. The world has twenty-four time zones with one hour's difference between each. A person traveling to a new time zone in the west will set his or her watch back. A person traveling to the east will set his or her watch ahead.

timpani

Timpani is the Italian name for kettle-drums. A kettle-drum is a large, copper, bowl-shaped instrument over which is stretched a calf-skin head. Usually numbering three or four in a modern symphony orchestra, they are the most important of all the percussion instruments. Timpani can be tuned to various ptiches and can vary greatly in volume from muted to thunderous.

tissue

Tissue is a group of cells of the same type that do the same job. For example, muscle tissue helps the body perform certain kinds of physical tasks. These groups of cells are called *tissues* because they often look flat and are very thin. *See cell.*

Titans

In Greek mythology, the Titans were the first race of beings who lived before the gods of Olympus. The first Titan was Gaea, the Earth, who gave birth to Uranus, the sky. They married and had many offspring, including Zeus, who deposed Uranus and became supreme ruler of the universe. *See Uranus.*

to/too/two

▷ *To* means "toward" or "in the direction of."
▷ *Too* means "also" or "very."
▷ *Two* is the written version of the number 2.

Example:
Too often, it takes more than two moves to parallel park.

Tokyo

Tokyo, the capital of Japan, is located on Honshu Island. One of the largest cities in the world, it has about 8.5 million people. Tokyo is the commercial, governmental, and financial center of Japan. *See Japan.*

tone

The writer's attitude or feeling toward his or her literary work, its characters, and events is called *tone*. Tone can be unemotional or passionate, serious or funny. The writer's tone creates the story's atmosphere. *See atmosphere.*

topic

The topic is the specific subject of a piece of writing.

topic sentence

The topic sentence is the sentence, generally near the beginning of a paragraph, that states the central idea of the paragraph and the writer's attitude toward that idea. *See central idea.*

topsoil

Topsoil is that part of the Earth's surface in which crops are grown. Farmers depend on the topsoil to grow their crops. The study of soil and what is in it is called pedology. *See erosion.*

tornado

A tornado is an extremely violent and destructive whirling wind. It looks like a mass of dark clouds in the sky with a twisting funnel attached. Tornadoes move over the ground in a narrow path.

torque

Torque is the measure of how strongly an object is turning or rotating. Torque is a factor of force and distance.

total fitness

Total fitness is the fitness of the whole person, including physical, mental, social, and emotional fitness. *See cardiovascular fitness and physical fitness.*

totalitarianism

Totalitarianism occurs when one group in a government has total control over the lives of all the other people. Fascist and some communist governments have had this type of control. For example, Joseph Stalin once ruled the former Soviet Union with complete and ruthless control. His government was a totalitarian government. *See fascism.*

totem

A natural object, often an animal, used as a symbol by a tribe or family is a totem. Native Americans of the Northwest carved huge totem poles to erect in front of their houses.

town meeting

A gathering of a community's people is a town meeting. New England colonists met and made decisions by voting. Some New England towns today continue this tradition. More often, town meetings are held for public discussion.

toxin

A toxin is any poison formed by an organism as a result of its metabolism.

trachea

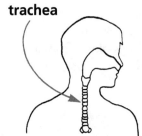

The tube that runs from a person's mouth down the throat to the lungs is the trachea. The trachea (windpipe) leads from the pharynx to the lungs.

trade wind

A trade wind is a steady wind that blows toward the equator from about 30° north latitude and about 30° south latitude.

tradition

The handing down of beliefs and customs from one generation to the next is tradition. In modern Japan, for example, people may wear traditional kimonos for special occasions, which is something their parents did before them.

tragedy

A tragedy is a piece of writing, especially a play, in which the events turn out badly for the characters. Tragedies have serious plots, exploring issues of morality and the meaning of human existence. *Antigone* was a Greek tragedy, *Othello* a Shakespearean tragedy, and *Mourning Becomes Electra* by Eugene O'Neill an American tragedy. *See comedy and drama.*

Trail of Tears

Between 1838 and 1839, the United States government ordered Native Americans to move west of the Mississippi River to a reservation in present-day Oklahoma. Because thousands of Cherokees died during the walk, the route is called the "Trail of Tears."

traitor

A person who betrays his or her country is a traitor. Benedict Arnold was considered a traitor for helping the British during the Revolutionary War. A traitorous act—that is, an act against one's country—is called *treason*. *See treason.*

transfusion

A transfusion is the process of taking blood from one person and giving it to another person. When someone loses blood from a wound or during surgery, he or she may need a blood transfusion.

transition

In writing, a transition is a word or phrase that serves as a bridge from one idea, point, or example to another. Often, transitions such as *first, next, then,* and *finally* connect paragraphs or sentences within paragraphs.

transposition

Transposition is the process of performing a musical selection in a key other than the key in which it is written.

trapezoid

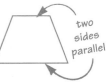

two sides parallel

A quadrilateral with one pair of parallel sides is a trapezoid. *See parallelogram and quadrilateral.*

treason

Treason is an act against or betrayal of one's own government. Helping the enemies of one's government is treason. During the Revolutionary War, Benedict Arnold committed treason when he tried to help the British instead of his own country, the United States. *See traitor.*

treaty

A formal agreement between two or more nations is a treaty. A treaty must be approved and signed by all of the nations involved. A treaty may be signed to settle a war, for example, or to solve a boundary dispute. A treaty may also be a peacetime arrangement, such as a trade agreement.

tremor

A tremor is a small earthquake. *See earthquake and fault.*

triangle

A triangle is a three-sided polygon. *See polygon and scalene triangle.*

triangles

tributary

A river or stream that flows into a larger stream or river is a tributary. For example, the Wabash River flows into the Ohio River, so it is a tributary of the Ohio. The Ohio River flows into the larger Mississippi River. The Ohio is, therefore, considered a tributary of the Mississippi.

triptych

A triptych is a set of three related paintings on three connected panels. Usually the main idea is placed on the center panel and an aspect of it on each side.

Trojan War

The Trojan War, which probably took place in the mid-1200s B.C., is the legendary war described by the Greek poet Homer in *The Odyssey*. Homer wrote that the Greeks gained entrance to the city of Troy by hiding inside a large wooden horse. Once the Trojans pulled the wooden horse inside the gates of their city, the Greeks came out of hiding at night and captured the city. *See Homer and Troy.*

trombone

The trombone is a brass orchestral and band instrument with a solemn, mellow sound. It is played by blowing into a cup-shaped mouthpiece while moving its long, curved section (the slide) in and out to change pitches. *See orchestra.*

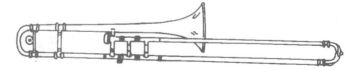

trompe l'oeil

The term *trompe l'oeil* is a French expression meaning "to trick the eye." In art, it is used to describe painting that tricks a viewer into thinking it might, indeed, be real.

tropical rain forest

The Earth is blanketed by millions of acres of tropical rain forest. Much of this forest region lies along the equator. The temperature in a rain forest averages 80° Fahrenheit. Because of the warm temperature and plentiful rain, plants grow wonderfully—layers and layers of them. Typically a rain forest has tall trees and several layers of smaller trees above a layer of ground plants. It has been estimated that between 37,000 and 150,000 acres of tropical rain forests are cleared and destroyed every single day. The forests— and the plants and animals that live in them—may never grow back again.

tropism

The response of a plant to stimulus that invokes growth movements is tropism. For example, when a plant is left near a window, the plant may begin growing, or leaning, in that direction. It grows toward the stimulus—the sunlight. The term *phototropism* refers to plants' tendency always to grow in the direction of available sunlight.

troposphere

troposphere

The troposphere is one of four layers of the atmosphere. It is the closest layer to the Earth. The air we breathe and weather conditions such as cloudiness and storms are all part of the troposphere. This area of the atmosphere varies from six to ten miles in thickness.

Troy

Troy was an ancient city in present-day Turkey. According to legend, the Greeks won the Trojan War by hiding soldiers inside a huge wooden horse sent to the Trojans as a "gift." Once the Trojans pulled the wooden horse inside the gates of their city, the Greeks came out of hiding at night and captured the city. The saying "Beware of Greeks bearing gifts" derives from this event. *See Trojan War.*

trumpet

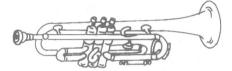

The trumpet is a brass instrument that is played by pressing one or more of its three valves to change pitch, while blowing into a cup-shaped mouthpiece and moving its long, curved section (the slide) in and out to change pitches. *See orchestra.*

Truth, Sojourner

Sojourner Truth (1790?-1883) was an abolitionist and civil rights activist. Born a slave in New York, she was freed in 1827. All of her life she spoke out for the rights of blacks and women. *See abolition.*

tsunami

A tsunami is a tidal wave caused by underwater earthquakes. Tsunamis travel at 400 to 500 miles per hour and can be devastating. In 1946, a tsunami hit Hilo, Hawaii, causing tremendous damage.

tuba

The tuba is the bass instrument of the brass orchestral family. Like the trumpet, it has a cupped mouthpiece and also employs four or five valves to change pitches. Because it is a very large horn, it is held in the lap with the bell upright.

Tubman, Harriet

Born into slavery, Harriet Tubman (1820?–1913) escaped in 1849 and became one of the best-known abolitionists. She returned again and again to the South to lead other slaves to freedom. *See abolition.*

tundra

A vast, dry, treeless plain in the arctic regions is a tundra. *See taiga.*

Turkey

Turkey is a country located in both southeastern Europe and southwestern Asia. Istanbul, its largest city, lies in the European part of the country. Turkey was the center of the Ottoman Empire from the 1300s to the early 1920s.

turpentine

Turpentine is a clear thinning solution for oil-based paints and a cleaner for paintbrushes. It is a by-product of pine trees.

Twain, Mark

Mark Twain is the pen name for the American writer, Samuel Langhorne Clemens. *See Samuel Langhorne Clemens.*

typewriter

The first typewriter was slow and difficult to use. The inventor, C. Latham Sholes, improved it until it was ready for public use. Before the invention of the typewriter, all correspondence had to be handwritten. The typewriter made written communication between people faster and clearer.

typhoon

A typhoon is a violent tropical storm that occurs in the western Pacific, chiefly between July and October. *See hurricane.*

ukulele

A ukulele is a four-stringed Hawaiian instrument, like a guitar but about half its size. It is easy to play and provides accompaniment for folk and popular singing. The strings are plucked with a plectrum (pick) or with the fingers.

umbilical cord

The umbilical cord connects an embryo (unborn baby) with the placenta of its mother. By connecting at the baby's belly button, the umbilical cord provides the way for the baby to receive oxygen and nutrition from the mother.

unanimous

If all parties to an election or referendum vote for the same side, the vote is unanimous. If an election, for example, is unanimous, all of the voters have chosen the same candidate.

Uncle Tom's Cabin

Published serially in 1851 and 1852, *Uncle Tom's Cabin* became internationally famous and, according to some historians, helped trigger the Civil War. Written by Harriet Beecher Stowe, it increased support for the abolitionists (those that opposed slavery) before the war. *See abolition.*

Underground Railroad

From 1830 to 1860, when slaves attempted to escape from the South to northern states, they traveled from one "safe" house to another. The abolitionists who helped slaves escape were called "conductors." They hid the slaves in safe places called "stations." This system was called the Underground Railroad to freedom. *See abolition.*

underlining

In any handwritten or typed piece of writing, underlining designates the use of italics. *See italics.*

union shop

A union is group of workers joined together for a common purpose. In some businesses, all workers must join the union. Such businesses are called union shops. In a union shop, the contract between the business and its workers requires that all employees join the union within a certain number of days of beginning work.

United Nations

The United Nations is an international organization of about 150 nations. They work to promote peace and good relations among all nations and to solve problems around the world. *See United Nations Security Council.*

United Nations Security Council

The United Nations has a body within it called the Security Council. It has five permanent member nations and ten members with two-year terms. The job of the security council is to decide how best to handle disputes around the world. Only the Security Council has the authority to send troops to end a dispute. The five permanent members of the Security Council are Britain, China, France, Russia, and the United States. *See United Nations.*

United States

The United States of America is a country in North America which lies south of Canada and north of Mexico. It is composed of fifty states including Alaska, located west and northwest of Canada, and Hawaii, an island group in the Pacific Ocean. The capital of the United States is Washington, D.C. *See North America and Washington, D.C.*

universe

The universe, which is unimaginably large, consists of everything that exists in space as well as in time. Edwin Hubble and Walter Baade were astronomers who tried to measure the universe with a telescope. *See telescope.*

unsaturated fat

Unsaturated fat is a nutrient found in many oils, such as olive oil and peanut oil. *See saturated fat.*

Uranus

In Greek mythology, Uranus, a Titan, was the ruler of the sky and the ancestor of other gods. He fathered Zeus. *See Titans.*

Uranus

Uranus is the seventh planet from the sun in our solar system. It does something no other planet does—it spins on its side. Uranus was discovered by Sir William Herschel in 1781. At first it was called "George's Star," after the King of England. But it was later decided that all planets should have names taken from mythology, so it was renamed Uranus.

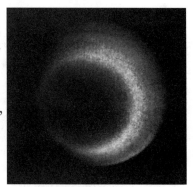

urban

The term *urban* means "characteristic of cities." *Urbanization* means "the growth of large-scale cities." *See rural.*

urine

Fluid waste from our bodies is urine. Urine contains water, salts, uric acid, and urea excreted from the body.

usage

Usage is the way in which language is used by people. Usage can be formal or informal. Formal usage is based on the rules of grammar. *See grammar.*

uterus

The hollow, pear-shaped female organ where a fertilized egg grows and develops is the uterus.

vaccine

A vaccine is a preparation of a weakened or killed bacteria or virus that when injected protects a person from a disease. The first vaccine was created by Edward Jenner in 1796. All over the world people dreaded being infected with smallpox, a disease that marked the a victim's face and killed its victims. A light case of smallpox was better than none at all, because a person who had gotten a light case never got the disease again. So Jenner injected a child with a weak solution containing cowpox, a disease similar to smallpox but less deadly. The light case of cowpox protected the boy from smallpox. A vaccine does the same thing: it gives someone a light case of a disease to protect the person from a severe case. *See Jonas Edward Salk and smallpox.*

vacuum

A vacuum is a space that contains no matter at all—nothing, not even air. Theoretically, a vacuum is completely empty. A complete vacuum, however, has never been achieved.

vagina

The passageway from the opening at the bottom of the uterus to the outside of a woman's body is the vagina. It is the birth canal. *See uterus.*

Valley Forge

Valley Forge is a village in Pennsylvania. During the Revolutionary War, General George Washington made his winter headquarters at Valley Forge in 1777–78. There his troops suffered greatly from the cold and lack of supplies. *See American Revolution.*

vanishing point

In a painting, the vanishing point is the point in perspective where parallel lines receding from the viewer appear to converge. *See perspective.*

variable

A letter or symbol used to represent a number is a variable.

Example:

$$7x + 3 = 24$$

variable

vascular system

The system of internal tubing in plants and animals is the vascular system. The vascular system transports blood in animals and sugars, water, and minerals in plants.

vein

A vessel that carries blood back to the heart is a vein. The vessels that carry blood away from the heart are arteries.

veld

The open, grass-covered plains of southern Africa are velds.

velocity

Velocity is the rate of motion—the speed of something expressed in distance and time, such as miles per hour. Measures of velocity indicate the rate of movement in one fixed direction. Speed indicates rate of motion in any direction.

veneer

A veneer is a thin sheet of fine wood glued over wood of lesser quality to give a smooth, beautiful appearance. Veneering is commonly used on furniture and paneling.

Venice

Venice is a city in northern Italy that is built on islands. By the eleventh century, it was a great center of trade and culture. Today, Venice's tourist attractions include its beautiful architecture, art treasures, canals, and gondola traffic. *See Italy.*

venom

Certain kinds of snakes produce venom, a toxic substance that is harmful. Snakes have glands with venom in their mouths. When snakes bite, the glands release venom through their fangs so it is injected into their victims. Some venoms attack nerves, paralyzing the victim. Other venoms affect the blood and blood vessels. *See snake bites.*

ventricle

The thick-walled chamber of the heart that pumps blood away from the heart is the ventricle.

verb

A verb is a word that shows action or a state of being. Action verbs may be transitive or intransitive. A transitive verb takes an object.

Example:

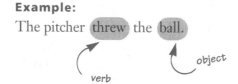

The pitcher (threw) the (ball.)

verb   object

An intransitive verb does not take an object.

Example:

The batter laughed. (The verb *laughed* has no object.)

An intransitive verb that shows state of being is called a *linking verb*. A verb may also be classified in terms of number, voice, and tense. *See linking verb, number, tense, and voice.*

verbal

A verbal is a verb form used as a noun or modifier. *See gerund, infinitive, and participle.*

vermilion

Vermilion is a bright, pure red color.

vernal equinox

About March 21 in the northern half of the world, there is an equal number of hours of daylight and of night. This date is referred to as the vernal equinox. *See equinox and solstice.*

Versailles

Versailles is an area outside Paris, France, that is the site of the Palace of Versailles. Built in the seventeenth century by King Louis XIV, the palace was the home of French kings for about 100 years. The Treaty of Versailles, signed at the palace in 1919, ended World War I. *See France.*

verse

Verse is a line of poetry that has a particular type of meter. *See blank verse, foot, free verse, meter, poetry, and rhythm.*

vertex

In geometry, the term *vertex* is used three ways.

A vertex is the common endpoint of two rays that form an angle.

A vertex is the point of intersection of two sides of a polygon.

A vertex is the point of intersection of the edges of a polyhedron.

vertebrates and invertebrates

Animals are classified into one of two major groups: vertebrates (animals with backbones) or invertebrates (animals without backbones). The invertebrate group is considerably larger than the vertebrate group. In fact, about 96 percent of all animals are invertebrates—that is, animals without backbones. This group includes such animals as sponges, snails, worms, jellyfish, starfish, and all insects. Humans, dolphins, and eagles, which have backbones, are all vertebrates. As a group, vertebrates tend to have more complex brains and behavior than invertebrates do.

Vespucci, Amerigo

Amerigo Vespucci (1454–1512) was an Italian explorer and merchant. Not long after Columbus, Vespucci sailed along the eastern coast of South America. Though some historians question it, he claimed to be the first European to set foot on that continent. A German mapmaker, charting the New World, named the land "America" in his honor.

veteran

A person who has served in the armed forces or a person who has had much experience in war is a veteran. Veterans of the United States are honored on Veterans Day, which is November 11.

veto

To veto a bill is to reject it. The president of a country or governor of a state has the authority to veto a bill if he or she does not support it. Lawmakers can then vote on the bill again and, if there are enough votes, pass the bill over the veto. *See bill.*

videodisk

A videodisk is a thin aluminum plate sandwiched between two layers of plastic. A single videodisk can store vast amounts of information—thousands of still pictures, large sections of encyclopedias, and so forth. Videodisks are used with computers so that people can look up any of the recorded information in any sequence.

Vietnam

Vietnam is a country located on the eastern coast of the Southeast Asian peninsula. Vietnam was divided into a communist North and anti-communist South from 1954 to 1976. *See Vietnam War.*

Vietnam War

The Vietnam War (1957–1975) was fought for control of Vietnam. Forces within Vietnam battled for years. Eventually, the United States entered the war. In the U.S., protesters opposed the war. Eventually, a cease-fire was negotiated, and the communist government the U.S. had opposed assumed power.

Vikings

Vikings were early Scandinavian traders, warriors, and explorers who established trade routes and settlements along many major European waterways. From the late 700s until about 1100, Vikings also explored the Atlantic coastline of North America. *See Scandanavia.*

viola

The viola is the alto member of the violin family quartet of instruments. It looks very much like a violin but it is a little larger. It is tuned a fifth lower than the violin but played in the same way. *See violin.*

violin

The violin, the soprano member of the stringed instrument family, usually carries the melody. It has a wide pitch range with tones from soft to brilliant. The violinist holds the body of the violin under the chin and fingers one or more of the four strings to control pitch while drawing a bow across the strings. *See orchestra.*

virtuouso

A virtuoso is a music performer with outstanding technical ability.

virus

A virus is an organism much smaller than a cell—thousands of times smaller. A virus latches onto a cell in order to reproduce and spread. When someone catches the flu or measles, for instance, the virus enters a cell, called the *host*, and reproduces. Pretty soon the person feels terrible because the virus has spread throughout his or her body.

viscosity

A liquid's resistance to flowing is its viscosity. A liquid that is thick and sticky, such as syrup, has a high viscosity. Liquids can be more or less viscous depending upon what temperature they are. For example, most of the time black tar is highly viscous and hard to stir. But once it's heated, tar becomes more fluid and less viscous.

vitamins

Vitamins are nutrients necessary for the growth and repair of body cells. Vitamins are essential to the healthy working of the body. The word vitamin comes from a combination of *vita*, which means "life" and *amine*, a particular chemical substance. Vitamins are, therefore, life's chemicals.

voice

In language, voice indicates whether a subject is doing the action or being acted upon. Active voice shows that the subject is doing the action.

Example:

Carlton threw the ball to second base. (The verb *threw* is active because it shows Carlton's action.)

Passive voice tells that the subject of the verb is being acted upon. Passive voice always includes a form of the verb *be*.

Example:

The ball was thrown to second base by Carlton. (The verb *was thrown* tells what was being done to the ball.)

Whenever possible, use the active voice because it is more direct and vivid. *See verb.*

volcano

A volcano is an opening in the Earth's surface through which rock fragments, hot gases, and lava erupt. At this time, there are approximately 455 active volcanoes throughout the world. Most of these volcanoes are located in what is known as the "Rim of Fire" in the Pacific. This string of volcanoes extends from the Philippine Islands north, along the coast of Japan, around the Alaskan peninsula, and down the west coast of the United States. The greatest volcanic eruption in history occurred on August 27, 1883. The island of Krakatoa in Indonesia exploded with the force of 20,000 megatons. It left a hole 1,000 feet below sea level where three mountains once stood. The eruption also created a tidal wave that killed more than 36,000 people. *See lava and magma.*

volt

A volt is a measure of electrical current. The term derives from the name of Alessandro Volta, an Italian scientist who discovered in the 1770s how to make an electric battery. By placing something moist between two different metals, he generated an electrical current.

volume

Volume is the amount of space an object takes up. Water, for example, takes up less volume than the same amount of ice. In geometry, the term *volume* is also used for the number given in cubic units that indicates the size of the inside of a solid figure.

voluntary muscles

Voluntary muscles are skeletal muscles, the activity of which a person can control. *See involuntary muscles.*

Vonnegut, Jr., Kurt

Kurt Vonnegut, Jr. (b. 1922) is an American novelist and short-story writer. His novels and short stories mix science fiction and fantasy with comic scenes and social commentary to produce a unique view of American life. *Slaughterhouse-Five*, his anti-war novel, is based on his experience as a prisoner of war during World War II. *See fantasy and science fiction.*

Walker, Alice

Alice Walker (b. 1944) is an American poet and novelist known for her portrayal of the experience of black families in America. Her novel *The Color Purple* won both the American Book Award and a Pulitzer Prize in 1983.

waltz

A waltz is a style of dance in graceful triple-time, popular since the early 1800s. Composers then and now have also used this form to write vocal and instrumental numbers, such as the Brahms *Liebeslieder Waltzes* for chorus.

Wars of the Roses

The various battles for the throne of England from 1455–1485 were known collectively as the "Wars of the Roses." Two branches of the royal family—one whose symbol was a white rose and one whose symbol was a red rose—fought and nearly destroyed each other. The winner, a Tudor who became King Henry VII of England, united both families and started a strong English dynasty. *See dynasty.*

warm-blooded animals

Most warm-blooded animals have thick skins or fur or feathers that help keep them warm in cold weather. The

WAIT, THERE'S MORE!

blood vessels of warm-blooded animals shrink when the temperature drops, which also helps prevent the loss of body heat. And, the food warm-blooded animals eat produces heat needed to maintain their body temperatures.

Washington, Booker T.

An American educator and author, Booker T. Washington (1856–1915) was a former slave who educated himself and became a teacher. In 1881 he founded the Tuskegee Institute, a college in Alabama for black students. Throughout his life he wrote and lectured about the problems faced by black people.

Washington, D.C.

Washington, D.C., is the capital of the United States of America. Located between Virginia and Maryland, it covers the federal District of Columbia. *See United States.*

Washington, George

American general, statesman, and first President of the United States, George Washington (1732–1799) led the colonial army to a difficult victory over the British in 1781. Called the "Father of Our Country," he was elected President in 1789. *See American Revolution and Yorktown.*

water pollution

Many times when garbage or sewage is dumped into water it causes algae to grow. When the algae die, the decaying process uses up much of the oxygen in the water of the stream or lake. This process removes the oxygen from the water that plants and other animals need to survive. As a result, they die. Eventually the water may become so polluted that no animal or plant life can survive. *See pollution.*

watercolor

Watercolors are transparent, water-based paints used to create paintings that are also called *watercolors*. Watercolor painting became highly popuar in England in the 1800s and has remained so since.

Waterloo, Battle of

The Battle of Waterloo (1815) caused the final defeat of Napoleon. European nations united to break Napoleon's stranglehold on the continent. The end came at Waterloo in Belgium. "Waterloo" has since come to mean a total defeat. *See Napoleon I.*

Watson and Crick

Crick

Watson

James Watson (b. 1928) was a child-genius who entered college at the age of fifteen. He graduated and went to Cambridge, England, in 1951 to continue his work. There he met Francis Crick (b. 1916), and together they began creating a model of a protein called DNA. This substance is important because it gives the genetic instructions to the body. DNA is located in a person's genes, which determine how tall a person is, what color eyes the person has, and so on. Watson and Crick's design of the DNA molecule was one of the most dramatic scientific discoveries ever made. *See DNA.*

Watt, James

James Watt (1736–1819), a Scottish engineer, created an efficient steam engine in 1769. His discovery led the way to creating larger and better machines, especially in factories. Eventually engines transformed the way work was done, because they could generate a lot of energy to do work simply.

wear/where

▷ *Wear* is a verb that usually means "to be dressed in."
▷ *Where* means "at" or "in what place."

Example:

Example:
Where did Bob buy that shirt he was wearing yesterday?

weather and climate

The climate of a place is the average weather conditions in a certain area over a long period of time. The study of weather includes changes in precipitation, barometric pressure, humidity, and temperature on a day-to-day basis. Both weather and climate are greatly affected by the location of an area on Earth, its elevation, and its closeness to large bodies of water.

weather/whether

▷ *Weather* is the atmospheric conditions and changes in a particular place.

▷ *Whether* means "which of two."

Example:
Whether the wedding is held inside or out depends upon the weather.

weathering

Rocks can change size and shape because of physical weathering. This process occurs when wind blows dust and sand against rocks. It can also occur when sand and silt in water wear away at rocks. Plants can cause weathering as well. As a plant's roots and stems grow, for instance, they can break rocks into smaller pieces.

Wells, H. G.

Herbert George Wells (1866–1946) was an English writer best known for his science fiction stories. *The Time Machine* is about time travel to the future. *The War of the Worlds* describes an invasion of the Earth by Martians.

westerlies

Global winds that move from the subtropical highs toward the poles are westerlies. They are responsible for some of the weather patterns we have in North America.

whale, blue

The blue whale, the largest animal to have lived on the Earth, is one of a number of endangered species. A blue whale can be 100 feet long and weigh 200 tons. Once there were hundreds of thousands of them in the seas, but by the 1960s, most of the blue whales had been killed. Since then, the number of blue whales has increased because they have been listed as a protected species. Now that they are "protected," anyone who kills or harms one is subject to severe penalties. *See endangered species.*

wheel

The invention of the wheel was very important for the advance of civilization. People in the Bronze Age first developed wheeled carts and pottery wheels. Other early inventions were windmills and pulleys. Even the most complex machines used today often depend on some form of the wheel.

white blood cell

A white blood cell is a nucleus-containing blood cell produced in bone marrow. White blood cells protect the body against diseases.

Whitman, Walt

Walt Whitman (1819–1892) was an American poet whose one book of poems, *Leaves of Grass,* is considered a classic. Whitman's poems most often praise democracy, the United States, and the American people. His flowing, rhythmic, unrhymed poetry, although not immediately accepted, had a strong influence on later poets.

Whitney, Eli

Eli Whitney (1765–1825) invented a cotton gin in 1793 that changed the cotton industry. The cotton gin could clean as much cotton in one hour as fifty people working by hand, thus saving farmers much labor. Today's cotton gin is basically Whitney's design. Whitney also invented the industrial production system of interchangeable parts, which led to mass production.

whole number

A whole number is one that is not a fraction or a mixed number. Examples of whole numbers are 0, 1, 2, 3, 4.

whose/who's

▷ *Whose* is the possessive form of the pronoun *who.*

Example:
Whose birthday is it today?

▷ *Who's,* the contraction of *who is* or *who has,* is always used in a question.
Example:
Who's going to the store to buy the milk?

Wilder, Thorton

Thornton Wilder (1897–1975) was an American novelist and playwright. Wilder's best-known play, *Our Town,* won the Pulitzer Prize in 1938. His play *The Skin of Our Teeth* and his novel *The Bridge of San Luis Rey* also won Pulitzer Prizes.

Williams, Tennessee

Thomas Lanier (Tennessee) Williams (1911–1983) was an American playwright. His most famous plays, *The Glass Menagerie* and *A Streetcar Named Desire,* deal with the loneliness of the individual in modern America. His play *Cat on a Hot Tin Roof,* like *A Streetcar Named Desire,* won a Pulitzer Prize.

wind

Wind is caused by changes in the air temperature. As warm air rises, cooler air rushes in to take its place. That cooler air begins to heat up and it, too, begins to rise. Then more cool air rushes in. This movement of air is what we refer to as wind.

wind speeds

Thunderstorms can become so powerful that updrafts, or wind speeds within a storm, can reach speeds of more than 65 miles per hour. On about 100 days each year, for instance, the wind speed on Mount Washington in New Hampshire reaches more than 70 miles per hour—or hurricane strength. In true hurricanes, wind speeds have been measured at 190 miles per hour. *See hurricane and thunderstorm.*

windmills

Windmills are used to provide power to pump water or generate electricity. Wind exerts force on the series of vanes on the windmill (that is, the parts that look like propeller blades). The vanes of the windmill are connected to an electric generator by a series of gears. The generator contains a coil of wires in a magnetic field. As the coil moves because of the wind, it starts an electric current flowing.

witch hunt

In political jargon, an effort to discover and expose disloyalty or dishonesty based on slight or non-existent evidence is a witch hunt. In politics, witch hunts are sometimes used to discredit an opponent. *See Salem Witch Trials.*

Wordsworth, William

William Wordsworth (1770–1850) was an English poet who wrote nature poems and sonnets. *Lyrical Ballads,* the collection of poems he wrote with Samuel Taylor Coleridge, is considered a milestone in English literature. *See Samuel Taylor Coleridge.*

work ethic

A work ethic is the belief that hard work and thriftiness is the way to a prosperous, satisfying life.

World War I

World War I (1914–1918) was a major war between the Allies, led by England, France, Russia, and the United States, and the Central Powers, led by Germany. Germany lost the long and bitter conflict that raged over much of Europe.

World War II

In World War II (1939–1945), Germany, Italy, and Japan (the Axis Powers) fought the Allies (a group of nations including the United States, Great Britain, France, and the Soviet Union). The primary issue behind the war was expansionism by the Axis Powers into smaller nations. Both sides suffered greatly before the Allies were victorious.

worms

Worms are mostly made up of blood vessels and skin. They have no lungs or backbone. Instead, they breathe through their skin. A slimy substance called mucous keeps their skin moist, which allows worms to take in oxygen from the air. Worms, which for the most part live in either water or soil, eat small plants and animals or live on decaying matter found, for example, in soil.

worm

Wounded Knee Massacre

The Wounded Knee Massacre (1890) was an attack by U.S. troops on the Sioux Indians in South Dakota. Fighting broke out when soldiers, sent to disarm the Indians, started firing in response to a rifle shot. More than two hundred Sioux were killed at Wounded Knee.

Wright brothers

Orville (1871–1948) and Wilbur (1867–1912) Wright were manufacturers and engineers. Working in their bicycle shop, they devised a lightweight engine that made flying machines possible. Their flight in an airplane at Kitty Hawk, North Carolina, in 1903 began the aviation age.

Orville

Wilbur

Wright, Richard

Richard Wright (1908–1960) was an American writer who spoke out strongly against racial discrimination in the United States. *Black Boy* is his autobiographical novel about growing up in the South. *Native Son* is his novel about a black man in Chicago who accidently commits murder and is sentenced to death.

writ of habeas corpus

A writ of habeas corpus is an order that a prisoner come before a court to decide whether he or she is being held lawfully. This writ protects someone from being held without evidence of guilt.

write-in candidate

In an election, a person who is not listed on the ballot but receives votes is a write-in candidate. The candidate's name has been written on the ballot. *See ballot.*

writing process

The writing process is the process a writer goes through in order to complete a piece of writing. The three major steps in the writing process are prewriting, writing, and revision. Each of these steps can include a variety of activities. *See prewriting and revision.*

X rays

One way to investigate inside the body is through X rays. They were identified by Wilhelm Roentgen in 1895. Although he started out investigating cathode rays, he found X rays by accident. He called them X rays because, in mathematics, x often stands for the unknown.

Yalta

Yalta, a city in the Ukraine, a former republic of the Soviet Union, was the site of a famous meeting in 1945 between Winston Churchill, Franklin D. Roosevelt, and Josef Stalin. At Yalta, these leaders talked about ending World War II and solving postwar problems. Differences about exactly how the war would be settled developed between Stalin and the other two leaders, who represented the major allied nations. *See World War II.*

yard

A yard is a unit for measuring length in the customary system. One yard equals three feet.

Yeats, William Butler

William Butler Yeats (1865–1939) was an Irish poet and playwright who won the Nobel Prize for literature in 1923. Many of his poems are based on Irish folklore. He is often considered the greatest poet of this century.

Yorktown

The final battle of the American Revolution was Yorktown, Virginia, in 1781. The leader of the English troops, General Cornwallis, surrendered to General George Washington at Yorktown, Virginia. The American colonies had won their independence at last. *See American Revolution.*

your/you're

▷ *Your* is the possessive form of the pronoun *you.*
▷ *You're* is a contraction of *you are.*

Example:

You're going to have to use your head if you expect to pass the test.

Zaire

Zaire is the largest country in Central Africa. The equator runs through Zaire, and almost a third of the country is covered by a tropical rain forest surrounding the Congo River. Zaire was formerly known as the Belgian Congo. *See Africa and Congo River.*

Zeno of Elea

Zeno of Elea (490?–430 B.C.) was an early Greek philosopher known for his paradoxes—that is, seemingly unsolvable puzzles. By presenting these puzzles for people to think about, Zeno extended human understanding about how the world worked.

Zeus

In Greek mythology, Zeus was the ruler of the gods of Olympus. His Roman name was Jupiter.

Zhou (Chou) Enlai

Zhou (Chou) Enlai (1898–1976) joined the Chinese Communists in 1931 and held party leadership for nearly fifty years. As premier and foreign minister, he helped bring China closer to the West.

Zindel, Paul

Paul Zindel (b. 1936) is an American writer best known for his young adult novels. His novels include *The Pigman* and *My Darling, My Hamburger.* His play *The Effect of Gamma Rays on Man-in-the-Moon Marigolds* won the Pulitzer Prize for drama in 1971.

zygote

A zygote is a fertilized egg.

Index

Art

aesthetics, 12
arabesque, 29
architect, 31
architecture, 31
arts and crafts, 34
asymmetry, 36
atelier, 36
Audubon, John James, 38
avant-garde, 40
background, 43
baroque, 46
Blake, William, 53
bronze, 61
brush, 62
calligraphy, 67
canvas, 68
caricature, 70
ceramics, 77
charcoal, 78
chiaroscuro, 78
chisel, 79
classicism, 85
clay, 85
color, 89
color spectrum, 90
cross section, 109
Cubism, 110
cyan, 112
da Vinci, Leonardo, 113
Daguerre, Louis, 113
daguerreotype, 114
design, 120
easel, 133
ebony, 133
enamel, 140
fin de siècle, 156
firing, 157
fluorescence, 159
focus, 159
foreground, 161
forgery, 161
fresco, 165
glaze, 173
Gothic, 176
graffito, 176
graphics, 177
graphite, 177
Gutenberg, Johannes, 181

Hellenic Period, 187
icon, 199
impressionism, 201
ivory, 213
kiln, 219
landscape, 222
lithography, 231
magenta, 237
marble, 219
mold, 255
mosaic, 258
motif, 259
movable type, 259
mural, 261
objet d'art, 275
palette, 283-84
panorama, 284
papier-mâché, 284
papyrus, 285
parchment, 286
pastel, 288
perspective, 293
pewter, 293
pigment, 296
plaster of Paris, 299
pop art, 304
porcelain, 305
portrait, 305
primary colors, 309
realism, 323
sculpture, 341
silkscreening, 348
sketch, 349
spectrum, 358
squeegee, 359
stenciling, 362
still life, 363
stucco, 364
texture, 375
triptych, 384
trompe l'oeil, 384
turpentine, 387
vanishing point, 393
veneer, 394
vermilion, 395
watercolor, 403

Computers

abacus, 3
Babbage, Charles, 42
binary code, 51
bit, 53
byte, 64
chip, 79

computer, 96-97
computer science, 97
CPU, 108
data, 115
database, 115
disk, 126
download, 129
E-mail, 131
file, 156
hacker, 182
keyboard, 219
laptop computer, 222
menu, 245
microchip, 249-50
microprocessor, 250
mouse, 259
network, 266
peripheral, 291
program, 311
software and hardware, 352
terminal, 374
videodisk, 397

Language Arts

Composition

argumentation, 32
audience, 38
body, 56
brainstorming, 60
central idea, 76
clustering, 86
coherence, 87
composition, 94
conclusion, 97
deduction, 117
description, 120
details, 120
focus, 159
free writing, 163
generalization, 170
induction, 203
introduction, 208
juxtaposition, 217
outline, 281
plagiarism, 297
premise, 308
prewriting, 308
proofreading, 311
purpose, 314
revision, 328
rhetorical question, 329
thesis statement, 376
topic, 380
topic sentence, 380

Music

Science

Earth Science

Physical Science

Social Studies

American History

Credits